NAG HAMMADI STUDIES

VOLUME X

NAG HAMMADI STUDIES

EDITED BY

MARTIN KRAUSE - JAMES M. ROBINSON
FREDERIK WISSE

IN CONJUNCTION WITH

ALEXANDER BÖHLIG - JEAN DORESSE - SØREN GIVERSEN
HANS JONAS - RODOLPHE KASSER - PAHOR LABIB
GEORGE W. MACRAE - JACQUES-E. MÉNARD - TORGNY SÄVE-SÖDERBERGH
WILLEM CORNELIS VAN UNNIK - R. McL. WILSON
JAN ZANDEE

X

VOLUME EDITOR

FREDERIK WISSE

LEIDEN

E. J. BRILL

1978

THE ENTHRONEMENT OF SABAOTH

Jewish Elements in Gnostic Creation myths

BY

FRANCIS T. FALLON

LEIDEN
E. J. BRILL
1978

ISBN 90 04 05683 1

TABLE OF CONTENTS

FOREWORD

This monograph grew out of a dissertation submitted to the faculty of the Harvard Divinity School as partial fulfilment of the requirements for the Doctorate of Theology. I wish to express on this occasion my sincere thanks to Professor Dieter Georgi, my thesis director, for his encouragement and critical advice; to Professor George MacRae, whose expertise in Gnosticism was a source of constant help; and to the other members of my committee and the faculty, Professors Frank M. Cross, Jr., Helmut Koester, and John Strugnell, for their generous assistance.

During the academic year 1972-73 I was the recipient of a scholarship from the Deutscher Akademischer Austauschdienst. I express my thanks to the German government and Professor Alexander Boehlig of Eberhard-Karls-Universität in Tübingen, with whom I had the privilege of studying during that year, as well as to his assistants at that time James Brashler and Dr. Frederik Wisse. While abroad that year I had the opportunity to visit Israel and to profit greatly from my discussion with Doctors Bentley Layton, Itthamar Gruenwald, and Michael Stone. To them also I extend my gratitude.

To Professor Philip King, who first stimulated my interest in biblical studies, and to the Archdiocese of Boston, which generously supported my graduate education, I also offer my sincere thanks. Lastly, I would thank Camilla Sieveking and Dorothy Riehm for their patience in typing this manuscript.

ABBREVIATIONS

A. GENERAL

Abhandl. phil.-philol. Classe Akad. Wiss.	*Abhandlungen der philosophischen-philologischen Classe der Akademie der Wissenschaften*
AJA	*American Journal of Archaeology*
AntuChrist	*Antike und Christentum*
APOT	R.H. Charles, ed., *The Apocrypha and Pseudepigrapha of the Old Testament*
BZNW	Beihefte zur *Zeitschrift für die neutestamentliche Wissenschaft*
CCSL	Corpus Christianorum, Series Latina
CSEL	Corpus Scriptorum Ecclesiasticorum Latinorum
DBSup	*Dictionnaire de la Bible, Supplément*
FRLANT	Forschungen zur Religion und Literatur des Alten und Neuen Testaments
Greg	*Gregorianum*
GCS	Die Griechischen Christlichen Schriftsteller
HzNT	Handbuch zum Neuen Testament
HTR	*Harvard Theological Review*
HTS	Harvard Theological Studies
HeyJ	*Heythrop Journal*
JCS	*Journal of Cuneiform Studies*
JNES	*Journal of Near Eastern Studies*
JQR	*Jewish Quarterly Review*
JTS	*Journal of Theological Studies*
LCL	Loeb Classical Library
NHS	Nag Hammadi Studies
NovT	*Novum Testamentum*
NovTSup	*Novum Testamentum*, Supplements
NumenSup	*Numen*, Supplements
OLZ	*Orientalistische Literaturzeitung*
OriensChrist	*Oriens Christianus*
PG	Migne, *Patrologia Graeca*
PW	Pauly-Wissowa, *Realencyclopaedie der classischen Altertums-wissenschaft*
RAC	*Reallexikon für Antike und Christentum*
RSR	*Recherches de science religieuse*
RB	*Revue biblique*
RTP	*Revue de théologie et de philosophie*
SBL	Society of Biblical Literature
SBLMS	Society of Biblical Literature Monograph Series
SC	Sources chrétiennes
SPB	Studia postbiblica
TDNT	G. Kittel and G. Friedrich, eds., *Theological Dictionary of the New Testament*
TLZ	*Theologische Literaturzeitung*
ThRu	*Theologische Rundschau*
TU	Texte und Untersuchungen

VT	*Vetus Testamentum*
VTSup	*Vetus Testamentum*, Supplements
VC	*Vigiliae Christianae*
ZNW	*Zeitschrift für die neutestamentliche Wissenschaft*
ZPE	*Zeitschrift für Papyrologie und Epigraphik*

B. GNOSTIC LITERATURE

ApocAd	*The Apocalypse of Adam* CG V, *5*
ApocryJas	*The Apocryphon of James* CG II, *1*
ApocryJn	*The Apocryphon of John* BG; CG II, *1*; III, *1*; IV, *1*
BG	*Papyrus Berolinensis Gnosticus 8502*
CG	Cairensis Gnosticus : Nag Hammadi
DialSav	*The Dialogue of the Saviour* CG III, *5*
Eug	*Eugnostos, the Blessed* CG III, *3*; V, *1*
GMary	*The Gospel of Mary* BG
GPh	*The Gospel of Philip* CG II, *3*
GTh	*The Gospel of Thomas* CG II, *2*
GTr	*The Gospel of Truth* CG I, *2*
GrPow	*The Concept of our Great Power* CG VI, *4*
GrSeth	*Second Treatise of the Great Seth* CG VII, *2*
NatArch	*The Nature of the Archons* CG II, *4*
OnOrgWld	*On the Origin of the World* CG II, *5*; XIII, *2*
OnRes	*The Treatise on the Resurrection* CG I, *3*
P.S.	*Pistis Sophia*
SJC	*The Sophia of Jesus Christ* BG; CG III, *4*
TestTr	*The Testimony of Truth* CG IX, *3*
ThCont	*The Book of Thomas the Contender* CG II, *7*
TriProt	*Trimorphic Protennoia* CG XIII, *1*

CHAPTER ONE

INTRODUCTION

In his introductory essay to the papers and discussions of the Messina Colloquium, Ugo Bianchi has aptly remarked :

> The studies which have been presented to this Colloquium confirm by their number and by the variety of subjects treated the legitimacy, the reality, and at the same time the difficulty of the theme of the origins of Gnosticism.[1]

Indeed, not only the Colloquium but also the scholarly debate during this century on the origins of Gnosticism witness to the difficulty of this theme.[2] Faced with this scholarly division of opinion and with the array of new material from Nag Hammadi, one can best further the discussion at this time by examining in detail the individual pericopes of these documents and the traditions in which they stand. Only later will a synthesis of these results and assessment of the

---

[1] U. Bianchi, "Le Problème des Origines du Gnosticisme", *Le Origini dello Gnosticismo*, Colloquio di Messina 13-18 April 1966, publ. U. Bianchi (NumenSup 12; Leiden 1967) 1; the translation here from the French and throughout this study from foreign languages is mine unless otherwise indicated.

[2] See, for example, from the viewpoint of the History of Religions W. Bousset, *Hauptprobleme der Gnosis* (FRLANT 10; Göttingen 1907); H. Jonas, *Gnosis und spätantiker Geist*, Bd. 1, 3te Aufl. (Göttingen 1964); R. Reitzenstein, *Das iranische Erlösungsmysterium* (Bonn 1921). Among those who considered Gnosticism as in essence a Christian heresy are to be numbered E. De Faye, *Gnostiques et Gnosticisme*, 2e édition (Paris 1925); F.C. Burkitt, *Church and Gnosis* (Cambridge 1932); A. D. Nock, "Review of Jonas, *Gnosis und spätantiker Geist,*" *Gnomon* 12 (1936) 605-12; now available as Nock, "The Milieu of Gnosticism," *Essays on Religion and the Ancient World*, ed. Z. Stewart, 2 vols. (Cambridge 1972) 1.444-51; and Nock, "Gnosticism," *HTR* 57 (1964) 255-79; now available as "Gnosticism" in *Essays on Religion*, 2.940-59. Other scholars have stressed the Jewish contribution to Gnosticism, e.g. R. McL. Wilson, *The Gnostic Problem* (London 1958) and *Gnosis and the New Testament* (Philadelphia 1968); G. Scholem, *Major Trends in Jewish Mysticism*, 3rd ed. (New York 1967) and *Jewish Gnosticism, Merkabah Mysticism, and Talmudic Tradition* (New York 1960). A further group of scholars has posited a Jewish origin for Gnosticism, e.g. R.M. Grant, *Gnosticism and Early Christianity* (1st ed. 1959; rev. ed. New York 1966); H.-M. Schenke, "Das Problem der Beziehung zwischen Judentum und Gnosis," *Kairos* 7 (1965) 124-33 and "Hauptprobleme der Gnosis," *Kairos* 7 (1965) 114-23; K. Rudolph, "Randerscheinungen des Judentums und das Problem der Enstehung des Gnostizismus," *Kairos* 9 (1967) 112-14; A. Böhlig, *Mysterion und Wahrheit* (Leiden 1968); G. MacRae, "The Apocalypse of Adam Reconsidered," *The Society of Biblical Literature*, One Hundred Eighth Annual Meeting, Seminar Papers, ed. Lane C. McGaughy (SBL 1972) 2. 573-80.

broader question of gnostic origins be possible. The following study is meant as a contribution to that initial examination.

We shall examine two related pericopes from Nag Hammadi documents to show first of all that they derive from a Jewish background, as a contribution to this wider scholarly discussion on the origins of Gnosticism and on the relationship of Judaism to Gnosticism. Secondly, we shall determine which segment or segments of Judaism have contributed to these pericopes. Thirdly, of course, we shall study these pericopes in terms of their relation to one another, the traditions upon which they draw, and their function within the given documents.

The pericopes which we have chosen to study are particularly interesting, since they are unique within gnostic literature. Although many gnostic documents contain creation myths, only the two documents that we shall study have pericopes in which the offspring of the evil creator repents and is enthroned in the heavens. The very uniqueness of these pericopes will enable us to delineate the theological issues being addressed by them, to date more precisely the documents in which these pericopes occur, and to determine more exactly the place of these documents within Gnosticism and the other gnostic influences which have shaped them.

A final word concerning a proposed Jewish background is appropriate here. To determine that a pericope derives from a Jewish background, one must first show positively that its motifs and traditions appear in Jewish literature and negatively that they appear only there or only there in their particular connections or that so many motifs and combinations of motifs can be found in Jewish tradition that another source is unthinkable. Secondly, since pagans were acquainted with the OT (e.g. Poimandres), it is necessary to show an acquaintance with traditions found only in the later, intertestamental literature in order to speak of a contribution from Judaism. Obviously, this then leaves open the question as to whether the pericope was formed and/or used in Jewish or Jewish-Christian circles as well as the question as to whether Gnosticism arose within Judaism or within Christianity. In either case, it shows the contribution of Judaism to Gnosticism.[3]

---

[3] Cf. the remark of Rudolph : "Naturally the usage of Israelite-Jewish traditions in no way signifies that Gnosticism as a whole must be a wild offspring of Judaism, but it is obvious that it presents this thesis as at least probable." Rudolph, "Randerscheinungen," 115. To prove the existence of Jewish Gnosticism, one naturally seeks a document of Jewish Gnosticism that is not Christianized or whose Christian additions are removable as secondary additions.

A. THE DOCUMENTS

The pericopes with which we are concerned are taken from two closely related documents of the Nag Hammadi Corpus, i.e. *The Nature of the Archons* (NatArch CG II, 4) and *On the Origin of the World* (OnOrgWld CG II, 5). NatArch[4] is a treatise, which is purportedly sent in response to enquiries concerning the reality of the heavenly authorities (86 [134]. 25ff.). There are two major parts within the treatise. The first contains a gnostic reinterpretation of the early chapters of Genesis through the story of the flood, and the second consists of a revelation discourse of the angel Eleleth to Norea, the sister of Seth and probable wife of Noah. In addition to Jewish elements, the document clearly exhibits a debt to Hellenistic syncretism and is Christian in its present form.[5]

Scholars have begun the analysis of this document by putting the customary, introductory questions to it. At present, it seems clear that NatArch was written originally in Greek and then translated into Coptic, since it follows the text of the LXX and retains the appropriate Greek inflection in some loan words even at the Coptic stage.[6] The

---

[4] Editions of NatArch are the following: R. A. Bullard, *The Hypostasis of the Archons*, with a contribution by M. Krause (Patristische Texte und Studien 10; Berlin 1970); P. Nagel, *Das Wesen der Archonten* (Wissenschaftliche Beiträge der Martin-Luther-Universität Halle-Wittenberg; Halle 1970); B. Layton, "The Hypostasis of the Archons or 'The Reality of the Rulers'," *HTR* 67 (1974) 351-426 and 68 (1976) 31-101. For the establishment of the text, see also R. Kasser, "L'Hypostase des Archontes: Propositions pour Quelques Lectures et Reconstitutions Nouvelles," *Essays on the Nag Hammadi Texts in honour of Alexander Böhlig*, ed. M. Krause (NHS 3; Leiden 1972) 22-35 and "Brèves remarques sur les caractéristiques dialectales du Codex Gnostique Copte II de Nag Hammadi," *Kemi* 20 (1970) 49-55; M. Krause, "Zur 'Hypostase der Archonten' in Codex II von Nag Hammadi," *Enchoria* 2 (1972) 1-20; B. Layton, "The Text and Orthography of the Coptic Hypostasis of the Archons (CG II, 4Kr.)," *ZPE* 11 (1973) 173-200 and "Critical Prolegomena to an Edition of the Coptic 'Hypostasis of the Archons' (CG II, 4)," *Essays on the Nag Hammadi Texts in Honour of Pahor Labib* (NHS 6; Leiden 1975) 90-109; P. Nagel, "Grammatische Untersuchungen zu Nag Hammadi Codex II," *Die Araber in der alten Welt* (Hrsg. F. Altheim and R. Stiehl; Berlin 1969) 2. 393-469; H.-M. Schenke, "Review of Bullard and Nagel," *OLZ* forthcoming. The edition and translation used here is that of Layton. The enumeration of the codex numbers, as currently ascertained by the UNESCO publications committee, is here followed rather than Labib's plate numbers found in the editions of Bullard, Nagel and Böhlig (for OnOrgWld cf. infra). For the sake of the reader, the plate numbers are also given in parentheses after the page numbers.

[5] Cf. Bullard, *The Hypostasis of the Archons*, 115.

[6] Cf. Nagel, *Das Wesen*, 16ff.

provenance of the tractate has not yet been decided;[7] nor has the
date for the tractate been established, except that it is, of course, prior
to the fourth century date of the codex. Scholarly attention has focused
more directly upon the question of the literary unity of NatArch,
although there is as yet no unanimity in answer. Schenke, Bullard
and Kasser have proposed that the two main parts of NatArch are
dependent upon two different written sources, which have been united
by a redactor.[8] However, it has been difficult to determine the exact
beginning of the second source.[9] Krause, on the other hand, has
suggested that three sources, all dealing with Norea (i.e. the race
of Seth and Norea, Norea and Noah's ark, Norea and Eleleth), have
been united by a redactor.[10] It is clear that a full literary analysis
of the text is necessary before this question can be finally answered.[11]

Related to the question of the literary unity of the tractate is the
issue as to whether non-Christian sources have been Christianized
by the redactor. Bullard has noted that the quotation of Eph 6:12
at 86(134).23-24 as well as the Christian allusions in 96(144).33-97
(145).21 belong to the redactor.[12] Again, as Krause has suggested,[13]

---

[7] H.-C. Puech has suggested Egypt as the possible place in "Les nouveaux écrits
gnostiques découvertes en Haute-Égypte," *Coptic Studies in honor of Walter Ewing
Crum* (Boston 1950) 122.

[8] H.-M. Schenke, "'Das Wesen der Archonten': Eine gnostische Originalschrift aus
dem Funde von Nag Hammadi," *TLZ* 83 (1958) 661; Bullard, *The Hypostasis of the
Archons*, 115; R. Kasser, "L'Hypostase des Archontes: Bibliothèque gnostique X,"
RTP 22 (1972) 169-74.

[9] Cf. Bullard, *The Hypostasis of the Archons*, 100, who emphasizes the startling
change from the third person singular to the first person singular as the possible
beginning of the second document. Schenke in his "Review of R. A. Bullard, *The
Hypostasis of the Archons*," in a forthcoming issue of *OLZ* has placed the caesura
at 92(140).18, the change from Norea and the ark of Noah to Norea and the rulers.

[10] Krause, "Zur 'Hypostase der Archonten'," 15-18.

[11] Scholars (e.g. Kasser, "L'Hypostase des Archontes: Bibliothèque gnostique X,"
169ff) have noted the unified purpose, which the redactor achieves in his use of sources
but have had difficulty in identifying the exact sources. As B. Layton has suggested
to me privately and if his restoration at 86(134).26 is correct (cf. "The Hypostasis of
the Archons 364f and 397)—i.e. [ⲁⲉⲓ-]ⲭⲉⲛⲉ ⲛⲁⲉⲓ "I have sent these"—then the
introduction of the first person singular in 93(141).13 is not so startling and can be
considered as merely a parenthetical remark of the composer. Secondly, it is difficult
to separate the story concerning Noah from that concerning Eleleth, since the mountain
(Mt. Seir) 92(140).14 functions as the customary site for a revelation in the literary
genre of a revelation discourse. Perhaps, then, to account for this achievement by
the composer, future analysis should focus on the possibility that the author is not
so much excerpting written documents as using material which is well-known to him
and which he is summarizing either from written sources or from memory.

[12] Bullard, *The Hypostasis of the Archons*, 48 and 113-14. Wilson has also raised
this possibility in *Gnosis and the New Testament*, 126.

[13] Krause, "Zur 'Hypostase der Archonten'," 20.

the full literary analysis of the text is necessary before the issue can be resolved.

A final introductory question with regard to NatArch is that of the gnostic school to which the document belongs. Scholars early noted the relationship of NatArch with the unnamed gnostics in Iren. *Adv. haer.* 1.30 and the sect called the Gnostics in Epiph. *Pan.* 26. On the basis of the title, Doresse then proposed that NatArch belonged to the Archontics of Epiph. *Pan.* 40.[14] Puech, however, suggested the Gnostics of Epiph. *Pan.* 26 because of the reference there to the book *Norea.*[15] Schenke, Jonas and Wilson considered the tractate as Barbelognostic because of the reference to Norea, Samael and Eleleth.[16] Bullard proposed that the first part stemmed from the Ophites, because of its relationship with Iren. *Adv. haer.* 1.30, and that the second part was influenced by Valentinianism.[17] Layton has assigned the document to the Sethians while Krause has left the question open until a full assessment of the relations of NatArch with other gnostic documents and the reports of the Father;[18] even more necessary before a final answer, however, is a reassessment of our customary division of gnostics into sects.[19]

OnOrgWld is a treatise[20] or, more precisely, a tract,[21] which claims to be written against the views of both the gods of the world and men in order to defend the thesis that before chaos something did in fact exist, namely, the light (97[145].24ff). OnOrgWld contains a gnostic interpretation of Genesis but only up to the expulsion from paradise and has no revelation discourse. With regard to the introduc-

---

[14] J. Doresse, *The Secret Books of Egyptian Gnostics*, tr. P. Mairet (New York 1960) 164.

[15] Puech, "Les nouveaux écrits gnostiques," 120-22.

[16] Schenke, "Das Wesen der Archonten," 662-63; Jonas, *Gnosis und spätantiker Geist*, l. 380, n. 1; Wilson, *Gnosis and the New Testament*, 125.

[17] Bullard, *The Hypostasis of the Archons*, 115.

[18] Layton, "The Hypostasis of the Archons," 371-72; Krause, "Zur 'Hypostase der Archonten'," 19-20.

[19] Cf. F. Wisse, "The Nag Hammadi Library and the Heresiologists," *VC* 25 (1971) 205-23.

[20] The edition of OnOrgWld is A. Böhlig and P. Labib, *Die koptisch-gnostische Schrift ohne Titel aus Codex II von Nag Hammadi* (Berlin 1962); the translation is mine.

[21] Böhlig, *Die koptisch-gnostische Schrift ohne Titel*, 19 and Wilson, *Gnosis and the New Testament*, 127. Puech had falsely identified it as an apocalypse in "Les nouveaux écrits gnostiques," 105. Doresse and Schenke had simply identified it as a treatise in Doresse, *The Secret Books of the Egyptian Gnostics*, 165 and H.-M. Schenke, "Vom Ursprung der Welt. Eine titellose gnostische Abhandlung aus dem Funde von Nag Hammadi," *TLZ* 84 (1959) 244.

tory questions, the source of its provenance is not definitely known. Its date is not certain, although its citation of other gnostic writings and its developed mythology would suggest a later date;[22] however, its mythology is less overgrown and therefore its date is probably earlier than *Pistis Sophia*.[23] In reference to literary unity, Böhlig has argued that two sources, characterized respectively by their use of *exousiai* and *archontes*, have been used by a redactor; he has also portrayed OnOrgWld as a compilation.[24] The separation into sources by means of these different terms, however, appears to be unsuccessful, since it is established on too narrow a base;[25] our own study and the study of M. Tardieu would also indicate the need to consider redaction and purposeful integration as well as mere compilation on the part of the composer.[26] Finally, while Schenke and Jonas have attributed the document to the Barbelognostics,[27] Puech has ascribed it to the Ophites and Tardieu has cautiously attributed it to the Archontics.[28] Böhlig, on the other hand, while recognizing the affinities with the Ophites, has wisely refrained from assigning the document to any one school, because of its composite nature.[29] Again, until our categories for division into gnostic sects are more firmly established, it is more appropriate merely to note the relations of the documents to the various sects rather than to assign it to one particular sect.

Both of the writings are cosmogonic works and so they follow a pattern, which is familiar in other gnostic pieces.[30] First, Wisdom[31]

---

[22] Cf. Böhlig, *Die koptisch-gnostische Schrift ohne Titel*, 31 ff, who suggests *Egypt* as the place but acknowledges the incertitude in this matter.

[23] Cf. Puech, "Les nouveaux écrits gnostiques," 122-23; Schenke, "Vom Ursprung der Welt," 244.

[24] Böhlig, *Die koptisch-gnostische Schrift ohne Titel*, 28-35.

[25] Cf. Bullard, *The Hypostasis of the Archons*, 43-44.

[26] M. Tardieu, *Trois mythes gnostiques: Adam, Éros et les animaux d'Égypte dans un écrit de Nag Hammadi (II, 5)* (Études Augustiniennes; Paris 1974), especially 44-48.

[27] Schenke, "Vom Ursprung der Welt," 246; Jonas, *Gnosis und spaetantiker Geist*, 1. 380, n. 1 and 383.

[28] Puech, "Les nouveaux écrits gnostiques," 122-23; Tardieu, *Trois mythes gnostiques*, 34-36.

[29] Böhlig, *Die koptisch-gnostische Schrift ohne Titel*, 35.

[30] Cf. G. MacRae, *Some Elements of Jewish Apocalyptic and Mystical Tradition and Their Relation to Gnostic Literature* (Ph. D. diss., Cambridge University, 1966), 81-84.

[31] In translating the term as Wisdom rather than transliterating as Sophia, we follow a suggestion of B. Layton. Although such is a departure from present scholarly convention, it commends itself for the following reasons. The term "Sophia" is obviously not a loan-word or foreign word when the document is written in Greek (cf. Achamoth, on the other hand). Secondly, transliteration can impede for us connotations that may be helpful in interpretation (cf. the connotation of a lack of continuity in speaking

falls—she wanted to fashion a product by herself without her partner (NatArch 94[142].5-7) or an image flowed out of Faith-Wisdom, which willed and became a work (OnOrgWld 98[146].13-16). Secondly, from the work of Wisdom there came into being matter and the Demiurge (NatArch 94[142].10ff//OnOrgWld 98[146].28-99[147].1; 99[147].17-22; 100[148].1-10). Thirdly, the demiurge arrogantly asserts that he is the only God (NatArch 94[142].21ff//OnOrgWld 100[148].29-34; 103[151]. 11-13; 108[156].1f). And lastly, there is a repentance; in both of these works and only in these works it is the repentance of Sabaoth rather than Wisdom (NatArch 95[143].13ff//OnOrgWld 104[152].26f).

That the two documents are closely related has already been noted by their respective editors in their commentaries. They contain points of contact not only in their cosmogonic elements (especially the accounts of Sabaoth, as we shall see) but also in their presentation of the creation of earthly man, the fall of Adam and Eve, their expulsion from paradise, and even the final re-integration into the light. The works are so close that Bullard has called for an examination of the exact relationship of the two works to one another.[32]

B. THE SABAOTH ACCOUNTS

Our concern in this study is with the parallel Sabaoth accounts in these documents, i.e. NatArch 95(143).13-96(144).3//OnOrgWld 103 (151).32-106(154).19. As the son of the Demiurge Ialdaboath, Sabaoth repents of his father's blasphemy, is snatched up into the heavens, instructed and given a name; whereupon he builds a chariot for himself (and dwelling place and throne in OnOrgWld) and creates angels before him. Then there follows a separation into right and left by which the images or prototypes of life (or justice) and injustice are established. In NatArch the account forms a distinct pericope within the cosmogonic myth. Similarly, in OnOrgWld the Sabaoth account is such a distinct pericope that Böhlig in his edition has proposed that it is an interpolation.[33]

---

of Wisdom in Jewish literature and the Sophia myth in Gnosticism). Although Sophia is a technical term for a heavenly figure in Gnosticism, this technical usage can be indicated in English by capitalization (Wisdom) just as easily as by transliteration. This principle will be applied in the following pages to other terms as well where it is considered feasible: e.g. Faith-Wisdom rather than Pistis-Sophia, Ruler rather than archon, Life rather than Zoe, etc.

[32] Bullard, *The Hypostasis of the Archons*, 115.

[33] Böhlig, *Die koptisch-gnostische Schrift ohne Titel*, 50.

In this study, we shall examine in the first chapter the relationship between these two accounts. By a detailed, synoptic comparison we shall demonstrate that both accounts draw upon the same tradition, that the additional features in OnOrgWld are redactional elements, and that thus the account in NatArch represents the typologically earlier form.

In our second chapter, we shall analyze the Sabaoth account in NatArch. In this analysis, our concern will be to show that the Sabaoth account derives from Judaism (mainly from Apocalyptic Judaism). Since J. Magne has proposed that Phil 2:6-11 and the NT in general, especially the passages on the enthronement of Christ (e.g. Acts 2:32-36; Eph 1:18-21; 4:7-16; Col 1:15-20) have drawn upon and been deeply influenced by the Sabaoth account in NatArch, we shall consider the relationship of the Sabaoth account to the NT and show that it has neither influenced nor been influenced by the NT.[34] Our further concern will be to exegete the passage. In our exegesis, we shall utilize the principles of tradition-criticism[35] and conclude that the Sabaoth account draws upon two Jewish traditions: heavenly enthronement and the ascent of the apocalyptic visionary to see the divine chariot and/or throne. We shall then propose that the Sabaoth account functions to justify the worth of certain parts of the OT and to evaluate more positively than some other gnostics in the late second century the God of the OT and the Jewish people. We shall also reflect upon the political consequences of maintaining that the ruler of this world is the son of an evil Demiurge. In order

---

[34] J. Magne, *La naissance de Jésus-Christ : L'exaltation de Sabaoth dans Hypostase des Archontes 143, 1-31 et l'exaltation de Jésus dans Philippiens 2, 6-11* (Cahiers du cercle Ernest-Renan, No 83; Paris 1973) especially 23-48. Magne has proposed that NatArch presents a partial rehabilitation of the God of the OT (Kyrios Sabaoth) under the name Sabaoth and Phil 2 a later, complete rehabilitation under the name Kyrios. While his proposal of a non-Christian Sabaoth account is theoretically possible, it is not shown to be historically probable. His study as a whole suffers from lack of proper, tradition-critical methodology and from working only with general patterns.

[35] By a tradition, we understand a recurrent sequence of motifs. The methodology of tradition-criticism then is to identify and trace a tradition by establishing a relationship among literary units on the basis of context, form, content, and function. Within content are included terminology (i.e. vocabularly, names, titles, specific terms), motifs (also particular combinations of motifs), and the pattern of the motifs. There is also a wider designation of the term tradition in scholarly usage and in our usage, e.g. the wisdom tradition, or apocalyptic tradition, or Jewish tradition, which we understand to mean the "handing on" of related conceptual materials within continuous circles of people.

to confirm our view, we shall consider related gnostic literature and the theological issues raised within them.

In our third chapter, we shall examine the Sabaoth account in OnOrgWld. Here we shall demonstrate that this Sabaoth account is more developed but uses the same Jewish traditions of heavenly enthronement and ascent of the visionary to the divine chariot and/or throne. Further, we shall show that this account—contrary to Böhlig— is not just an interpolation but a carefully redacted piece, which suits the author's purpose. We shall conclude that in accord with influence from Valentinianism the Sabaoth account serves in this document an anthropological function, i.e. to represent a particular class of men, rather than a theological function, and probably dates from the first half of the third century. By his heavenly enthronement, Sabaoth is validated as divinely appointed ruler, but only of the psychic class of men. Since the psychic class of men form the Christian church, we shall see that Sabaoth's enthronement in the seventh heaven has ecclesiological as well as political implications. We shall again investigate possible relations of this Sabaoth account with the NT. Lastly, we shall consider whether the specific tradition of these Sabaoth accounts is found in other gnostic documents, since such an analysis can be of assistance not only in understanding these Sabaoth accounts but also in tracing the development of this particular tradition and in classifying into groups in a preliminary way the literature of Gnosticism.

CHAPTER TWO

THE RELATIONSHIP OF THE TWO ACCOUNTS:
A COMMON TRADITION

A. A COMMON TRADITION

Before analyzing in detail the individual pericopes, it is appropriate to consider the relationship between the accounts as wholes in these documents. As we have previously remarked, the parallels between the accounts indicate that there is a relationship. Specifically, the Sabaoth accounts in NatArch and OnOrgWld share the same tradition. The data, however, are insufficient to determine whether this tradition consisted of oral or written elements or a combination thereof. The conclusion that a common tradition is being used, though, is justified first of all because of the identity of topic considered in both accounts, namely, Sabaoth. Although the conception of Sabaoth as one of the offspring of the Demiurge is familiar in gnostic thought (e.g. Iren. *Adv. haer.* 1. 30), the conception of Sabaoth as enthroned above him is not.

This conclusion is further justified because the structure or sequence in the accounts is the same. It appears as follows:

1) the repentance of Sabaoth—95(143).13-18//103(151).32-104(152).6
2) the ascent and enthronement of Sabaoth—95(143).19-25//104(152).6-31
3) creation of the throne/chariot of Sabaoth—95(143).26-28//104(152).31-105(153).16
4) creation of the angels—95(143).28-31//105(153).16-106(154).3
5) the instruction of Sabaoth—95(143).31-34//104(152).26-31 and 106(154).3-11
6) the separation into right and left—95(143).34-96(144).3//106(154).11-19

There are two minor elements, which disturb this identity of sequence. First, the giving of a name of Sabaoth appears in NatArch as part of section "2", the ascent and enthronement, whereas in OnOrgWld it appears within "1" the repentance of Sabaoth. Second, section "5" the instruction of Sabaoth is reduplicated in OnOrgWld; it appears once within the enthronement of Sabaoth and then again later at the point corresponding to NatArch. It will be argued shortly that within OnOrgWld the giving of a name to Sabaoth and the first occurrence of the instruction of Sabaoth can be explained as intentional alterations on the part of the redactor. If such be true, these minor differences in sequence would not militate against the use of the same tradition but would rather presuppose it. The second occurrence of the instruction of Sabaoth, it will be then argued, is another piece of tradition introduced by the redactor into the account.

The conclusion that the same tradition is being used in both documents is also justified by the verbal identity between the two accounts, an identity which is visible even in the Coptic, although both documents are probably translations from the Greek.[1] Some sixty words of the account in NatArch—and therefore approximately 50% of its account—are shared by OnOrgWld. Since OnOrgWld is a longer account, these same sixty words represent only approximately 14% of its total. The following synopsis shows clearly the amount of detail that is common to both accounts (underscored in unbroken lines are elements that are identical and in broken lines are elements that are common but exhibit a different form or position within the account).

1) The Repentance of Sabaoth—95(143).13-18//103(151).32-104(152).6

ΠΕϥϢΗΡΕ ΔΕ ΣΑ	ΣΑΒΑϢΘ ΔΕ ΠϢΗΡΕ
14 ΒΑϢΘ ΝΤΑΡΕϥΝΑΥ ΑΤΑΥΝΑΜΙΣ ΜΠΑΓ	33 ΝΙΑΛΛΑΒΑϢΘ ΝΤΑΡΕϥΣϢΤΜ [Ν]Τ
15 ΓΕΛΟΣ ΕΤΜΜΑΥ ΑϥΜΕΤΑΝΟΕΙ ΑϥΡΚΑ	34 ΣΜΗ ΝΤΠΙΣΤΙΣ Αϥ2ΥΜΝΕΙ ΕΡΟ[Σ Αϥ]
16 ΤΑΓΕΙΝϢΣΚΕ ΜΠΕϥΕΙϢΤ ΜΝ ΤΕϥΜΑΑΥ	35 ΚΑΤΑΓΕΙΝϢΣΚΕ ΜΠΕΙϢΤ [ΜΝ ΤΜΑΑΥ]
17 ΘΥΛΗ ΑϥΣΙΧΑΝΕ ΕΡΟΣ ΑϥΡ2ΜΝΕΙ ΔΕ	1 ΕΧΝ ΠϢΑΧΕ ΝΤΠΙΣΤΙΣ [Αϥ]† ΕΟΟΥ ΝΑΣ
18 Ε2ΡΑΙ ΕΤΣΟΦΙΑ ΑΥϢ ΤΕΣϢΕΕΡΕ ΝΖϢΗ	2 ΧΕ ΑΣΤΑΜΟΟΥ ΑΠΡϢΜΕ [Ν]ΑΘΑΝΑΤΟΣ
	3 ΜΝ ΠΕϥΟΥΟΕΙΝ ΤΠΙΣΤΙΣ ΔΕ ΤΣΟΦΙΑ ΑΣ
	4 ΣϢΤ ΜΠΕΣΤΗΗΒΕ ΕΒΟΛ ΑΣΠϢ2Τ ΑΧϢϥ
	5 ΝΟΥΟΕΙΝ ΕΒΟΛ 2Μ ΠΕΣΟΥΟΕΙΝ ΑΥΚΑ
	6 ΤΑΚΡΙΜΑ ΜΠΕϥΕΙϢΤ

2) The Ascent and Enthronement of Sabaoth—95(143).19-25//104(152). 6-31

	ΣΑΒΑϢΘ ΘΕ ΝΤΑ
	7 ΡΕϥΧΙ ΟΥΟΕΙΝ ΑϥΧΙ ΟΥΝΟ6 ΝΕϪΟΥΣΙΑ
	8 Ε2ΟΥΝ ΕΝΑΥΝΑΜΙΣ ΤΗΡΟΥ ΜΠΧΑΟΣ
	9 ΧΙΜ Π2ΟΟΥ ΕΤΜΜΑΥ ΑΥΜΟΥΤΕ ΕΡΟϥ ΧΕ
	10 ΠΧΟΕΙΣ ΝΝΒΟΜ ΑϥΜΕΣΤΕ ΠΕϥΕΙϢΤ ΠΚΑ
	11 ΚΕ ΑΥϢ ΤΕϥΜΑΑΥ ΠΝΟΥΝ ΑϥΣΙΧΑΝΕ Α
	12 ΤΕϥΣϢΝΕ ΠΜΕΕΥΕ ΜΠΑΡΧΙΓΕΝΗΤϢΡ
	13 ΠΕΤΝΝΑ ΕΤΝΝΗΥ 2ΙΧΝ ΜΜΟΟΥ ΕΤΒΕ

---

[1] Cf. Nagel, *Das Wesen der Archonten*, 15ff and Böhlig, *Die koptisch-gnostische Schrift ohne Titel*, 17.

19 ⲁⲩⲱ ⲁⲧⲥⲟⲫⲓⲁ ⲙⲛ ⲍⲱⲏ <u>ⲧⲟⲣⲡϥ ⲉⲍⲣⲁⲓ ⲁⲩ</u>
20 ⲕⲁⲑⲓⲥⲧⲁ ⲙⲙⲟϥ ⲉ<u>ⲭⲛ ⲧⲙⲉⲍⲥⲁϣϥⲉ ⲙⲡⲉ</u>
21 ⲡⲥⲁ ⲙⲡⲓⲧⲛ ⲙⲡⲕⲁⲧⲁⲡⲉⲧⲁⲥⲙⲁ ⲟⲩⲧⲉ
22 ⲡⲥⲁ ⲛⲧⲡⲉ ⲙⲛ ⲡⲥⲁ ⲙⲡⲓⲧⲛ ⲁⲩⲱ ⲁⲩⲙⲟⲩ
23 ⲧⲉ ⲉⲣⲟϥ <u>ϫⲉ ⲡⲛⲟⲩⲧⲉ ⲛⲛⲁⲩⲛⲁⲙⲓⲥ ⲥⲁ</u>
24 ⲃⲁⲱⲑ ϫⲉ ⲉϥⲙⲡⲥⲁ ⲛⲧⲡⲉ ⲛⲛⲁⲩⲛⲁⲙⲓⲥ
25 ⲙⲡⲭⲁⲟⲥ ϫⲉ ⲁⲧⲥⲟⲫⲓⲁ ⲕⲁⲑⲓⲥⲧⲁ ⲙⲙⲟϥ

14 ⲡⲉϥⲟⲩⲟⲉⲓⲛ ⲇⲉ ⲁⲛⲉϫⲟⲩⲥⲓⲁ ⲧⲏⲣⲟⲩ ⲕⲱⲍ
15 ⲉⲣⲟϥ ⲛⲧⲉ ⲡⲭⲁⲟⲥ ⲁⲩⲱ ⲛⲧⲁⲣⲟⲩϣⲧⲟⲣⲧⲣ
16 ⲁⲩⲉⲓⲣⲉ ⲛⲟⲩⲛⲟϭ ⲙⲡⲟⲗⲉⲙⲟⲥ ϩⲛ ⲧⲥⲁϣ
17 ϥⲉ ⲙⲡⲉ ⲧⲟⲧⲉ ⲧⲡⲓⲥⲧⲓⲥ ⲧⲥⲟⲫⲓⲁ ⲛⲧⲁⲣⲉⲥ
18 ⲛⲁⲩ ⲁⲡⲡⲟⲗⲉⲙⲟⲥ ⲁⲥϫⲟⲟⲩ ⲛⲥⲁⲃⲁⲱⲑ
19 ⲉⲃⲟⲗ ϩⲙ ⲡⲉⲥⲟⲩⲟⲉⲓⲛ ⲛⲥⲁϥϥ ⲛⲁⲣⲭⲁⲅ
20 ⲅⲉⲗⲟⲥ ⲁⲩⲧⲟⲣⲡϥ ⲉⲍⲣⲁⲓ ⲉⲧⲙⲁⲍⲥⲁϣϥⲉ ⲙ
21 ⲡⲉ ⲁⲩⲱϩⲉ ⲉⲣⲁⲧⲟⲩ ϩⲓⲧⲉϥϩⲏ ϩⲱⲥ ⲇⲓⲁⲕⲟ
22 ⲛⲟⲥ ⲡⲁⲗⲓⲛ ⲁⲥϫⲟⲟⲩ ⲛⲁϥ ⲛⲕⲉϣⲟⲙⲧ
23 ⲛⲁⲣⲭⲁⲅⲅⲉⲗⲟⲥ ⲁⲥⲥⲙⲛ ⲧⲙⲛⲧⲉⲣⲟ ⲛⲁϥ
24 ⲛⲧⲡⲉ ⟨ⲛ⟩ⲟⲩⲟⲛ ⲛⲓⲙ ϫⲉⲕⲁⲁⲥ ⲉϥⲛⲁϣⲱⲡⲉ
25 ⲙⲡⲥⲁ <u>ⲛϩⲣⲉ ⲙⲡⲙⲛⲧⲥⲛⲟⲟⲩⲥ ⲛⲛⲟⲩⲧⲉ</u>
26 ⲙⲡⲭⲁⲟⲥ ⲛⲧⲁⲣⲉⲥⲁⲃⲁⲱⲑ ⲇⲉ ϫⲓ ⲡⲧⲟⲡⲟⲥ
27 ⲛⲧⲁⲛⲁⲩⲡⲁⲩⲥⲓⲥ ⲉⲡⲙⲁ <u>ⲛⲧⲉϥⲙⲉⲧⲁⲛⲟⲓⲁ</u>
28 ⲉⲧⲓ ⲁⲧⲡⲓⲥⲧⲓⲥ † ⲛⲁϥ ⲛⲧⲉⲥϣⲉⲉⲣⲉ ⲛϩⲱⲏ
29 ⲙⲛ ⲛⲟⲩⲛⲟϭ ⲛⲉϫⲟⲩⲥⲓⲁ ϫⲉⲕⲁⲁⲥ ⲉⲥⲛⲁ
30 ⲧⲁⲙⲟϥ ⲁⲛⲉⲧϣⲟⲟⲡ ⲧⲏⲣⲟⲩ <u>ϩⲛ ⲧⲙⲁϩ</u>
31 <u>ϣⲙⲟⲩⲛⲉ</u>

3) Creation of the Throne/Chariot of Sabaoth—95(143).26-28//104 (152).31-105(153).16

26 <u>ϩⲟⲧⲓ ⲇⲉ ⲁⲛⲁⲉⲓ ϣⲱⲡⲉ ⲁϥⲧⲁⲙⲓⲟ ⲛⲁϥ</u>
27 <u>ⲛⲟⲩⲛⲟϭ ⲛϩⲁⲣⲙⲁ ⲛⲭⲉⲣⲟⲩⲃⲓⲛ ⲉϥⲟ ⲛ</u>
28 <u>ϥⲧⲟⲟⲩ ⲙⲡⲣⲟⲥⲱⲡⲟⲛ</u>

                    ϩⲱⲥ ⲉⲩⲛⲧⲁϥ ⲇⲉ ⲛⲟⲩⲉϫⲟⲩⲥⲓⲁ
32 ⲁϥⲧⲁⲙⲓⲟ ⲛⲁϥ ⲛϣⲟⲣⲡ ⲛⲟⲩⲙⲁ ⲛϣⲱ
33 ⲡⲉ ⲟⲩⲛⲟϭ ⲡⲉ ⲉϥⲧⲁⲉⲓⲏⲩ ⲉⲙⲁⲧⲉ ⲉϥⲟ ⲛ
34 [ⲥⲁϣ]ϥ ⲛⲕⲱⲃ ⲡⲁⲣⲁ ⲛⲉⲧϣⲟⲟⲡ ⲧⲏⲣⲟⲩ
35 [ϩⲛ ⲧⲥ]ⲁϣϥⲉ ⲙⲡⲉ ⲙⲡⲙⲧⲟ ⲇⲉ ⲉⲃⲟⲗ
1 ⲙⲡⲉϥⲙⲁ ⲛϣⲱⲡⲉ <u>ⲁϥⲧⲁⲙⲉⲓⲟ</u> ⲛⲟⲩⲉⲣⲟ
2 ⲛⲟⲥ ⲉⲩⲛⲟϭ ⲡⲉ ⲉϥϩⲓϫⲛ ⲟⲩϩⲁⲣⲙⲁ ⲉϥⲟ
3 ⲛϥⲧⲟⲟⲩ ⲙⲡⲣⲟⲥⲱⲡⲟⲛ ⲉⲩⲙⲟⲩⲧⲉ ⲉⲣⲟϥ
4 ϫⲉ ⲭⲉⲣⲟⲩⲃⲓⲛ ⲡⲭⲉⲣⲟⲩⲃⲓⲛ ⲇⲉ ⲟⲩⲛⲧⲁϥ
5 ⲙⲙⲁⲩ ⲛϣⲙⲟⲩⲛⲉ ⲙⲙⲟⲣⲫⲏ ⲕⲁⲧⲁ ⲡϥ
6 ⲧⲟⲩⲕⲟⲟϩ ϩⲙⲙⲟⲣⲫⲏ ⲙⲙⲟⲩⲉⲓ ⲁⲩⲱ ϩⲙ
7 ⲙⲟⲣⲫⲏ ⲙⲙⲁⲥⲉ ⲁⲩⲱ ϩⲙⲙⲟⲣⲫⲏ ⲣⲣⲱ
8 ⲙⲉ ⲙⲛ ϩⲙⲙⲟⲣⲫⲏ ⲛⲁⲉⲧⲟⲥ ϩⲱⲥⲧⲉ ⲙⲙⲟⲣ
9 ⲫⲏ ⲧⲏⲣⲟⲩ ⲥⲉⲉⲓⲣⲉ ⲛⲥⲉⲧⲁϥⲧⲉ ⲙⲙⲟⲣⲫⲏ
10 ⲁⲩⲱ ⲥⲁϣϥ ⲛⲁⲣⲭⲁⲅⲅⲉⲗⲟⲥ ⲉⲩⲁϩⲉⲣⲁⲧⲟⲩ
11 ϩⲓⲧⲉϥϩⲏ ⲛⲧⲟϥ ⲡⲉ ⲡⲙⲁϩϣⲙⲟⲩⲛ ⲉⲩⲛ
12 ⲧⲁϥ ⲉϫⲟⲩⲥⲓⲁ ⲙⲙⲟⲣⲫⲏ ⲧⲏⲣⲟⲩ ⲥⲉⲉⲓⲣⲉ
13 ⲛϣⲃⲉⲥⲛⲟⲟⲩⲥ ⲉⲃⲟⲗ ⲅⲁⲣ ϩⲙ ⲡⲉⲉⲓϩⲁⲣⲙⲁ
14 ⲁⲩϫⲓ ⲧⲩⲡⲟⲥ ⲛϭⲓ ⲡϣⲃⲉⲥⲛⲟⲟⲩⲥ ⲛⲛⲟⲩ
15 ⲧⲉ ⲁⲩϫⲓ ⲧⲩⲡⲟⲥ ⲁⲧⲣⲟⲩⲣⲁⲣⲭⲉⲓ ⲉϫⲛ ⲧϫⲃⲉ
16 ⲥⲛⲟⲟⲩⲥ ⲛⲁⲥⲡⲉ ⲛⲛϩⲉⲑⲛⲟⲥ

4) Creation of the Angels—95(143).28-31//105(153).16-106(154).3

                           ϩⲓϫⲛ ⲡⲉⲣⲟ
17 ⲛⲟⲥ ⲇⲉ ⲉⲧⲙⲙⲁⲩ ⲁϥⲧⲁⲙⲓⲉ ϩⲛⲕⲉⲁⲅⲅⲉ

            ⲘⲚ ⲜⲚⲀⲅⲅⲈⲖⲞⲤ

29 ⲈⲚⲀϢⲰⲞⲨ ⲈⲘⲚⲦⲞⲨ ⲎⲠⲈ ⲈⲦⲢⲞⲨⲢⲢⲨ

30 ⲠⲎⲢⲈⲦⲈⲒ

18 ⲖⲞⲤ ⲘⲘⲞⲢⲪⲎ ⲚⲀⲢⲀⲔⲰⲚ ⲈⲨⲘⲞⲨⲦⲈ ⲈⲢⲞ

19 ⲞⲨ ϪⲈ ⲤⲀⲢⲀⲪⲒⲚ ⲈⲨϮ ⲈⲞⲞⲨ ⲚⲀϤ ⲚⲚⲀⲨ

20 ⲚⲒⲘ ⲘⲚⲚⲤⲰⲤ ⲀϤⲦⲀⲘⲒⲞ ⲚⲞⲨⲈⲔⲔⲖⲎⲤⲒⲀ

21 ⲚⲀⲅⲅⲈⲖⲞⲤ ⲢⲚϢⲞ ⲘⲚ ⲢⲚⲦⲂⲀ ⲈⲘⲚⲦⲞⲨ

22 ⲎⲠⲈ ⲈⲤⲦⲚⲦⲞⲚⲦ ⲈⲦⲈⲔⲔⲖⲎⲤⲒⲀ ⲈⲦⲢⲚ

23 ⲦⲘⲀⲢϢⲘⲞⲨⲚⲈ ⲀⲨⲰ ⲞⲨϢⲢⲠⲘⲘⲒⲤⲈ

24 ⲈⲨⲘⲞⲨⲦⲈ ⲈⲢⲞϤ ϪⲈ ⲠⲒⲤⲢⲀⲎⲖ ⲈⲦⲈ ⲠⲀⲈⲒ

25 ⲠⲈ ⲠⲢⲰⲘⲈ ⲈⲦⲚⲀⲨ ⲈⲠⲚⲞⲨⲦⲈ ⲀⲨⲰ ⲔⲈ

26 ⲞⲨⲀ ϪⲈ ⲒⲎⲤ ⲠⲈⲬⲤ ⲈϤⲦⲚⲦⲰⲚ ⲈⲠⲤⲰⲦⲎⲢ

27 ⲈⲦⲢⲒ ⲠⲤⲀ ⲚⲦⲠⲈ ⲚⲦⲘⲀⲢϢⲘⲞⲨⲚⲈ ⲈϤ

28 ⲢⲘⲞⲞⲤ ⲢⲒ ⲞⲨⲚⲀⲘ ⲘⲘⲞϤ ⲢⲒϪⲚ ⲞⲨⲐⲢⲞ

29 ⲚⲞⲤ ⲈϤⲦⲀⲈⲒⲎⲨ ⲢⲒ ϬⲂⲞⲨⲢ ⲆⲈ ⲘⲘⲞϤ ⲈⲤ

30 ⲢⲘⲞⲞⲤ ⲚϬⲒ ⲦⲠⲀⲢⲐⲈⲚⲞⲤ ⲘⲠⲠⲚⲀ ⲈⲦⲞⲨ

31 ⲀⲀⲂ ⲢⲒϪⲚ ⲞⲨⲐⲢⲞⲚⲞⲤ ⲈⲤϮ ⲈⲞⲞⲨ ⲚⲀϤ

32 ⲀⲨⲰ ⲤⲈⲀⲢⲈⲢⲀⲦⲞⲨ ⲢⲒⲦⲈⲤⲈⲢⲎ ⲚϬⲒ ⲦⲤⲀ

            ⲀⲨⲰ ⲢⲘⲮⲀⲖⲦⲎⲢⲒⲞⲚ ⲘⲚ ⲢⲚ

31 ⲬⲒⲐⲀⲢⲀ

33 ϢⲞⲨ̣⟨ϥ̣⟩Ⲉ ⲘⲠⲀⲢⲐⲈⲚⲞⲤ ⲈⲨⲘ ⲘⲀⲀⲂⲈ ⲚϬⲒ̣[Ⲑ]Ạ̣

34 Ṛ̣Ạ ⲚⲦⲞⲞⲦⲞⲨ ⲘⲚ ⲢⲘⲮⲀⲖⲦⲎⲢⲒⲞⲚ [ⲘⲚ]

1 ⲢⲚⲤⲀⲖⲠⲒⲄⲜ ⲈⲨϮ ⲈⲞⲞⲨ ⲚⲀϤ ⲀⲨⲰ ⲚⲤⲦⲢⲀ

2 ⲦⲈⲨⲘⲀ ⲦⲎⲢⲞⲨ ⲚⲚⲀⲅⲅⲈⲖⲞⲤ ⲤⲈϮ ⲈⲞⲞⲨ ⲚⲀϤ

3 ⲀⲨⲰ ⲤⲈⲤⲘⲞⲨ ⲈⲢⲞϤ

5) The Instruction of Sabaoth—95(143).31-34//104(152).26-31 and 106 (154).3-11

                            ⲈϤⲢⲘⲞⲞⲤ ⲆⲈ ⲢⲒϪⲚ ⲞⲨ

4 ⲐⲢⲞⲚⲞⲤ ⟨ⲢⲚ ⲞⲨ⟩ⲞⲨⲞⲈⲒⲚ ⲚⲚⲞϬ ⲚⲔⲖⲞⲞⲖⲈ

                                   ⲈⲤⲤⲔⲈ

          ⲀⲨⲰ ⲀⲦⲤⲞⲪⲒⲀ ϤⲒ ⲦⲈⲤϢⲈⲈⲢⲈ Ⲛ

32 ⲌⲰⲎ ⲀⲤⲦⲢⲈⲤⲢⲘⲞⲞⲤ ⲢⲒ ⲞⲨⲚⲀⲘ ⲘⲘⲞϤ

33 ⲈⲦⲢⲈⲤⲦⲀⲘⲞϤ ⲀⲚⲈⲦϢⲞⲞⲠ [Ⲣ][Ⲛ] ⲦⲘⲀⲢ

34 ϢⲘⲞⲨⲚⲈ

5 ⲠⲀⲤⲈ ⲘⲘⲞϤ ⲀⲨⲰ ⲚⲈⲘⲚ ⲖⲀⲀⲨ ⲚⲘⲘⲀϤ

6 ⲢⲚ ⲦⲈⲔⲖⲞⲞⲖⲈ ⲈⲒⲘⲎⲦⲒ ⲀⲦⲤⲞⲪⲒⲀ ⲦⲠⲒⲤⲦⲒⲤ

7 ⲈⲤⲦⲤⲈⲂⲞ ⲘⲘⲞϤ ⲀⲚⲈⲦϢⲞⲞⲠ ⲦⲎⲢⲞⲨ ⲢⲚ ⲦⲘⲀⲢ

8 ϢⲘⲞⲨⲚⲈ ϪⲈⲔⲀⲀⲤ ⲈⲨⲚⲀⲦⲀⲘⲈⲒⲞ ⲚⲚⲦⲞⲚ

9 ⲦⲚ ⲚⲚⲎ ϢⲒⲚⲀ ⲦⲘⲚⲦⲈⲢⲞ ⲈⲤⲚⲀⲘⲞⲨⲚ ⲈⲂⲞⲖ

10 ⲚⲀϤ ϢⲀ ⲦⲤⲨⲚⲦⲈⲖⲈⲒⲀ ⲚⲘⲠⲎⲨⲈ ⲘⲠⲬⲀⲞⲤ

11 ⲘⲚ ⲚⲞⲨⲆⲨⲚⲀⲘⲒⲤ

6) The Separation into Right and Left—95(143).34-96(144).3//106(154). 11-19

                            ⲦⲠⲒⲤⲦⲒⲤ ⲆⲈ ⲦⲤⲞⲪⲒⲀ ⟨Ⲁ⟩Ⲥ

          ⲀⲨⲰ ⲠⲒⲀⲅⲅⲈⲖⲞ[Ⲥ ⲚⲦⲈ ⲦⲞ]Ⲣ̣

5 ⲄⲎ ⲀⲤⲔⲀⲀϤ ⲢⲒ ⲢⲂⲞⲨⲢ ⲘⲘⲞϤ [ϪⲒⲘ ⲪⲞ]

6 ⲞⲨ ⲈⲦⲘⲘⲀⲨ ⲀⲨⲘⲞⲨⲦⲈ ⲀⲦ̣[ⲈϤⲞⲨⲚⲀⲘ]

1 ϪⲈ ⲌⲰⲎ ⲀⲨⲰ Ⲧ̣ⲢⲂⲞ[Ⲩ]Ṛ̣ ⲀⲤϢⲰⲠⲈ ⲚⲦⲨⲠⲞⲤ

2 ⲚⲦⲀⲆⲒⲔⲒⲀ ⲚⲦⲘⲚⲦⲀⲨⲐⲈⲚⲦⲎⲤ ⟨ⲈⲦ⟩ ⲘⲠⲤⲀ Ⲛ

3 ⲦⲠⲈ ⲚⲦⲀⲨϢⲰⲠⲈ ⲢⲀⲦⲞⲨⲈⲢⲎ

12 ⲠⲞⲢϪϤ ⲈⲠⲔⲀⲔⲈ ⲀⲤⲘⲞⲨⲦⲈ ⲈⲢⲞϤ ⲈⲞⲨⲚⲀⲘ

13 ⲘⲘⲞⲤ ⲠⲀⲢⲬⲒⲄⲈⲚⲈⲦⲰⲢ ⲆⲈ ⲀⲤⲔⲀⲀϤ ⲢⲒ ϬⲂⲞⲨⲢ

14 ⲘⲘⲞⲤ ϪⲒⲘ ⲪⲞⲞⲨ ⲈⲦⲘⲘⲀⲨ ⲀⲨⲘⲞⲨⲦⲈ ⲈⲞⲨ

15 ⲚⲀⲘ ϪⲈ ⟨Ⲧ⟩ⲆⲒⲔⲀⲒⲞⲤⲨⲚⲎ ϬⲂⲞⲨⲢ ⲆⲈ ⲀⲨⲘⲞⲨ

16 ⲦⲈ ⲈⲢⲞⲤ ϪⲈ ⲦⲀⲆⲒⲔⲒⲀ ⲈⲦⲂⲈ ⲠⲀⲈⲒ ϬⲈ ⲀⲨϬⲒ

17 ⲦⲎⲢⲞⲨ ⲚⲞⲨⲔⲞⲤⲘⲞⲤ ⲚⲦⲈⲔⲔⲖⲎⲤⲒⲀ ⲚⲦⲀⲆⲒⲔⲀⲒ

18 ⲞⲤⲨⲚⲎ ⲘⲚ ⲦⲀⲆⲒⲔⲒⲀ ⟨ⲈⲤ⟩ⲀⲢⲈ Ⲉ⟨Ⲣ⟩ⲢⲀⲒ̈ ⲈϪⲚ

                                   ⲞⲨⲤⲰⲚⲦ

19 {ⲦⲎⲢⲞⲨ}

When one extracts from the two accounts the common elements, one can see clearly the amount of shared tradition. The following presents the wording common to both accounts but follows the order of NatArch. Understood in broken lines are words which although common, are not identical either in their placement within the narrative or their form.

13	пєсωнрє ⲇє ⲥⲁⲃⲁⲱⲑ	Now his offspring Sabaoth
14	ⲛⲧⲁⲣєⲥ	when
15	ⲁⲥⲙⲉⲧⲁⲛⲟⲉⲓ	he repented (repentance),
	ⲁⲥⲣ̅ⲕⲁⲧⲁⲅⲉⲓⲛⲱⲥⲕⲉ	he condemned
16	ⲙⲡⲉⲥⲉⲓⲱⲧ ⲙⲛ ⲧⲉⲥⲙⲁⲁⲩ	his father and his mother
17	ⲁⲥⲥⲓⲭⲁⲛⲉ ⲁⲥⲣ̅ϩⲩⲙⲛⲉⲓ	he loathed he sang songs of praise
18	ⲉϩⲣⲁⲓ ⲉⲧⲥⲟⲫⲓⲁ	to Wisdom (her)
19	ⲧⲟⲣ̅ⲡⲥ ⲉϩⲣⲁⲓ	they caught him up
20	ⲧⲙⲉϩⲥⲁⲱϥⲉ ⲙⲡⲉ	the seventh heaven
21		
22	ⲁⲩⲱ ⲁⲩⲙⲟⲩⲧⲉ	and they called
23	ⲉⲣⲟϥ ⲭⲉ ⲡ————ⲛⲛⲁⲩⲛⲁⲙⲓⲥ	him the God (Lord) of the Forces
24	ⲙⲡⲥⲁ ⲛⲧⲡⲉ (ⲛϩⲣⲉ)	above
25	ⲙⲡⲭⲁⲟⲥ	of chaos
26	ⲁϥⲧⲁⲙⲓⲟ ⲛⲁϥ	He made himself
27	ⲛⲟⲩⲛⲟϭ ⲛϩⲁⲣⲙⲁ ⲛⲭⲉⲣⲟⲩⲃⲓⲛ ⲉϥⲟ ⲛ	a huge chariot of Cherubim
28	ϥⲧⲟⲟⲩ ⲙⲡⲣⲟⲥⲱⲡⲟⲛ ⲙⲛ ϩⲛⲁⲅⲅⲉⲗⲟⲥ	four-faced and angels
29	ⲉⲙⲛⲧⲟⲩ ⲏⲡⲉ	infinitely many
30	ϩⲙ̅ⲯⲁⲗⲧⲏⲣⲓⲟⲛ ⲙⲛ ϩⲛ	and harps
31	ⲕⲓⲑⲁⲣⲁ ⲁⲩⲱ ⲁⲧⲥⲟⲫⲓⲁ	lyres. And Wisdom
	ⲧⲉⲥⲱⲉⲉⲣⲉ ⲛ	her daughter
32	ⲍⲱⲏ ϩⲓ ⲟⲩⲛⲁⲙ ⲙⲙⲟϥ	Life on his right
33	ⲉⲧⲣⲉⲥⲧⲁⲙⲟϥ ⲁⲛⲉⲧⲱⲟⲟⲡ [ϩ][ⲛ]ⲧⲙⲁϩ	to teach him about what exist
34	ⲱⲙⲟⲩⲛⲉ	in the Eighth
35	ⲁⲥⲕⲁⲁϥ ϩⲓ ϩⲃⲟⲩⲣ	she placed him on his
	[ⲭⲓⲙ ⲫⲟ]	left. Since
36	ⲟⲩ ⲉⲧⲙⲙⲁⲩ ⲁⲩⲙⲟⲩⲧⲉ	that day his right has
	ⲁ[ⲧⲉⲥⲟⲩⲛⲁⲙ]	been called
1	ⲧϩⲃⲟ[ⲩ]ⲣ̣	the left
2	ⲛⲧⲁⲇⲓⲕⲓⲁ	unrighteousness

From this identity of topic (Sabaoth), identity of sequence and identity of wording, one can conclude to the use of a common tradition. On the other hand, the lack of more extensive and more continuous verbal identity and the greater length and detail of OnOrg-Wld prevent one from concluding to literary dependence of OnOrgWld on NatArch or vice versa.

B. Possible Identifications of the Common Tradition

At this point we must consider the possibility that the common tradition behind NatArch and OnOrgWld is part of the book entitled *Norea*, which is referred to by Epiphanius. In his *Panarion* 26.1.3-9,[2] Epiphanius speaks of this book *Norea* and presents the story connected with this mythological figure Norea. Because of the impressive list of parallels between the contents of NatArch and the story of Norea, scholars have been divided in their assessment of the relationship between NatArch and this book entitled *Norea*:

1) Puech considered them identical.[3]
2) Doresse considered much of NatArch as an abridgement of this book *Norea*.[4]
3) Schenke denied the identity between the two.[5]
4) Böhlig denied the identity between the two and suggested that NatArch knew this book *Norea* and/or its traditions but that it was impossible to decide whether the source of NatArch and this book *Norea* were exactly the same.[6]
5) Bullard suggested that the revelation section of NatArch was once "an independent Revelation of Norea, but that it was not the same as that referred to by UW (OnOrgWld) or by Epiphanius."[7]

Surely Böhlig is right in denying that the present form of NatArch can be said to be identical with the *Norea* in Epiphanius. In his reference to this book *Norea*, Epiphanius merely relates the myth associated with the person of Norea. He does not indicate the genre, the limits or necessarily the full contents of this book.[8] Thus, it is impossible to say whether or not this *Norea* mentioned by Epiphanius contained a gnostic reinterpretation of Genesis, as the first half of NatArch does. If with Bullard one considers the possibility that the latter half of NatArch, the revelation section, is identical with *Norea*, the parallels are indeed striking. The following are the details mentioned by Epiphanius and found in NatArch 92(140).3-18 :

1) Norea is the wife of Noah.
2) She fights against the Ruler, the creator of the world.

---

[2] Ed. K. Holl 1 (GCS 25; Leipzig 1915) 27f.
[3] H.-C. Puech, "Les nouveaux écrits gnostiques," 120-22.
[4] J. Doresse, *The Secret Books of the Egyptian Gnostics*, 163.
[5] H.-M. Schenke, "Das Wesen der Archonten," 662-63.
[6] Böhlig, *Die koptisch-gnostische Schrift ohne Titel*, 31f.
[7] Bullard, *The Hypostasis of the Archons*, 101.
[8] I am grateful to B. Layton for calling this point to my attention.

3) Her husband, Noah, obeys the Ruler.
4) She reveals the existence of the powers above.
5) The creator seeks to destroy her in the flood.
6) She is not allowed to enter the Ark.
7) She burns the Ark three times (only two are recounted in NatArch).
8) Noah must rebuild it.

However, there are also differences in the source of Epiphanius, which must be noted :

1) Barbelo is the name of the mother above rather than Wisdom.
2) There is no mention of the repentance, ascent and enthronement of Sabaoth, the offspring of Ialdabaoth.
3) Norea teaches that what has been stripped from Barbelo, the mother above, must be regathered from the rulers. This motif is missing in NatArch.

Thus, it is clear that the revelation section of NatArch, even if it existed as an independent Revelation of Norea, is not the same as *Norea* in Epiphanius. Rather, one would have to say that both the Revelation of Norea and the book *Norea* in Epiphanius stem from the same stream of gnostic tradition. Thus also, for the purposes of our own concern here, the Sabaoth account in NatArch and OnOrgWld is not a part of the *Norea* referred to in Epiphanius.

A final possibility that we must consider here is that the common tradition about Sabaoth behind NatArch and OnOrgWld is part of the *First Book of Norea* or the *First Logos of Norea*, referred to in OnOrgWld 102(150).10f. and 24f. First, as Böhlig has suggested, these references are well taken as applied to the same piece.[9] Second, neither NatArch nor any of its parts is this *First Book or Logos of Norea*, since the further and more exact knowledge concerning the names and occupants of the seven heavens, supposed to be found in it, is not in NatArch. Third, it appears more probable that this *First Book or Logos of Norea* is not identical with NatArch or its parts but uses the same tradition. Thus, again, the *First Book or Logos of Norea* cannot be proved to be the written source behind the common tradition concerning Sabaoth in NatArch and OnOrgWld.

C. The Earlier Stage of the Tradition

If the two accounts derive from the same tradition, a further question is raised. Which account reflects a stage in the tradition,

---

[9] Böhlig, *Die koptisch-gnostische Schrift ohne Titel*, 32.

which is historically earlier? The mere observation that OnOrgWld is longer and fuller by no means establishes it as later. In the following pages it will be argued that OnOrgWld represents the later stage since its account contains internal contradictions and variations which can be identified as redactional elements. NatArch, on the other hand, presents a simpler, more consistent account in which the variations from OnOrgWld cannot be identified as redactional elements and therefore represents an earlier stage of the tradition.

As we begin our detailed analysis of the various sections, we turn first to the section on the repentance of Sabaoth. According to NatArch 95(143).14f it is "the strength of that angel" which prompted the repentance of Sabaoth, whereas in OnOrgWld 103(151).33f it is "the voice of Faith." This phrase in OnOrgWld exhibits secondary elements of the author and therefore represents the later stage of the tradition. *Sophia*, a single designation, had been the name of the OT hypostasis of Wisdom since the LXX translation (e.g. Prov 8:22-31; Sir 24:1-7; Wis 8:2ff). Through association with πίστις, although the reason for that association is as yet unclear,[10] Wisdom received a double name Faith-Wisdom, e.g. in NatArch 87(135).7-8; 94(142).5-6; 95(143).6. The origin of the name is still remembered in the formula "Wisdom, she who is called Faith" which occurs in NatArch 94(142). 5-6; Eug CG III, *3* : 82.5-6; and SJC BG 8502 : 103.7-9). In OnOrgWld, on the other hand, the origin has been forgotten so that the formula is inverted to "Faith, she who is called Wisdom" (98[146].13-14) and Faith alone can function as the name, as here (cf. also 99[147].2 etc.). NatArch, on the other hand, does not use the title Faith alone.

The "voice" of Faith is also redactional since it refers to the previous utterance of Faith concerning the immortal Light-Man, who is a major element in the author's own theology (103[151].15-28; cf. 104[152].2-3). To demonstrate this, we must first discuss the motif of light—and its opposite, darkness—in the treatise as a whole. This contrast between light and darkness expresses the basic dualism of the author's theology. In enunciating its central theme, the treatise has argued that something did exist before chaos (97[145].24ff). If one will grant the author that chaos is darkness and therefore a shadow, he believes that he can prove that the light existed previously (98[146].23-27):

> the Aeon (αἰών) of truth has
> no shadow within, for

---

[10] Cf. Gal 3 for the hypostatization of Faith.

the light (ογοειν) which has no measure
is throughout it. Its outside
is shadow. It is called darkness (κακε).

This theme, then, of the contrast between light and darkness pervades
the text. The term "light" (ογοειν) occurs 41 times and "darkness"
(κακε) 17 times in the text. Within the Sabaoth account alone light
occurs 6 times (and once more in the phrase "to receive light," χι
ογοειν) and darkness twice. On the other hand, in NatArch the
basic contrast is not between light and darkness. The realm above the
veil is termed imperishability (τμν̄ταττακο) rather than light—e.g.
94(142).4f.[11] That which is below the veil is termed more frequently
matter (ὕλη) than darkness—e.g. 94(142).4-12. Naturally enough,
though, such a familiar contrast as light versus darkness is presupposed
and does occur, e.g. 94(142).30-34. The motif of light occurs 7 times
and that of darkness 4 times—but note that in 3 of the 4 instances
the term appears in the phrase "the authorities or rulers of darkness"
rather than in contradistinction to the light: 86(134).22; 87(135).14;
92(140).23; and 94(142).33. However, neither term occurs in the Sabaoth account of NatArch.

One further illustration may show that the theme of light vs. darkness is part of the author's own theology and contribution to his
treatise. This illustration derives from the pericope concerning the
tree of the knowledge of good and evil in NatArch and OnOrgWld.
NatArch draws upon the biblical texts (Gen 2:17; 3:15, 22) and
speaks of the tree of knowledge of good and evil at 88(136).28-30
and inverts the order to evil and good at 90(138).1,10. Similarly,
OnOrgWld at 119(167).2-4 maintains the inversion and speaks about
knowing the difference between evil and good men. But at 120(168).
26-29 OnOrgWld diverges from both the biblical text and NatArch
to state that Adam knows the difference between "light and darkness."

In addition to and related to the importance of light for the
author of OnOrgWld is the importance of the immortal Light-Man.
Faith in OnOrgWld 103(151).19-28 in her response to the blasphemy
of the Demiurge proclaims that this Light-Man will appear in his
fashioning and trample upon him.[12] Sabaoth praises Faith that she

---

[11] Cf. also 87(135).1, 2, 12, 20; 88 (136).18; 93(141).29; 94(142).5. Even in 96(144).22
where the light occurs, it is the imperishable light and the light is opposed to matter
rather than darkness (96[144].18f).

[12] A further indication that this pericope derives from the hand of the redactor is
the occurrence of the term συντέλεια to indicate the end of time. It occurs frequently

has instructed him about this immortal Light-Man (104[152].1-3). Later that light does come from the Eighth, with the form of a man in it, and that angel is henceforth called the Light-Adam (108[156].2-22). After revealing himself upon the earth, the Light-Adam returns toward the light (111[159].29-112[160].1) but is unable to enter the Eighth because of the fault with which his light has been mixed. Therefore, he builds a great Aeon which is in a boundless region between the Eighth and chaos (112[160].10-22), i.e. the middle. In addition to this Light-Adam, the author distinguishes the psychic and choic Adams (117[165].28-36). Then, in accord with this description of the three Adams, for the author there are also three kinds of men and their races until the end of the world: the pneumatic of the Aeon, the psychic and the earthly (122[170].6-9). All souls are at first captured and enclosed in the bonds of matter (114[162].14ff). It is the light of gnosis, however, which makes one aware of the true situation (119[167].12-15). To complete his light theology, the author then adds that at the end of time the light will return to its root (127[175].4f) and the perfect ones will go to the unbegotten (127[175].5ff). Thus, the "voice" of Faith is redactional in this pericope, since it alludes to this theology of the immortal Light-Man, which is characteristic of the redactor's own theology.

Within this section on the repentance of Sabaoth the repetitive statement concerning "the condemnation (or hate) of the father" in OnOrgWld is also a later stage of the tradition. In NatArch (95[143]. 15f) the condemnation of the father is mentioned only once, and the father is simply to be identified as Ialdabaoth (95[143].2ff). OnOrg Wld (103[151].35) uses the exact same terms (καταγινώσκειν and πειωτ), and the father is probably to be identified here as well as Ialdabaoth (101[149].23; 102[150].11ff). The idea is repeated a few lines later (104[152].5f) in a synonymous phrase (ⲁⲩⲕⲁⲧⲁⲕⲣⲓⲙⲁ ⲙⲡⲉϥⲉⲓⲱⲧ). It is to be noted that here the father is left unidentified and that what makes possible the condemnation of the father is the light from Faith-Wisdom (lines 3ff). Again the idea is repeated in the clause "he hated his father" (ⲁϥⲙⲉⲥⲧⲉ ⲡⲉϥⲉⲓⲱⲧ 104[152].10). The motif of light has also been recalled as the source of this hate (line 7),

---

throughout the work in this usage in the phrase ⲧⲥⲩⲛⲧⲉⲗⲉⲓⲁ ⲙⲡⲁⲓⲱⲛ (seven times: 110[158].13; 114[162].24; 121[169].26f; 122[170].6, 33; 123[171].30; 125[173].32); ⲧⲥⲩⲛ-ⲧⲉⲗⲉⲓⲁ ⲙⲡⲕⲟⲥⲙⲟⲥ (122[170].7f); ⲧⲥⲩⲛⲧⲉⲗⲉⲓⲁ ⲅⲁⲣ ⲛⲛⲉⲧⲛϩⲃⲏⲩⲉ (103[151].25), ⲧⲥⲩⲛⲧⲉⲗⲉⲓⲁ alone (117[165].11; 123[171].19), and ⲧⲥⲩⲛⲧⲉⲗⲉⲓⲁ ⲛⲙⲡⲏⲩⲉ ⲙⲡⲭⲁⲟⲥ ⲙⲛ ⲛⲟⲩⲇⲩⲛⲁⲙⲓⲥ (106[154].10f).

and here the father is identified as darkness. As the previous discussion would indicate, the contrast between light and darkness suggests redactional expansion. Thereby, the repetition of the condemnation of the father can be understood—to incorporate the earlier tradition and at the same time to articulate the redactor's own dualistic contrast.

In the section concerning the ascent and enthronement of Sabaoth there are also several indications that NatArch represents the earlier stage of the tradition. In NatArch (95[143].22-24) Sabaoth receives a name "God of the Forces" as part of his enthronement and after he has been placed in charge of the seventh heaven. In OnOrgWld (104[152].3-10) Sabaoth receives his name "Lord of the Forces" prior to his ascent. The giving of the name appears to be more appropriate after the installation and as part of the enthronement (cf. Phil 2:6-10). Also, it is again the light from Faith-Wisdom, which gives him the great authority over the powers of chaos, which is thus the cause of his name, and which enables him to hate his father, the darkness. Since the redactional element of light versus darkness is present in the motif, it seems more probable that NatArch has preserved the earlier order. Thirdly, in our later discussion we shall see that the odd formulation "God of the Forces" is purposely constructed in NatArch in order to serve the original function of the Sabaoth account, i.e. Sabaoth is to be the *God* of the OT, a lower *God* beneath the transcendent God of the Eighth. OnOrgWld, on the other hand, has lost sight of this original function and thus returned to the customary name "Lord of the Forces."

The discrepancy over who "catch up" Sabaoth also provides an insight into the earlier stage of the tradition. NatArch 95[143].19f provides—quite consistently with the context—that Wisdom and Life catch him up. In OnOrgWld 104(152).17-21, on the other hand, Wisdom sends seven archangels, who have not been previously mentioned, to catch up Sabaoth. This sudden introduction of the seven archangels intrudes in the narrative; also since the seven archangels are necessary in another passage of the work (105[153].10-16) to reach the number of the seventy-two languages and gods, they appear as part of the interest of the author and thus as redactional elements in this passage. Another indication that the seven archangels derive from the redactor's hand is the presence of the motif of light. It is because of the light, which Sabaoth has, that the powers of chaos make war; and then it is because of the war that Faith-Wisdom from her light sends the seven archangels.

The pericope in OnOrgWld 104(152).22-26 concerning the three further archangels, who are sent to Sabaoth that he might be over the twelve gods of chaos, also represents the redactor's contribution. First, it is not clear why these three other archangels are then sent to Sabaoth; the figure may be a remnant of other calculations.[13] But, just as the seven previous archangels may be attributed to the redactor, so the inclusion of these further archangels is appropriately ascribed to the redactor. Secondly, the motif that Sabaoth has the "kingdom" occurs not only here (line 23) but also in another passage (106[154]. 9-11), which we shall identify as redactional.

One final pericope in this section concerning the ascent and enthronement of Sabaoth indicates that OnOrgWld represents the later stage of the tradition. At this point in the narrative, OnOrgWld 104(152).28-31 has Faith give her daughter Life to Sabaoth in order to instruct him concerning things in the Eighth. In similar wording (ⲧⲉⲥϣⲉⲉⲣⲉ ⲛ̄ⲍⲱⲏ ... ⲧⲁⲙⲟϥ ⲁⲛⲉⲧϣⲟⲟⲡ ... ϩⲛ̄ ⲧⲙⲁϩϣ̄ⲙⲟⲩⲛⲉ) NatArch 95(143).31-34 places this incident after the creation of the throne/ chariot. There are two signs of redactional elements in OnOrgWld —the name Faith alone (cf. above) and the phrase "with a great authority" (line 29). The phrase occurs in connection with the motif of the light, and the authority itself is derived from the light in 104 (152).4-8—again a sign of the redactor's hand. It is the authority then which is emphasized as the source of Sabaoth's ability to create his throne, chariot and other accoutrements (104[152].31). The instruction concerning the Eighth is later alluded to in the angelic church, which is "like the church in the Eighth" (105[153].20-23). If in fact the placement of the instruction of Sabaoth in OnOrgWld is due to the redactor, he accomplishes two things. He explains the source of Sabaoth's creative capacity; but by specifically directing Sabaoth's authority and knowledge to this ability, he also softens the importance of that knowledge for men. In discussing the function of the Sabaoth accounts, we shall see more completely the significance of that change. Briefly, in NatArch the instruction of Sabaoth concerning what exist in the Eighth serves to insure that the God of the OT has communicated some worthwhile revelation in the books of the OT; in OnOrgWld,

---

[13] Cf. ApocryJn BG 39.10-19 and CG III, *1* : 16.8-13 in which each authority under Ialdabaoth has seven angels and three powers or forces. In the BG version the number of angels is then given as 360, although the exact number of tabulation is not clear.

on the other hand, this function is bypassed and Sabaoth serves as king over all below him and as the type of the psychic class of men.

The section on the throne of Sabaoth in OnOrgWld is obviously longer. Use of the motif of the seven archangels here and also in 104(152).19f indicates that the section is an expansion of what is found in NatArch rather than that NatArch is a contraction of what is found in OnOrgWld.

In the section on the creation of the angels, OnOrgWld presents a fuller account with its reference first to the creation of Seraphim and then to the creation of the angelic church. There is no clear sign that the material on the Seraphim is a redactional addition to the earlier tradition. However, in the material on the creation of the angelic church there is one indication that OnOrgWld represents the later stage of the tradition. In NatArch 95(143).29-30 the angels are said to "minister" to Sabaoth (ὑπηρετεῖν). The term occurs only once in NatArch and therefore does not appear to be redactional. This same term occurs elsewhere in OnOrgWld at 102(150).23 and 123 (171).7, where Ialdabaoth is the recipient of the service, but in the parallel passage on the creation of the angels the expression is "to give him glory" (ϯ ⲉⲟⲟⲩ). The presence of this expression in the passage previously identified as reflecting the author's own theology (104 [152].1-3 "he gave her glory for she instructed them about the immortal Man and his light") and its frequency throughout the work suggest that it is a part of the redactor's material.[14]

Also within this section on the creation of the angels in OnOrgWld, the pericope concerning the creation of Jesus Christ (105[153].25-33) appears as part of the redactor's contribution. It is not necessary to the context. Rather, introduction of the right/left schema with Christ and the Holy Spirit overloads the scene and appears as a later development based on the righteousness or life/unrighteousness set. Elsewhere in the treatise the author refers to Christ (114[162].17) or the Savior (124[172].33) and alludes to the NT (125[173].14-19). Also, of course, there is no creation of Jesus Christ at this point in NatArch.

As we previously suggested, NatArch 95(143).31-34 preserves the earlier placement in the tradition of the section on the instruction of

---

[14] It is not possible, however, to separate ὑπηρετεῖν as preserved for Ialdabaoth and ϯ ⲉⲟⲟⲩ as preserved for figures associated with the light. To be sure, Faith at 104(152).1, Sabaoth at 105(153).19, 31 and 106(154).1, 2, and Adam after he has received a breath from Wisdom-Life at 115(163).23 are given glory. But Ialdabaoth can also be said to "receive glory" as at 103(151).5, 8; cf. 120(168).33f.

Sabaoth, as opposed to the first report of it in OnOrgWld 104(152).26-31. The second report in OnOrgWld 106 (154).3-11 then appears as another piece of tradition, which the redactor has incorporated into his text. First of all, the pericope is obviously a reduplication. Secondly, it contradicts the preceding report in that the former states that Life was given to Sabaoth to instruct him, while this latter pericope introduces the motif of the cloud and states that no one was within the cloud with him except Faith-Wisdom, whose role was to instruct him. Thirdly, it contradicts the following pericope as well, which states that rather than being alone, Sabaoth also has Ialdabaoth beside him. Fourthly, only in this pericope is the title rendered as Wisdom-Faith rather than Faith-Wisdom. This is particularly strange in a work where the title has been explained as "Faith, she who is called Wisdom" (98[146].14) rather than the customarily opposite—as we have previously discussed. Thus, the pericope is clearly an extra piece of tradition that interrupts the context. However, the pericope is also manifestly the work of the redactor rather than a later interpolator. The second purpose clause—"so that the kingdom might remain for him until the consummation (συντέλεια) of the heavens of the chaos and their powers"—betrays the theological concern and the terminological usage of the author in the term συντέλεια.[15] Thus, at least this second purpose clause stems from the hand of the redactor.

In the final section concerning the separation into right and left, NatArch 95(143).31-34 again exhibits the earlier stage of the tradition. It is consistent with the preceding account that Life and the angel that cast Ialdabaoth into Tartarus are seated at the right and left. The right was then called Life and the left became a type of unrighteousness. On the other hand, OnOrgWld 106(154).11-18 begins with a contradiction. Faith-Wisdom is said to separate Sabaoth from the darkness (line 11 f), although he has previously already been snatched up by the seven archangels (104[152].19-21). One notes also in the phrase "from the darkness" the hand of the redactor. Thirdly, introduction of the motif of righteousness appears as a slight interruption in the narrative since it has not been previously mentioned. Further, the term is significant for the author of OnOrgWld, since the righteousness is later said to fashion Paradise (110[158].2-13) within which grows the olive tree which will cleanse the kings and high priests of righteousness (111[159].2ff).

---

[15] Cf. supra, n. 12.

In conclusion, then, NatArch exhibits the earlier form of the tradition, which is common to it and to OnOrgWld. In the two interruptions in sequence—the giving of the name and the instruction of Sabaoth—NatArch preserves the earlier form. OnOrgWld, on the other hand, shows clearly a greater number of internal contradictions and redactional touches and thus must be deemed the later form of the tradition. In the following chapters, then, we shall exegete first the Sabaoth account in NatArch and then that in OnOrgWld in order to understand more precisely the motifs which are used, the traditions which are drawn upon, and the functions which are assigned to these Sabaoth accounts.

CHAPTER THREE

THE SABAOTH ACCOUNT IN NATARCH

A. Exegesis

In NatArch the Sabaoth account is set within the revelation discourse of the Angel Eleleth to Norea. The discourse itself follows the pattern : [1]

1) a mountain is the scene of the revelation 92(140).14
2) the appearance of the revealing angel from heaven 93(141).2-3
3) his self-presentation 93(141).6-10, 19
4) the revelations occur mainly in question and answer form 93(141).32ff

In response to the request of Norea that he teach her about the authorities—their capacity, their matter, and their creator—he reveals the myth of Wisdom (94[142].4ff). Imperishability exists above in the infinite aeons. Ultimately, because Wisdom desired to fashion a product alone, there came forth a shadow which became matter. From this matter the Demiurge took shape. For his blasphemy the Demiurge Ialdabaoth is at first rebuked by a voice from above (94[142].23ff). He then builds a great aeon and begets seven offspring (94[142].34ff). Because of his second blasphemy, he is cast into Tartarus (95[143].4ff). The Sabaoth account then follows, after which Ialdabaoth begets envy and thereby enables all of the heavens of chaos to be filled (96 [144].3ff). Then the angel Eleleth responds to questions of Norea as to whether she belongs to matter and how long a time must pass (96[144].17ff).

Within this discourse and within the presentation of the myth itself, the Sabaoth account forms a distinct unit. Since Sabaoth is presented as a child of Ialdabaoth, this unit is tied with what precedes it; and yet the focus of interest is now different—Sabaoth rather than Ialdabaoth. The unit closes when Ialdabaoth returns as the center of interest in 96(144).3.

---

[1] In this particular revelation discourse, the revelation is not accompanied by signs of theophany nor is there a curse formula at the end, as one might expect (cf. the description of the pattern by H. Koester in H. Koester and J. M. Robinson, *Trajectories Through Early Christianity* [Philadelphia 1971] 194-95).

1. *The Repentance of Sabaoth* 95(143).13-18

ΠЄϤϢΗΡЄ ΔЄ ϹΑ	Now (δέ) when his offspring
14 ΒΑϢΘ ΝΤΑΡЄϤΝΑΥ ΑΤΔΥΝΑΜΙϹ ΜΠΑΓ	Sabaoth saw the force (δύναμις) of
15 ΓЄΛΟϹ ЄΤΜ̄ΜΑΥ ΑϤΜЄΤΑΝΟЄΙ ΑϤΡΚΑ	that angel (ἄγγελος), he repented (μετανοεῖν) and
16 ΤΑΓЄΙΝⲰϹΚЄ Μ̄ΠЄϤЄΙⲰΤ Μ̄Ν ΤЄϤΜΑΑΥ	condemned (καταγινώσκειν) his father, and his mother,
17 ΘΥΛΗ ΑϤϹΙΧΑΝЄ ЄΡΟϹ ΑϤΡ̄ⲄΥΜΝЄΙ ΔЄ	matter (ὕλη). He loathed (σικχαίνειν) her. But he sang songs of praise (ὑμνεῖν) up
18 ЄⲀΡΑⲒ ЄΤϹΟΦΙΑ ΑΥⲰ ΤЄϹϢЄЄΡЄ Ν̄ⲌⲰΗ	to Wisdom (σοφία) and her daughter Life (ζωή).

The particle δέ links this new section with the preceding material. Sabaoth is here presented as one of the seven offspring of Ialdabaoth (95[143].2-3, 11), who represent the seven planets of astrology.[2] Unlike OnOrgWld 101(149).21 ff and Iren. *Adv. haer.* 1. 30, the names of the other offspring are not given. Although there is no hint within this section itself that Sabaoth is androgynous, all of the offspring have previously been identified as such (95[143].3). In the clause, "when he saw the strength of that angel," the author then refers to the previously related punishment of Ialdabaoth (lines 10-13) as the motive for the repentance of Sabaoth.

In this pericope as well as in the tractate as a whole, Ialdabaoth emerges from the conflation of three figures: that of the God of the OT, the leader of the fallen angels and the god ʿÔlam. First of all, Ialdabaoth is clearly identified as the God of the OT. In his mouth there is placed the claim of Yahweh to be the only God, a claim found in Deut 4:35 and 32:39 and frequently in 2 Isa (e.g. 43:10f; 44:6; 45:5f, 18, 21f; 46:9; cf. also Exod 20:5 and Joel 2:27).[3] Here the claim is considered as blasphemy and bespeaks the devaluation of that OT God.

Secondly, Ialdabaoth is also clearly identified as the leader of the fallen angels. He is called Samael (94[142].25), a name which is given to one of the fallen angels and/or their leader in the intertestamental literature and the Targumim (e.g. as the angel of death in TargPs-Jon on Gen 3:6; as a tempter in Mart Isa 1:8, 11f; 2:1ff; and as the equal to Satan in Asc Isa 2:1 and 3 Bar 4:8).[4] Further, motifs that are

---

[2] Cf. Bullard, *Hypostasis of the Archons*, 103-07.

[3] This same adscription is given to God at Qumran 1QS 11:18; 1QH 7:32; 10:9; 12:10.

[4] Cf. W. Bousset and H. Gressmann, *Die Religion des Judentums*, 4te Aufl. (HzNT 21; Tübingen 1966) 254, n. 1. In Iren. *Adv. haer.* 1.30.9 the serpent cast down is called Michael and Samael (ed. W. W. Harvey 1857; reprint Ridgewood 1965; 1. 236).

appropriate to the leader of the fallen angels are applied to him. His sin, for example, is that of blasphemous rebellion (94[142].21ff and 95[143].4ff). In late Jewish tradition, the fall of the angels was originally associated with Gen 6:1-4 and the $b^e n\hat{e}$ '$\hat{e}l\hat{i}m$, who took to wife the daughters of men; but their sin was that of lust for women and the revelation of the heavenly secrets (1 Enoch 6:2; 9:6f). Subsequently, because of influence from the tradition about Lucifer the sin was considered as blasphemous rebellion. In its origin, the tradition about Lucifer derives from that of Athtar of ancient Canaanite myth, who attempted to fill the throne of Baal but was found inadequate and therefore had to descend and rule in the underworld, just as the morning star retreats before the rising sun.[5] Isa 14:12-20 uses this tradition in its taunt against the king of Babylon and brings out the blasphemy in verse 14b: "I will make myself like the Most High" (cf. Ezek 28).[6] This same tradition is then applied to the rebellion of the leader of the fallen angels in *Vita Adae et Evae* 15:2f, as Michael speaks to the devil:

> And Michael saith, "Worship the image of God but if thou wilt not worship him, the Lord God will be wrath with thee." And I said, "If He be wrath with me, I will set my seat above the stars of heaven and will be like the Highest."[7]

Again this tradition occurs in 2 Enoch 29:4f (Rec. A):

> And one from out of the order of angels, having turned away with the order that was under him, conceived an impossible thought, to place his throne higher than the clouds above the earth, that he might become equal in rank to my power. And I threw him out from the height.[8]

It was but a short step for the gnostic then to change this rebellious assertion from the claim to be equal to God to the claim to be the only God. In particular, as the God of the OT was devalued, this step was

---

[5] L. R. Clapham, *Sanchuniathon: The First Two Cycles* (Ph.D. diss., Harvard University 1969) 150-53. He draws principally here upon Ugaritic Text 6.I (49.I).

[6] Clapham, *Sanchuniathon*, 152f. The otherwise helpful articles of W. Förster are deficient in that they do not take into account the Ras Shamra material: G. von Rad and W. Förster, διάβολος, *TDNT* 2 (1964) 71-81; W. Förster, σατανᾶς *TDNT* 7 (1971) 151-63.

[7] Text in W. Meyer, "Vita Adae et Evae," *Abhandl. phil-philol. Classe Akad. Wiss.* 14 (Munich 1878) 226. Translation from R. H. Charles, *APOT* 2. 137.

[8] *APOT* 2. 447. In Apoc Abr 14; 2 Enoch 7:3 (Rec. A); and 2 Enoch 18:3 the motif of rebellion is present, but the blasphemous desire to be equal to or higher than God is not present; in Asc Isa 4:1-8 Beliar uses the claim, which appears in the mouth of Ialdabaoth in gnostic writings. Cf. also Bousset, *Die Religion des Judentums*, 335.

made easier by considering the Yahwistic claim "to be the only God" as the blasphemy itself.

In reference to the origin of Gnosticism, we note that this motif of the blasphemous rebellion of the leader of the fallen angels derives not from the OT but from later Judaism. Further, this motif cannot be said to have influenced or to have been derived from the NT, since it is lacking there.[9]

A further motif appropriate to the leader of the fallen angels is that he is "bound and cast into Tartarus" (95[143].11f). Frequently in the intertestamental literature, the leader of the fallen angels is portrayed as bound and cast into the abyss, e.g. 1 Enoch 88:1 :

> And I saw one of those four who had come forth first, and he seized that first star which had fallen from the heaven, and bound it hand and foot and cast it into an abyss.[10]

Bullard in his commentary has correctly noted that Tartarus in this context is somewhat strange.[11] Usually, the fallen angels are kept in a place of internment (e.g. the desert in 1 Enoch 10:4 or the abyss in Jub 5:5f; 10:7-9; 1 Enoch 14:5; 88:3) and only at the end of time are they cast into the lower part of the abyss, the place of punishment (e.g. 1 Enoch 21:7-10; 90:24ff). However, the prior consignment of the fallen angels to Gehenna or Tartarus is not completely unattested. It occurs in the hymn of chapter 60 of Ps.-Philo's *Liber Antiquitatum Biblicarum*, a hymn which shows such close affinities to gnostic language (vv. 2f) :

> There were darkness and silence before the world was, and the silence spoke, and the darkness became visible. And then was thy name created, even at the drawing together of that which was stretched out, whereof the upper was called heaven and the lower was called earth. And it was commanded to the upper that it should rain according to its season, and to the lower that it should bring forth food for man that should be made. And after that was the tribe of your spirits made. Now therefore, be not injurious, whereas thou are a second creation, but if not, then remember Hell (lit. be mindful of Tartarus) wherein thou walkedst. Or is it not enough for thee to hear that by that which resoundeth before thee I sing unto man? Or forgettest thou that out of a rebounding echo in the abyss (or chaos) thy creation was born?[12]

---

[9] W. Förster, σατανᾶς, *TDNT* 7 (1971) 156-58.

[10] R. H. Charles, *The Book of Enoch*, 2d ed. (Oxford 1912) 189.

[11] Bullard, *The Hypostasis of the Archons*, 109.

[12] Text in G. Kisch, *Pseudo Philo's Liber Antiquitatum Biblicarum* (Publications in Medieval Studies 10; Indiana 1961) 261. Translation from M. R. James, *The Biblical Antiquities of Philo* (New York 1917) 232-33. Marc Philonenko ("Remarques sur un

As a final motif, the motif that from him comes death is also appropriate to the leader of the fallen angels.[13] As we previously mentioned, Samael can also be considered as the angel of death. Of course, the difference is that in this gnostic text death is considered as an offspring of Ialdabaoth.

Lastly, the figure of Ialdabaoth arises from the tradition concerning the god *'Ōlam/Aiōn* of ancient Canaanite theogonic myth. In a recent dissertation L. R. Clapham has demonstrated the reliability of the account of Sanchuniathon, translated by Philo Byblos and preserved in Eusebius' *Praeparatio evangelica* 1.10, for reconstructing ancient Canaanite theogonic myth.[14] He has been able to do so by an examination of new material—the Ras Shamra tablets, a newly-found Babylonian theogony,[15] the Hittite myths,[16] the Sefire treaty[17]—as well as by a reconsideration of biblical material—Gen 1 and the theogonic witnesses to covenant lawsuits, e.g. Mic 6:2a.

In the ancient Canaanite myths there is to be distinguished first of all the theogonic myth from the cosmogonic myth.[18] In the former the origin of the gods is presented and the myth is characterized by the language of procreation, by pairs whose names are abstract or natural opposites, and by gods whose abode is now the netherworld. They are the old gods, the dead gods, whose influence nevertheless is still felt in this world. In the latter type of myth the conflict or war is presented from which the victory of life and order comes. These are the younger or executive gods, whose cult is at present observed. Conflict among the gods can occur between the succeeding

---

hymn essénien de caractère gnostique," *Semitica* 11 [1961] 43-54) has argued that the hymn is both Essene and gnostic. However, he has only succeeded in showing an affinity of language between the hymn and Gnosticism.

[13] Cf. Bousset, *Die Religion des Judentums*, 253, n. 2.

[14] L. R. Clapham, *Sanchuniathon: The First Two Cycles.*

[15] W. G. Lambert and P. Walcot, "A New Babylonian Theogony and Hesiod," *Kadmos* 4 (1965) 64-72. The tablets date from the 7th-4th c. B.C. according to the authors.

[16] Especially the works of H. G. Guterbock: *Kumarbi: Mythen von churritischen Kronos, aus den hethitischen Fragmenten zusammengestell, übersetzt und erklärt*, (Istanbuler Schriften, No. 16; Zürich-New York 1946); "The Hittite Version of the Hurrian Kumarbi Myths: Oriental Forerunners of Hesiod," *AJA* 52 (1948) 123-34; "The Song of Ullikummi: Revised Text of the Hittite Version of a Hurian Myth," *JCS* 5 (1951) 135-61; 6 (1952) 8-42. These Hittite tablets date from 1400-1200 B.C.

[17] J. A. Fitzmyer, *The Aramaic Inscriptions of Sefire* (Rome 1967). The three steles and the treaties upon them date from the 8th c. B.C.

[18] I am indebted in what follows to the as yet unpublished paper of F. M. Cross, Jr., "Canaanite Myth and Hebrew Epic." Cf. also his book *Canaanite Myth and Hebrew Epic: Essays in the History of the Religion of Israel* (Cambridge 1973) 40-43.

generations in the theogony or between the younger gods and the old gods—especially between the head of the younger gods and the old gods. When the old gods are bound and cast into the netherworld, the victory for the young gods and for life and order is achieved.

In Canaanite myth then one can reconstruct that the promordial pair consisted of the East Wind (*Qodm*) and Chaos (*Bahot*). From the desire and union of East Wind with Chaos there resulted the second pair *ʿOlamu and *ʿOlamtu, the masculine and feminine forms of the epithet "Ancient" or "Eternal." In Greek the term is translated as *Aiōn* and can be seen, for example, in Euseb. *Praep. evang.* 1.10.7:

> Then, he says, there was begotten of the wind Kolpia (κολπία) and his wife Baau (βάαυ) (this, he explains, is Night) Aiōn.[19]

The final pair of the theogony then was Heaven and Earth. Thereupon the cosmogonic gods, El, Dagon (Baal) and Ashtarte followed.

In this gnostic text the similarity in basic principles to the Canaanite myth is striking. Wisdom takes the place of East Wind (94[142].5). However, this is not surprising in the light of late Jewish presentation of Wisdom as a spirit (e.g. Wis 1:6f; 7:22-24) and of gnostic exegesis of the *ruʿḥ* of Gen 1, e.g. ApocryJn BG 44:19-45:10:

> Then the mother began (ἄρχεσθαι)
> to move (ἐπιφέρεσθαι)
>   when she knew
> her fault, that
> her partner (σύζυγος) had not
>   agreed (συμφωνεῖν) with her
> when she was damaged (ψέγειν)
> in her fulness.
> But (δέ) I said, "Christ, what
> is 'to move' (ἐπιφέρεσθαι)?"
>   But (δέ) he
> laughed. He said, "Do you think
> that it is as Moses said
> 'over the waters?' No!"[20]

---

[19] Cf. Clapham, *Sanchuniathon*, 80ff for an analysis of this passage as well as the translation. In these pages Clapham follows the suggestion of Albright that ΚΟΛΠΙ is a corruption of ΚΟΔΜ, the figure of Canaanite myth; *Baau* he then derives from *Bohu*.

[20] Text from W.C. Till, *Die gnostischen Schriften des koptischen Papyrus Berolinensis 8502* (TU 60; Berlin 1955) 128-31; cf. CG II, *1*: 13.13-21; CG IV, *1*: 20.29-21.8; in CG III, *1* pages 19 and 20, where this account would appropriately fall, are missing. Cf. also the identification of Wisdom and the Spirit in the Barbelognostics in Iren. *Adv. haer.* 1.29.4 (ed. Harvey 1. 225). Cf. also O. Betz, "Was am Anfang Geschah," *Abraham unser Vater: Festschrift für Otto Michel*, ed. O. Betz, M. Hengel and P. Schmidt (Leiden 1963) 34-39.

The second principle is the shadow, which became matter and equals chaos. Because of Wisdom's will or desire, from that chaos comes Ialdabaoth (94[142].4-95[143].11).

As Clapham has pointed out, the name Ialdabaoth probably comes from two parts, *Ialda* and *baoth*, which mean "son of chaos." *Ialda* then would come from the root *yld* with a frozen accusative ending upon it and *baoth* would come from the same root as biblical *bōhû*. Originally the form of *bōhû* was **buhwu* in Hebrew or **bahwu* in Phoenician. By the process of normal vowel development in Phoenician, the final short vowel would be dropped and the first vowel **a* would be lengthened by stress to *ō* to produce *bōhw⟩bōhû*. Similarly, *baoth* in the gnostic name probably represents the feminine form of the same noun : **bahwatu⟩bahwat⟩bahwṓt⟩bahṓt*, which corresponds to Greek βαώθ.[21]

Lastly, Ialdabaoth is overcome and cast into the netherworld (95[143]. 11-13). In the Greek mythology, which is dependent upon the Semitic myths,[22] the old gods are bound and cast into the netherworld, which is explicitly identified as Tartarus, e.g. Hes. *Theog.* 713-35, 850-68.[23] Therefore, Ialdabaoth in this gnostic document is formed from the fusion of three figures. Or, better said, the God of the OT has been devalued by identifying him with the evil leader of the fallen angels and with the old, dead god Ialdabaoth and thereby presented as the source of this evil world.[24]

Before we can rest with this assertion, it is necessary to consider the possibility of influence from Canaanite myth upon a gnostic document because of the obvious and lengthy time span involved. First of all, it must be said that the myths were still known in the Graeco-Roman period. Philo Byblos lived from A.D. 64-140. Further elements of Canaanite myth are also preserved by Damascius in *De princ.* 125.3 and attributed to Mochus and Eudemus.[25] Secondly, recent studies have focused on the recrudescence of myth in apocalyptic. P. Hanson, for example, has shown the resurgence of Canaanite myth

---

[21] Clapham, *Sanchuniathon*, 39 ff.

[22] Cf. Lambert and Walcot, "A New Babylonian Theogony and Hesiod."

[23] Hesiod, "Theogony," *The Homeric Hymns and Homerica*, ed. and tr. H. G. Evelyn-White (LCL; Cambridge 1959) 130-33 and 140-43.

[24] Bullard's statement is thus true that this episode of the Demiurge is "the result of Jewish legend being worked into a previously existing myth" (*The Hypostasis of the Archons*, 50 f). But it should be modified somewhat in that the myth itself is also adapted to the legend.

[25] Damascius, *Problèmes et Solutions touchant Les Premiers Principes*, trad. A.-Ed. Chaignet (reprint Bruxelles 1964) 2.129-30.

in 3 Isa and Zech 9.[26] Similarly, scholars have concluded to the ancient
Canaanite myth concerning El and Baal as the most probable history-
of-religions background to the Ancient of Days of the Son of Man
in Dan 7.[27] Thirdly, on philological grounds the name Ialdabaoth
derives from West Semitic lore. Fourthly, it is important to note that
the genre is the same—a theogonic and cosmogonic myth. Lastly, just
as the royal cult carried mythical elements which were used in apocalyptic, so the apocalyptic groups could have carried these same
elements to the gnostics.[28] On these grounds it seems reasonable then
to postulate that ancient Canaanite myth, transmitted over the centuries,
has influenced this gnostic document.

It is necessary to note, however, that these myths not only re-surface
but that they are also reformulated and re-applied and thus, to this
extent, can be said to be secondary myth.[29] As we mentioned previously, Wisdom takes the place of East Wind in relation to chaos. Further,
as in the biblical transformation of the ancient cosmogonic myth,
there is a first principle, the Great Invisible Spirit (93[141].21-22)
or the Father (96[144].19-20), who is superior to Wisdom and chaos.
Further, Wisdom is here considered as androgynous.[30] Her desire
then is not a hetero-sexual one for chaos; it is rather the aberrant will
to make a work alone without her partner in the Ogdoad (94[142].6-7).
The result of this errant desire is then matter, which is chaos and out
of which Ialdabaoth proceeds. Next, it is Wisdom who by her angel
defeats Ialdabaoth; he is not defeated by one of his own offspring
or one of the younger gods as in Canaanite myth. We shall see the re-
application when we discuss the function of the Sabaoth account.

Recently, an alternate hypothesis to the preceding has been offered
by G. Scholem.[31] In his article he has criticized sharply those scholars

---

[26] P. Hanson, *The Dawn of Apocalyptic* (Philadelphia 1975); idem, "Jewish Apocalyptic Against its Near Eastern Environment," *RB* 78 (1971) 31-58; idem, "Old
Testament Apocalyptic Reexamined," *Interpretation* 25 (1971) 454-79.

[27] J. A. Emerton, "The Origin of the Son of Man Imagery," *JTS* N.S. 9 (1958)
225-42; C. Colpe, ὁ υἱὸς τοῦ ἀνθρώπου, *TDNT* 8 (1972) 400-30; F. M. Cross, Jr.,
Canaanite Myth and Hebrew Epic; Essays, 16-17.

[28] Hanson, "Jewish Apocalyptic Against its Near Eastern Environment," 34ff.

[29] Cf. Jonas, "Delimitation of the Gnostic Phenomenon," *Le Origini dello Gnosticismo*, 100-01.

[30] For the significance of the myth of the androgyne, see M. Eliade, *Mephistopheles
and the Androgyne: studies in Religious Myth and Symbol*, tr. J. M. Cohen (New York
1965) 78-124.

[31] G. Scholem, "Jaldabaoth Reconsidered," *Mélanges d'Histoire des Religions offerts
à Henri-Charles Puech* (Paris 1974) 405-21.

who derive Ialdabaoth from "son of chaos." He accuses them of philological inexactness in deriving the terms from non-existent Hebrew or Aramaic words. He then notes that in the Nag Hammadi documents (e.g. NatArch and OnOrgWld) chaos is called the mother of Samael, but the name Ialdabaoth is not used in these pericopes. Lastly, Scholem proposed that Ialdabaoth derives from two terms : the Aramaic active participle *yālēd* meaning "to beget" and the personal name Abaoth which originated as an abridged form or substitute of Sabaoth and which was used in magical circles. Ialdabaoth then is the secret name of Samael and means "the begetter of [S]abaoth" or "the begetter of Abaoth." The name for Scholem is probably connected with the fact that Ialdabaoth creates six or seven powers in the gnostic sources. Of these Scholem contends that Sabaoth or Abaoth was important since he occupied the main role among the powers and since the word sums up all the powers. The tale of Sabaoth's repentance is also taken by Scholem as a sign of Sabaoth's importance.

In response, one should note that Scholem does not consider the possible Canaanite background or the philological analysis of Clapham, who has recourse to the Phoenician rather than Hebrew or Aramaic language. Here one must grant to Scholem that Clapham's analysis ultimately rests on a hypothetical feminine form of the noun. Secondly, while Scholem is correct in observing that the *name* Ialdabaoth is not used, for example in NatArch 87(135)6-8, it is still remarkable that the *figure* known ultimately as Samael/Saklas/Ialdabaoth is here associated with origin from chaos, i.e. a son of chaos. Thirdly, it is not clear that Sabaoth is the most important of the powers for all the gnostics. For some gnostics Adonaios can be the most important power (e.g. GrSeth CG VII, 2; cf. ch. 4). The repentance of Sabaoth also does not prove that Sabaoth is the main figure among the powers, if our interpretation of the Sabaoth passage is correct. Rather, Sabaoth's repentance answers a particular need in the late second century for some gnostics (see infra). Lastly, Scholem's proposal involves a play upon words whether Sabaoth or Abaoth was the term combined with *yālēd*. If Sabaoth was used, it is indeed conceivable that Sabaoth could function as both the personal name of one god and the plural noun for many powers or gods. But then the omission of the "S" in Sabaoth is to be explained in Ialdabaoth. If Abaoth was used, it is clear that Abaoth could function as the personal name of one god (as Scholem has demonstrated) but it is less clear that Abaoth would have the further connotation of a plural noun for many powers or gods in the name Ialdabaoth. In conclusion, then, the origin of the name Ialdabaoth from the terms meaning "son of chaos" still seems to us the more likely hypothesis in accord with the interpretation of Clapham.

Sabaoth also arises from the conflation of three figures: those of the God of the OT, the leading angels, and the apocalyptic visionary. First of all, the name is clearly drawn from the OT God, Yahweh Sabaoth, as well as, of course, the portrayal of him upon a chariot of cherubim (Ezek 1, 10; Isa 6).

Secondly, the tradition concerning a leading angel, especially Michael, has influenced the figure of Sabaoth. In NatArch, Sabaoth is presented as a figure less than the high God who is against Satan (Ialdabaoth) from primordial time, enthroned, bears the name of the God of the OT, has power over chaos, and is the maker—and thus leader—of angels. In later Judaism similar features are ascribed to Michael or a leading angel. For example, Michael is the prince over Israel (Dan 10:13, 21; 12:1; 1 Enoch 20:5) and is the opponent of Satan—e.g. T Dan 6:1-4 (cf. NatArch 95[143].20ff):

> And now, fear the Lord, my children, and beware of Satan and his spirits. Draw near unto God and unto the angel that intercedeth for you, for he is a mediator between God and man, and for the peace of Israel he shall stand up against the kingdom of the enemy. Therefore is the enemy eager to destroy all that call upon the Lord. For he knoweth that upon the day on which Israel shall repent, the kingdom of the enemy shall be brought to an end.[32]

In the teaching of Qumran he is also the "Prince of Light," the "Spirit of Truth," who from primordial time is opposed to the "Prince of Darkness," and the "Spirit of Error" (1 QS 3:13-25).[33] He also appears at Qumran (1 QM 17:6-8), at least in the eschatological battle, as the angel who is installed in power over Satan, the Prince of Darkness (cf. NatArch 95[143].20ff):

---

[32] Text in R. H. Charles, *The Greek Versions of the Testaments of the Twelve Patriarchs* (Darmstadt 1960) 140 and translation from Charles, *APOT* 2. 335. Cf. W. Lueken, *Michael* (Göttingen 1898) 24-30 (cf. also Adam and Eve 12-17).

[33] For the identification of Michael as the Prince of Light, cf. F. M. Cross, Jr., *The Ancient Library of Qumran and Modern Biblical Studies* (rev. ed. New York 1961) 210-16 and Y. Yadin, *The Scroll of the War of the Sons of Light*, tr. B. and C. Rabin (Oxford 1962), 235f and O. Betz, *Der Paraklet* (Arbeiten zur Geschichte des Spätjudentums und des Urchristentums 2; Leiden 1963) 64-69.

6. He will send eternal assistance to the lot to be redeemed by Him through the might of an angel: He hath magnified the authority of Michael through eternal light

7. to light up in joy the house of Israel, peace and blessing for the lot of God, so as to raise amongst the angels the authority of Michael and the dominion

8. of Israel amongst all flesh.[34]

Although Michael does not bear the name of the God of the OT, in late Judaism a leading angel can be so described. Thus the angel Yaoel appears in the Apoc Abr 10 : "Go, Jaoel, and by means of my ineffable name raise me yonder man, and strengthen him (so that he recover) from his trembling."[35] Further, the "lesser Yahweh" of 3 Enoch 12:5; 48C:7; 48D:1, 102 and *Pistis Sophia* l. 7 both derive ultimately from Jewish speculation upon an angel bearing that name.[36] However, it must be admitted that there is no evidence of a leading angel who bears the name of Sabaoth.[37]

Michael is lastly the master over chaos (1 Enoch 20:5; cf. NatArch 95[143].23-25) and leader of the angels (1 QM 17:7; cf. NatArch 95[143].28).[38] In conclusion, then, it seems clear that the figure of a leading angel, especially Michael, has contributed to the portrayal of Sabaoth in this account.

Thirdly, the figure of the apocalyptic visionary has influenced the portrayal of Sabaoth. Later, in considering the tradition underlying this pericope, we shall discuss in greater detail the terminology and the pattern of motifs within the tradition concerning the apocalyptic visionary. For the moment it can be summarily stated that in apocalyptic the seer is taken up, receives a vision of the divine throne and/or chariot, and is then given revelation concerning secret mysteries. The seer himself can also be installed in heaven in a position of authority (e.g. Enoch in 1 Enoch 69-71; cf. also 2 Enoch 20-22). In the related traditions concerning Moses, he can sit upon the divine throne (e.g. Ezekiel the Tragedian in Euseb. *Praep. evang.* 9.29) and also be called God and king (*theos kai basileus*, Philo *De vita Mosis* 1.158). Similarly,

---

[34] Yadin, *The Scroll of the War*, 340f.

[35] G. H. Box, *The Apocalypse of Abraham* (London 1919) 46.

[36] Cf. Odeberg, *3 Enoch*, 188-92 for discussion of the matter. The references to the "little Yao" may be found in C. Schmidt-W. C. Till, *Koptisch-gnostische Schriften*, 3. Aufl. (GCS 45; Berlin 1962).

[37] However, cf. in Josh 5:14-15 the śar sᵉbā' YHWH. This reference was pointed out to me by Professor Cross.

[38] Cf. Lueken, *Michael*, 32-43.

Sabaoth is taken up, placed in charge of the seventh heaven, receives the name God of the Forces, fashions his own chariot, and then receives a revelation from Life.

In conclusion, then, Sabaoth has been formed from these three figures. Or, perhaps again better said, in these gnostic documents the God of the OT has been split in two—into a father who is totally evil and into an offspring, who is rehabilitated through Wisdom.

To return to the text from these lengthy discussions of Ialdabaoth and Sabaoth, we note that since Sabaoth had seen the angel cast his father down to Tartarus (95[143].10-15), he repented. In this context, the "strength of that angel" serves to terrify Sabaoth, to instill fear in him. Here, then, "to repent" (μετανοεῖν) is used in the sense familiar to Diaspora Judaism of a religio-ethical conversion, a change in one's relation to God.[39] In this case, however, there is no sin on the part of Sabaoth but rather his turning away from the blasphemous claim of Ialdabaoth and his turning toward Wisdom.

Besides repenting, Sabaoth condemned his father, namely, Ialdabaoth (95[143].2f).[40] Further, matter is identified as his mother and equally condemned as hostile to the heavenly realm. The metaphor that "matter is a mother" is not present in the OT or NT. However, in Plato's *Timaeus* within the universe the principle which receives forms is described as Μητὴρ τοῦ γεγονότος (51A) and also as τιθήνη (49A and 52D).[41] Then, Philo in a section alluding to the *Timaeus* draws upon this metaphor and identifies the receptive principle as matter. He utilizes the metaphor in *De ebrietate* 61 in an ethical context, in which he allegorically discusses the soul. Noticeable here, however, is the depreciation of matter as something negative. In sections 56-64 Philo is treating of the soul (ψυχή) and its relation with apparent goods. He admires the soul that confesses that it cannot withstand these but praises the mind (διάνοια), such as Sarah, who has no part with the mother's side and has only male parentage (Gen 20:12). Then in section 61 Philo describes Sarah in these words:

---

[39] Instead of ἐπιστρέφειν, μετανοεῖν becomes the translation equivalent of the OT שׁוּב in the later translations of the OT and in the later translations and/or compositions of the apocrypha and pseudepigrapha. Cf. J. Behm and E. Würtheim, μετανοέω, μετάνοια, *TDNT* 4 (1967) 989-95.

[40] Although the term καταγινώσκειν is rare in the LXX, it occurs at Deut 25:1 in the sense of courtroom condemnation.

[41] Plato, *Timaeus*, tr. R. G. Bury (LCL; Cambridge 1966) 112-13, 118-19, and 124-25.

She is not born of that material substance perceptible to our senses, ever in a state of formation and dissolution, the material (ὕλη) which is called mother (μητήρ) or foster-mother or nurse of created things by those in whom first the young plant of wisdom grew; she is born of the Father and Cause of all things.[42]

Similarly, in *Leg all* 2.51, when speaking about Levi, Philo uses this same metaphor of matter as a mother but in this case with the mind (νοῦς) considered as the father. Here it should also be noted that Levi leaves both father and mother since his portion is God. Philo writes :

This man forsakes his father and mother (μητήρ), his mind and material (ὕλη) body, for the sake of having as his portion the one God, "for the Lord himself is his portion" (Deut 10.9).[43]

Although this metaphor of "matter as a mother" then is not ultimately from Judaism, its usage by Philo indicates that its presence in this gnostic document could be mediated through Jewish circles.[44]

Next, Sabaoth is said to loathe (σικχαίνειν) his mother matter.[45] Then, in contrast, he is said to sing songs of praise up to Wisdom and her daughter Life. Usually in the OT it is God who is the object of praise, except for Prov 1:20 and 8:3 where Wisdom in the LXX is praised.[46] In this change in object from the usual, one sees in miniature the significance of Wisdom for Gnosticism.[47] Further, if in fact the Sabaoth account derives mainly from apocalyptic literature, we already see mirrored in this pericope a contributing factor to the rise of Gnosticism—the combination of wisdom and apocalyptic traditions.

---

[42] Philo, *De ebrietate* 61, ed. L. Cohn and P. Wendland (Berlin 1897) 2. 181; translation F. H. Colson and G. H. Whitaker, LCL (1960) 3. 349.

[43] Text in Cohn-Wendland, 1. 100 and translation from LCL (1962) 1. 257.

[44] Cf. also NatArch 94(142).12-18 in which matter is also considered as feminine and produces the abortion, who is Ialdabaoth. I am grateful to B. Layton for refining my understanding of these passages.

[45] The term σικχαίνειν does not appear in the LXX, Philo, or NT but does appear in the tranlation of Aquila.

[46] The Hebrew רן "to cry out" is rendered passively so that Wisdom is praised. Cf. G. Delling, ὕμνος κτλ, *TDNT* 8 (1972) 493-98. Also in the NT it is God who is either explicitly or implicitly the object of praise (Matt 26:30; Mark 14:26; Acts 16:25; Heb 2:12).

[47] Cf. U. Wilckens, σοφία, *TDNT* 7 (1971) 509, who writes that the Wisdom myth belongs to the basic foundation of the gnostic systems. However, this remark is appropriate only to certain systems based on a female principle within the Jewish and Christian forms of Gnosticism; cf. the systems based on a male principle in Jonas, *Gnosis und spätantiker Geist*, l. 335-51.

2. *The Ascent and Enthronement of Sabaoth* 95(143).19-25

19 ⲁⲩⲱ ⲁⲧⲥⲟⲫⲓⲁ ⲙⲛ̄ ⲍⲱⲏ ⲧⲟⲣⲡϥ ⲉ2ⲣⲁⲓ̈ ⲁϥ	And Wisdom and Life caught him up and
20 ⲕⲁⲑⲓⲥⲧⲁ ⲙ̄ⲙⲟϥ ⲉ.ⲭⲛ̄ ⲧⲙⲉ2ⲥⲁϣϥⲉ ⲙ̄ⲡⲉ	gave him charge (καθιστάναι) of the seventh heaven
21 ⲡⲥⲁ ⲙ̄ⲡⲓⲧⲛ̄ ⲙ̄ⲡⲕⲁⲧⲁⲡⲉⲧⲁⲥⲙⲁ ⲟⲩⲧⲉ	below the veil (καταπέτασμα)
22 ⲡⲥⲁ ⲛⲧⲡⲉ ⲙⲛ̄ ⲡⲥⲁ ⲙ̄ⲡⲓⲧⲛ̄ ⲁⲩⲱ ⲁⲩⲙⲟⲩ	between Above and Below. And they called[48]
23 ⲧⲉ ⲉⲣⲟϥ ϫⲉ ⲡⲛⲟⲩⲧⲉ ⲛ̄ⲛ̄ⲇⲩⲛⲁⲙⲓⲥ ⲥⲁ	him God of the Forces (δύναμις) Sabaoth,
24 ⲃⲁⲱⲑ ϫⲉ ⲉϥⲙ̄ⲡⲥⲁ ⲛⲧⲡⲉ ⲛ̄ⲛ̄ⲇⲩⲛⲁⲙⲓⲥ	because it is above the Forces (δύναμις) of
25 ⲙ̄ⲡⲭⲁⲟⲥ ϫⲉ ⲁⲧⲥⲟⲫⲓⲁ ⲕⲁⲑⲓⲥⲧⲁ ⲙ̄ⲙⲟϥ	the Chaos (χάος) that he is because Wisdom put him in charge (καθιστάναι).

Now that Sabaoth has repented and praised Wisdom and Life, they catch him up and place him in charge of the seventh heaven, where he is given a divine name and later fashions a chariot for himself and receives instruction concerning the eighth heaven. When we ask what tradition or traditions lie behind this material, the answer must be that two traditions from Judaism have been conflated here: the tradition concerning the apocalyptic visionary and the tradition concerning heavenly enthronement.

We begin with the tradition concerning the ascent of the apocalyptic visionary. First of all, we note that the term "to catch up" or "to snatch up" (ⲧⲱⲣⲡ ⲉ2ⲣⲁⲓ ἁρπάζειν)[49] is used in apocalyptic contexts for the translation to heaven (e.g. Enoch in Wis 4:11; Adam in Apoc Mos 37) or for the mystic rapture of the visionary (e.g. Paul in 2 Cor 12:2, 4).[50] Next, as for the chariot and instruction or revelation by Life, ultimately the material derives from the prophets Ezekiel (1, 10 and 43:3) and Isaiah (6), who have a vision of the divine chariot (מרכבה/ ἅρμα) and/or throne (כסא/θρόνος). But, then, within apocalyptic Judaism, the visionary is first snatched up or taken up, given a vision of the divine throne and/or chariot and then provided with a revelation concerning secret mysteries. For example, in 1 Enoch, Enoch in his dream vision is lifted up into heaven by the winds (14:8) and brought into a house within a house where he saw "a lofty throne: its

---

[48] The active translation "they called him" seems to me preferable to the passive translation "he is called" proposed by Layton, since the other verbs in the pericope are active, since the tense is perfect, since Wisdom and Life are available as the subjects and since the giving of the name seems to be part of the enthronement scene. If the verb were to be translated as "he is called," I should think that one would expect a present tense as in the clause "since he is up above the Forces of chaos."

[49] Cf. W. E. Crum, *A Coptic Dictionary* (Oxford 1962) 430b.

[50] See also 1 Thess 4:17 and Rev 12:5. Cf. W. Förster, ἁρπάζω, *TDNT* 1 (1964) 472-73. Note that in Wis 4:11 the verb refers not to the death (sic Förster 472, n. 2) but to the translation of Enoch.

appearance was as crystal, and the wheels thereof as the shining sun; and there was the vision of cherubim" (14:18).[51] As in Ezechiel, the association here of wheels and a throne indicates that the motifs of chariot and throne have been united. Enoch then receives revelation first in the form of audition. He is charged to bring the word of the Lord to the Watchers (14:24-16:4). Then he receives revelation in the form of vision and interpretation. He is taken through the cosmos and through Sheol in order to see the hidden places and treasuries, while the angel accompanying him explains all to him (17-36). Similarly, in the T Levi, in a dream-vision Levi ascends to heaven at the bidding of an angel (2:7). As he ascends through the three heavens their contents are revealed to him and explained by the accompanying angel (2:8-3:10). Upon arriving at the highest heaven, he is given a vision of the Most High upon his throne of glory (5:1). Then Levi receives the revelation that is more important for this document: "Levi, I have given thee the blessings of the priesthood until I come and sojourn in the midst of Israel" (5:2; cf. 8:2-19; 14:7; 16:1; 17-18).[52] Again in 2 Enoch, Enoch is taken up by angels (3:1) through the various heavens (3:2-19:6). Through vision and audition the contents of these heavens are revealed to him by the angels. Then finally he beholds the throne of the Lord and the glory of his face (20-22). Enoch himself is then transformed from his earthly garments (22:4-12). He is instructed first by the angel Pravuil or Vretil (23:1-6); then, after being seated at the left of the Lord near Gabriel, he is given the major revelation as he is instructed by the Lord concerning the origins of the cosmos (24-33).

Also in Apoc Abr one finds this pattern. In c. 15 Abraham is taken up by an angel and given a vision of the divine throne and chariot (17-18):

"And as I stood alone and looked, I saw behind the living creatures a chariot with fiery wheels, each wheel full of eyes round about; and over the wheels was a throne; which I saw, and this was covered with fire, and fire encircled it round about, and lo! an indescribable fire environed a fiery host. And I heard its holy voice like the voice of a man."[53]

In both vision and instruction by the Lord, the universe and also the history of mankind are then revealed to Abraham (19-29). Interestingly enough, for our purposes, the vision of mankind consists of multitudes of people on the right and multitudes on the left (21-22, 27). The

---

[51] Charles, *APOT*, 2. 197.
[52] Charles, *APOT*, 2. 307.
[53] Box, *The Apocalypse of Abraham*, 63.

history of the world is then told from this perspective with those of the right representing the people of God and those of the left representing the nations (21-29), some of whom are to be saved, and some damned (22).

Likewise in Test Abr this pattern is discernible. Abraham is lifted up by Michael into the heavens (10, Rec. A; 8, Rec. B) and receives a vision of a throne. However, here there are two thrones, one for Adam (11, Rec. A; 8, Rec. B) and one for Abel (12-13, Rec. A; cf. also 11, Rec. B, where the second throne, however, is not explicitly mentioned). Also through vision and through the instruction of Michael a revelation is given to Abraham, especially about the judgment of souls after death (11-14, Rec. A; 8-12, Rec. B). Again, for our purpose, it is important to note that there is an angel on the right who represents the righteous and an angel on the left who represents the wicked (12-14, Rec. A).[54] From these two late pieces of apocalyptic literature, Apoc Abr and Test Abr,[55] one can conclude that the motif of separation into right and left became incorporated as a final part of this tradition concerning the ascent of the apocalyptic visionary in late Judaism.

As one considers this pattern of the ascent of the apocalyptic seer, his vision of the throne/chariot and reception of revelation, it is important to note that there are variations. The seer may behold not only God upon his throne but also some other important figure upon a throne (e.g. Adam or Abel in Test Abr 11-12, Rec. A). Secondly, the seer himself may be transformed into one like an angel and seated in heaven (Enoch in 2 Enoch 22). Or the seer may be himself installed in a position of power, i.e. enthroned (e.g. Enoch in 1 Enoch 69-71). The revelation may then consist in a vision of the judgment that is given by the enthroned figure (e.g. Test Abr 11-12, Rec. A). Lastly,

---

[54] This same pattern can be found in Christian apocalyptic material. For example, in Rev John ascends (4:1), sees the throne (4:2-11) and then receives revelation by vision and audition (5:1-22:7). In Asc Isa after Isaiah ascends (7:2f), he sees the praise of the Lord but not the glory of the Lord itself (10:1-3) and then receives the revelation concerning the future descent of Christ into the world, his life and death and reascent (10:7-11:36).

[55] Box dates the Apoc Abr between the fall of Jerusalem and the early decades of the second century (*The Apocalypse of Abraham*, XVI) and the Text Abr in its original form to the first half of the first century A.D. (G.H. Box, *The Testament of Abraham*, London 1927, XXVIII). Schmidt dates the short recension of Test Abr to the same period and proposes the first half of the second century A.D. for the longer recension (F. Schmidt, *Le Testament d'Abraham*, Diss. Strasbourg 1971, 1. 119-20).

the judgment upon men may be made in terms of a distinction between right and left (e.g. Apoc Abr 21-39; Test Abr 12-14, Rec. A).

It is clear then that the Sabaoth account draws upon this tradition of the ascent of the apocalyptic seer. The terminology is the same (ⲧⲱⲣⲡ ⲉϩⲣⲁⲓ/ἁρπάζειν, ἅρμα). The sequence of motifs is the same: ascent, the chariot/throne, revelation by instruction and the separation into right and left. Here Sabaoth not only ascends but is also installed in a position of power. As we have seen, the variety within the tradition of the apocalyptic seer also provides examples of this possibility.

While the main and direct influence upon the Sabaoth account derives then from apocalyptic literature, we would not exclude but rather include further influence from Diaspora Judaism. Specifically, some traditions concerning Moses, which are themselves related to the traditions found in apocalyptic literature, portray Moses as seated upon God's own throne (Ezekiel the Tragedian in Euseb. *Praep. evang.* 9.29) and given the name of God and king (Philo *De vita Mosis* 1.158). However, in these passages the reference is to a throne rather than chariot and there is no mention of separation into right and left.

Specifically new in the Sabaoth account are the context of time (i.e. as the origin of the universe), the application of this tradition to the son of the Demiurge rather than to a mortal, his repentance prior to ascent, and the fashioning of rather than simply the vision of the chariot. Also new is the fact that Wisdom and Life take Sabaoth aloft rather than an angel or angels as in apocalyptic literature (e.g. Apoc Abr 15). Again, in this alteration we see in miniature the confluence of the wisdom and apocalyptic traditions.

After his ascent, Sabaoth is placed in charge of the seventh heaven. In translating the phrase as "installed him over the seventh heaven," Bullard [56] has failed to see that underlying the Coptic usage ⲕⲁⲑⲓⲥⲧⲏⲙⲓ ⲉⲝⲛ is the Greek idiom καθίστημι ἐπί "to place in charge of."[57]

---

[56] Bullard, *The Hypostasis of the Archons*, 37.

[57] καθίστημι appears frequently in the Hellenistic period in the sense of "to place in charge of," or "to set in an office" or "to install" (cf. W. Bauer, *Griechisch-deutsches Wörterbuch zu den Schriften des Neuen Testaments und der übrigen urchristlichen Literatur*, 5. Aufl. (Berlin 1958) 771. The verb can be used absolutely with only an accusative object, e.g. Tit 1:5, but appears more frequently with the preposition ἐπί (cf. A. Oepke, καθίστημι, *TDNT* 3 [1965] 444-47). This idiom καθίστημι ἐπί is then rendered as ⲕⲁⲑⲓⲥⲧⲙⲓ ⲉⲝⲛ in the Sahidic NT at Matt 25:21. Besides installation as king, e.g. Ps 2:6 LXX, the term can apply to other offices (e.g. high priest 1 Macc 10:22 LXX) or responsibilities (e.g. Matt 25:21).

Subsequently Sabaoth will receive a name, fashion a chariot, and henceforth have the right hand called life and the left hand called unrighteousness.

It seems to us that the Sabaoth account here conflates the tradition concerning heavenly enthronement with that of the ascent of the apocalyptic visionary.[58] When Sabaoth is placed in charge of the seventh heaven, he is installed as king although he is not given the title. We shall see that Sabaoth then functions to rule over those who are not gnostics, while the gnostics belong to the "kingless race" (97[145].4-5).

Recent studies, especially those of P. Hanson, have strikingly illuminated the myth and ritual pattern which underlies enthronement material in Judaism.[59] Basically the myth relates that in response to a threat the divine warrior appears, defeats his enemies, returns to assume his kingship which is evidenced in the building of his temple, and then manifests his reign. Within the Mesopotamian realm

---

In the NT καθίστημι also appears frequently in the same senses noted above. However, it does not occur in the scenes of heavenly enthronement (e.g. Phil 2:9 ὑπερυψοῦν; Eph 1:22 ὑποτάσσειν; δίδωμι κεφαλήν; Heb 1:3 καθίζειν ἐν δεξιᾷ).

[58] By heavenly enthronement, I mean installation in heaven in royal power, whether in fact the person sits on a throne or not. For the sake of terminological clarity, I also follow the distinctions of G. W. E. Nickelsberg, Jr., who writes: "Hereafter, I use 'exaltation' to mean exaltation to authority, 'assumption' to mean the translation of the soul or spirit to heaven immediately upon death, and 'ascension' and 'elevation' to mean a literal going up to heaven, with no specification of time (before death, immediately after death, or at the time of a future resurrection)." His remarks are found in *Resurrection, Immortality, and Eternal Life in Intertestamental Judaism* (HTS 26; Cambridge 1972) 82, n. 134. To this list of terms one should also add "installation of a prophet" as the transfer of authority to the prophet. It would be further helpful to distinguish not only the terms but also the traditions of enthronement, installation as prophet, and exaltation. Besides over-utilization of Mesopotamian parallels and under-utilization of Canaanite material, the basic flaw, for example, in Geo Widengren's book *The Ascension of the Apostle and the Heavenly Book* (Acta Universitatis Upsaliensis 7; Uppsala 1950) is the failure in the period of the classical prophets to distinguish installation of a prophet from enthronement of a king. In this regard, he is followed by J. P. Schultz, "Angelic Opposition to the Ascension of Moses and the Revelation of the Law," *JQR* 61 (1971) 282-308. On the installation of a prophet, see F. M. Cross, Jr., "The Council of Yahweh in Second Isaiah," *JNES* 12 (1953) 274-77; G. E. Wright, "The Lawsuit of God: A Form Critical Study of Deuteronomy 32," *Israel's Prophetic Heritage: Essays in Honor of James Muilenburg*, ed. B. W. Anderson and W. Harrelson (New York 1962) 41-43; K. Baltzer, "Considerations Regarding the Office and Calling of the Prophet," *HTR* 61 (1968) 567-81. For the tradition of exaltation, particularly in some intertestamental texts, see Nickelsberg, *Resurrection, Immortality and Eternal Life*.

[59] P. Hanson, *The Dawn of Apocalyptic*; idem, "Jewish Apocalyptic Against its Near Eastern Environment"; idem, "The Old Testament Apocalyptic Reexamined."

the classical statement of this myth occurs in the Enūma Eliš.[60] This same mythical pattern is found as well in a simplified form in the Apsu-Ea conflict of tablet I : i.e. threat (37-58), combat-victory (59-70), and temple built (71-77).[61] Also in the Baal cycle from Ugarit, Hanson has found the same ritual structure as the most common reconstruction of the Baal-Yam conflict.[62]

Israel as well drew upon the myth and ritual pattern of this material but directed it towards its own historical experience. Thus, Israel interpreted the Conquest in terms of the triumph of Yahweh as the Divine Warrior. In one of the earliest examples of Israelite poetry, Exodus 15, we find this same pattern in a hymn from the League, which celebrates the ritual conquest. Specifically, as Hanson suggests, the pattern is as follows :[63]

Combat-Victory (vv. 1-12)
Theophany of Divine Warrior (8)
Salvation of the Israelites (13-16a)
Procession and Building of Temple (16b-17)
Manifestation of Yahweh's Universal Reign (18)

---

[60] Hanson presents the pattern in detail as follows in *The Dawn of Apocalyptic*, 302 :
Threat (I : 109-II : 91)
Combat-Victory (IV : 33-122)
Theophany of Divine Warrior (IV : 39-60)
Salvation of the Gods (IV : 123-46; VI : 1-44; cf. VI : 126-27, 149-51)
Fertility of the Restored Order (V : 1-66; cf. VII : 1-2, 59-83)
Procession and Victory Shout (V : 67-89)
Temple Built for Marduk (V : 117-56; VI : 45-68)
Banquet (VI : 69-94)
Manifestation of Marduk's Universal Reign (anticipated : IV : 3-18; manifested : VI : 95-VII : 144)
[61] Hanson, *The Dawn of Apocalyptic*, 303.
[62] In detail Hanson provides the following pattern in *The Dawn of Apocalyptic*, 302 :
Threat (2.1[137])
Combat-Victory (2.4[68])
Temple Built (4[51])
Banquet (4.6.39 ff.[51])
Manifestation of Baal's Universal Reign (anticipated : 2.4.9-10[68]; manifested : 4.7.9-12[51])
Theophany of Divine Warrior (4.7.27-39[51])
Fertility of Restored order (anticipated : 4.5.68-71[51]; effected : 4.7.18-30[51]; cf. 6.3.6-7, 12-13[49]).
[63] Hanson, *The Dawn of Apocalyptic*, 301. Cf. F. M. Cross, Jr., and D. N. Freedman, "The Song of Miriam," *JNES* 14 (1955) 237-50; and Cross, *Canaanite Myth and Hebrew Epic, Essays*, 16-17.

The psalms, and particularly the enthronement psalms (Ps 47, 93, 95-99) demonstrate that the old mythic patterns were kept alive in the royal cult at Jerusalem. Thus in Ps 47, for example, the victory of Yahweh is portrayed in the opening verses (2-5). The procession or ascent of the Lord (v. 6) is followed by the acclamation of Yahweh as king (vv. 7-8). In the following verses (9-10), then, his universal reign is made manifest.[64] Similarly, in the royal psalm, Ps 2, this pattern is maintained with the added motif that the Davidic king has been adopted by Yahweh as his son (v. 7; cf. also Ps 110).

Within proto-apocalyptic this material again re-surfaces. As Hanson has shown, the oracle in Zech 9 recapitulates the ancient myth and ritual pattern and the League pattern of ritual conquest.[65] In his dissertation, W. Millar has extended this analysis to the cycles of the Isaiah Apocalypse (Isa 24-27) and shown that the same pattern is visible in this material, i.e. Yahweh's battle and victory (Isa 24:1-13, 18c-23; 25:10-12; 26:1-27:1), the procession with the Ark to the temple (26:1-8), and the beginning of reign with the victory feast upon the mount (Isa 25:6-8).[66]

It is also now clear that the dream-vision of Dan 7, an example of full-blown apocalyptic, reflects ancient Canaanite myth. The picture of the transcendent God, the Ancient of Days, has been presented in El-language, while the one like a son of man, the symbol for the true Israel in v. 27, has been presented in Baal-language.[67] However, the pattern remains the same.[68] The threat to the divine council is present in the emergence of the four beasts from the sea (vv. 3-8). The victory occurs through the judgment and destruction of the beasts (vv. 9-12). The enthronement of this one like a son of man and the manifestation of his reign occur through his presentation to the Ancient

---

[64] Hanson, *The Dawn of Apocalyptic*, 307.

[65] Specifically, he sets forth its pattern as follows in *The Dawn of Apocalyptic*, 315f:
Conflict-Victory (vv. 1-7)
Temple Secured (8)
Victory Shout and Procession (9)
Manifestation of Yahweh's Universal Reign (10)
Salvation: Captives Released (11-13)
Theophany of Divine Warrior (14)
Sacrifice and Banquet (15)
Fertility of Restored Order (16-17)

[66] W. R. Millar, *Isaiah 24-27 and the Origin of Apocalyptic* (Ph.D. diss., Harvard University 1970) 95ff, 156-75, 190ff.

[67] Emerton, "The Origin of the Son of Man Imagery"; Colpe, ὁ υἱός τοῦ ἀνθρώπου; Cross, *Canaanite Myth and Hebrew Epic*; *Essays*, 16-17.

[68] Hanson, "Old Testament Apocalyptic Reexamined," 474ff.

of Days and installation in royal power : "And he came to the Ancient of Days and was presented before him. And to him was given dominion and glory and kingdom, that all peoples, nations, and languages should serve him; his dominion is an everlasting dominion, which shall not pass away, and his kingdom one that shall not be destroyed" (Dan 7:13b-14).

The vision of 1 Enoch 71, with its Son of Man and Head of Days, is apocalyptic and obviously draws consciously upon Dan 7. Here the apocalyptic seer Enoch, after being translated in spirit to heaven and being shown by Michael the temple of the Lord and his throne, is proclaimed to be the Son of Man. He is the one who is enthroned as the Son of Man;[69] he is the one who is installed in this position of power and authority. His reign then is characterized by peace, righteousness and length of days :

> He proclaims unto thee peace in the name of the world to come;
> For from hence has proceeded peace since the creation of the world,
> And so shall it be unto thee for ever and for ever and ever.
> And all shall walk in *thy* ways since righteousness never forsaketh *thee* :
> With *thee* will be their dwelling-places, and with *thee* their heritage,
> And they shall not be separated from *thee* for ever and ever and ever.
> And so there shall be length of days with that Son of Man,
> And the righteous shall have peace and an upright way
> In the name of the Lord of Spirits for ever and ever"
>
> (vv. 15-17)[70]

In this passage concerning Enoch, then, we see the conflation of two traditions, that of the ascent of the apocalyptic seer and vision of the throne of the Lord and that of the heavenly enthronement. It is because of the conflation of these two tradition that the motifs of the threat, battle and victory of the Divine Warrior, are omitted in favor of the ascent of the apocalyptic visionary from this scene of heavenly enthronement.

In two other instances we find the conflation of these two traditions outside apocalyptic literature but within the literature of Diaspora Judaism. In both cases, it is Moses who is the seer. The first instance

---

[69] V. 14a perhaps echoes the adoption formula of Ps 2:7.

[70] Charles, *The Book of Enoch* (1912) 145-46. At the underlined *thee* or *thy*, I have followed the reading of the text rather than Charles' emendation and translation into the third person, *him* or *his*. 2 Enoch 22:6, Targ Ps-Jon on Gen 5:24 and 3 Enoch witness the possibility of such an exaltation of Enoch; cf. also Bousset, *Die Religion des Judentums*, 353-54, who has argued for the reading of the text rather than for emendation.

occurs in Ezekiel the Tragedian, probably an Alexandrian dramatist of the 2d c. B.C.,[71] wherein Moses recounts to his father-in-law a dream that he has had:

> Methought upon Mount Sinai's brow I saw
> A mighty throne that reached to heaven's high vault,
> Whereon there sat a man of noblest mien
> Wearing a royal crown; whose left hand held
> A mighty sceptre; and his right to me
> Made sign, and I stood forth before the throne.
> He gave me then the sceptre and the crown,
> And bade me sit upon the royal throne,
> From which himself removed. Thence I looked forth
> Upon the earth's wide circle, and beneath
> The earth itself, and high above the heaven.
> Then at my feet, behold! a thousand stars
> Began to fall, and I their number told,
> As they passed by me like an armed host:
> And I in terror started up from sleep.[72]

The biblical starting point for this composition by Ezekiel is obviously the ascent of Moses on Mt. Sinai to receive the Law from God (Exod 19f and 24). However, equally clearly, Ezekiel has expanded upon that biblical incident by presenting God there as sitting upon a throne with crown and sceptre[73] and by portraying Moses as receiving these emblems of royalty, a vision of the universe and the homage of the stars. Cerfaux has seen in this passage an influence from Orphism.[74] However, in the proposed Orphic fragments there is neither

---

[71] Fragments from Ezekiel's drama *The Exodus* were taken over by Alexander Polyhistor (80-40 B.C.) and thence preserved in Eusebius, *Praep. evang.* 9.29 and Clement of Alexandria, *Stromateis* 1.23.155. Cf. E. Schürer, *Geschichte des jüdischen Volkes im Zeitalter Jesu Christi*, 4. Aufl. (Leipzig 1909) 3.502 and W. Meeks, *The Prophet-King: Moses Traditions and the Johannine Christology* (NovTSup 14; Leiden 1967) 149. In what follows I am also indebted to the seminar paper of J. Robertson, "Ezekiel the Tragedian: Scholia," N.T. Seminar Papers, Harvard Divinity School, May 8, 1970.

[72] Text in Eusebius, *Die Praeparatio Evangelica*, hrsg. K. Mras (GCS 43.1; Berlin 1954) 529; trans. from E. H. Gifford, *Eusebii Pamphili, Evangelicae Praeparationis*, vol. 3, part 1 (Oxford 1903) 470. J. Strugnell in "Notes on the Text and Metre of Ezekiel the Tragedian's 'Exagoge'," *HTR* 60 (1967) 451, n. 6, suggests plausibly that the text in line 11 should be emended from παρέδωκε to πάρδωκε in order to secure the proper metre.

[73] The "man of noblest mien" must represent God; cf. the Ancient of Days in Dan. 7.

[74] L. Cerfaux, "Influence des Mystères sur le Judaisme Alexandrin avant Philon," *Le Muséon* 37 (1924) 54-58. As Orphic fragments, he refers in this article (pp. 36ff) to ps-Justin, *Cohortatio ad Graecos* 15 and *De Monarchia* 2; Clement of Alexandria,

a parallel in form nor in content.[75] On the other hand, the influence of biblical and apocalyptic tradition upon this scene is clear. Regarding the form of this passage, one should first note the dream with its interpretation by another person in Gen 37:9f (cf. the allusion here to Joseph's dream in the motif of the "stars" paying homage to Moses) and by an angel in Dan 7 as well as the dream-vision in 1 Enoch 14. In drawing upon this form from biblical and apocalyptic tradition Ezekiel Tr has retained it here, since it is also appropriate to Greek drama.[76] Concerning its content, like the apocalyptic seer, Moses after his ascent sees the divine throne and then receives as his revelation a vision of what is upon the earth, beneath the earth, and above the heaven (cf. 1 Enoch 14ff; 2 Enoch 3ff). Probably the motif of homage of the stars derives from Gen 37:9, while the motif of the stars which form the host of heaven and whose number can be told comes from Isa 40:26. In his wide-ranging study, Meeks has shown that the motif of Moses' ascent on Mt. Sinai as his enthronement as king occurs not only in intertestamental literature but also in Rabbinic and Samaritan literature and plausibly suggests an early exegetical tradition as the source of these disparate phenomena.[77]

The function of the dream-vision is then made clear in the interpretation rendered by Moses' father-in-law :

Stromateis 5.14.123-24; and Eusebius, *Praep. evang.* 13.13.12.5. He is followed in this view by E. R. Goodenough in *By Light, Light: The Mystic Gospel of Hellenistic Judaism* (New Haven 1935) 290f and in *Jewish Symbols in the Greco-Roman Period* (New York 1964) 9. 101.

[75] The form of the Orphic fragments is not that of a dream as here in Ezekiel Tr. The Orphic fragments contain a vision of the Lord upon his heavenly throne; however, there is no enthronement of the seer.

[76] A. Kappelmacher in "Zur Tragödie der hellenistischen Zeit," *Wiener Studien: Zeit. für klassische Philologie* 44 (1924-25) 78f has provided examples of the use of dreams in Greek dramas (e.g. the dream of Atosia in Aeschylus, *Persians*) but also noted that interpretation of the dream *by another person* is not customary. Rather, dreamers usually interpret their own dreams. For interpretation by another person he can only point to one drama, *Brutus* of Accius; in addition he refers to the Roman *Praetextata* and Cicero, *De divinatione* 1.44. Cf. also B. Snell, "Ezechiels Moses-Drama," *Antike und Abendland* 13 (1967) 154-55, who points to the dream of Jacob or Joseph as the inspiration of this passage, since the dreams of Greek drama are those of ill fate rather than heavenly enthronement. Meeks, however, only points to Greek tragedy, *The Prophet-King*, 148.

[77] Meeks, *The Prophet-King*, 194; cf. Deut 33:5 as a scriptural starting point for Moses as king. For the motif of sitting upon the throne of Yahweh, can the inspiration be such a passage as 1 Chr 29:23 (cf. 1 Chr 28:5), when transposed to a heavenly setting (cf. Dan 7)?

> This sign from God bodes good to thee, my friend.
> Would I might live to see thy lot fulfilled!
> A mighty throne shalt thou set up, and be
> Thyself the leader and the judge of men!
> And as o'er all the peopled earth thine eye
> Looked forth, and underneath the earth, and high
> Above God's heaven; so shall thy mind survey
> All things in time, past, present and to come.[78]

Moses is to set up a "mighty throne." We suggest the hypothesis that this "mighty throne" represents not only the dynasty but also the kingdom or nation, which Moses is ultimately to found when he leads the people out of Egypt (cf. 2 Sam 3:10 and 1 Kgs 2:4). This throne is to be more than just the men whom he will "lead and judge"; it is to be the enduring Jewish nation, to which even the diaspora Jew was related.[79] For Ezekiel Tr the Jewish people are not only God's chosen people (cf. *Praepar. evang.* 9.29.8; Mras [GCS 43.1] 530.23-27), but also by the heavenly enthronement of Moses the nation is validated as divinely established. Although Moses sits upon the throne and receives the emblems of kingship, he does not receive the title king, probably in order to remain closer to the biblical text and also to reserve the title king for the king of Egypt (e.g. *Praepar. evang.* 9.29.8; Mras [GCS 43.1] 530.30f).[80]

---

[78] Text Mras (GCS 43.1) 529-30; tr. Gifford, *Eusebii Pamphili*, 470.

[79] Cf. the similar idea in Aristobulus: τὴν ἐξαγωγὴν τὴν ἐξ Αἰγύπτου τῶν Ἑβραίων, ἡμετέρων δὲ πολιτῶν—Eusebius, *Praepar. evang.* 13.12.1; Mras (GCS 43.1) 190f.

[80] In the final scene of the drama, a marvelous bird—most probably the phoenix— appears. It is difficult to find the exact reason for the appearance then of this bird, and thus various suggestions for it have been made in the past. R. Van den Broek on the basis of his extensive study *The Myth of the Phoenix according to Classical and Early Christian Traditions* (Études Préliminaires aux Religions Orientales dans l'Empire Romaine 24; Leiden 1972) 122, has offered the most plausible explanation, i.e. the appearance of the phoenix marks the beginning of a new era (his use, here, however, of the much later Coptic Sermon on Mary as an interpretative aid is methodologically questionable). In support of this interpretation, one may point to the appearance of the phoenix at the re-accession of Seleucus I to power in 312 B.C. and the inauguration of the Seleucid era (cf. Pliny, *Historia naturalis* 10.4-5; tr. H. Rackham, LCL, Cambridge 1940, 3. 294-95) and at the attempt to introduce a new calendar during the reign of Ptolemy III Euergetes (cf. Tacitus, *Annals* 6.28; tr. J. Jackson, LCL, Cambridge 1937, 3. 200-03; cf. also Van den Broek, 103-09). If this interpretation is correct, it would seem to tie together the beginning (the enthronement scene) and the end of the drama. Although it is true that only in later literature does the phoenix appear in order to mark the accession of a new king (cf. Van den Broek, 115ff), yet here it is probably the installation of Moses as king, the choice of a people, and the foundation of the nation by the events of the *Exodus*, which together mark the inauguration of the new era. In *Praepar. evang.* 9.29.16 (Mras [GCS 43.1] 538.2f) this bird is described as the βασιλεὺς δὲ πάντων ὀρνέων, behind whom all the other

The interpretation, which Moses' father-in-law gives to the vision, also provides an insight into a further function of this scene. The vision by Moses of what is upon the earth, under the earth, and above the heaven is interpreted to mean that Moses' mind will survey "all things in time past, present, and to come." It is important to note the change in this interpretation from the vertical to the horizontal, from the cosmological to the historical. We suggest that Ezekiel has incorporated the apocalyptic tradition's interest in cosmological secrets in the dream-vision but re-interpreted that material and applied it to Moses' legacy to his people, the Law. As in a similar interpretation in Philo, which we shall see presently, "the things in time past" refer to Genesis; those in "the present" to Exodus through Deuteronomy; and those "to come" at least to the foretelling of his death in Deut 31 and the future events for the twelve tribes in Deut 33. Just as the vision of the apocalyptic seer validates not only himself but also his words and the books that circulate in his name (cf. Dan 12:4, 9; 1 Enoch 104:9-13; 2 Enoch 33:3-10; 36:1-2), so the vision of Moses authenticates him and the books that circulate in his name, i.e. the Pentateuch.[81] Thus, through this scene of heavenly ascent and enthronement those whom Moses leads out of Egypt and their descendants are guaranteed to be the divinely founded nation and God's chosen people with His sacred scriptures.

The second instance within diaspora Judaism of the ascent and enthronement of Moses occurs in Philo's treatise *De vita Mosis* 1.158:

> Again, was not the joy of his partnership with the Father and Maker of all magnified also by the honor of being deemed worthy to bear the same title? For he was named god and king of the whole nation, and entered, we are told, into the darkness where God was, that is into the unseen, invisible, incorporeal and archetypal essence of existing things. Thus he beheld what is hidden from the sight of mortal nature, and, in himself and his life displayed for all to see, he has set before us, like some well-wrought picture, a piece of work beautiful and godlike, a model for those who are willing to copy it. Happy are they who imprint, or strive to imprint,

---

birds hovered in fear. Is this a symbolic statement that the new nation of Israel is to rule over the other peoples?

[81] W. Meeks, in his essay "Moses as God and King," *Religions in Antiquity : Essays in Memory of Erwin Ramsdell Goodenough*, ed. J. Neusner (Leiden 1968) 367-69, stresses the function of the ascent and vision as the validation of the prophet and the guarantee of esoteric tradition attached to his name. We would extend that insight and apply it to exoteric material as well as to books, which circulate in the prophet or seer's name. Thereby, the books, which diaspora Judaism particularly revered, the Pentateuch, are given the same guarantee.

that image in their souls. For it were best that the mind should carry the form of virtue in perfection, but, failing this, let it at least have the unflinching desire to possess that form.[82]

Once again the biblical starting point is the ascent of Moses upon Mt. Sinai. As in Ezekiel Tr, this ascent of Moses is considered as his enthronement. Strikingly new is the fact that Moses receives a name and that name is "god." From *De sac.* 8f we can see that Philo's exegetical basis for attributing this name to Moses was Exod 7:1 "See I make you as God to Pharaoh"[83] and that Philo attributed this name quite seriously to him.[84] In *De sac.* 8f Philo argues against attributing to Moses the common biblical phrase "N. died and was added to his people." His reason is that since God cannot be added to and since Moses is God, therefore Moses cannot be added to. However, in *Quod det.* 161-62 Philo uses this same scriptural text to demonstrate that the usage here is not literal : "when Moses is appointed 'a god unto Pharaoh,' he did not become such in reality, but only by a convention is supposed to be such."[85] Rightly then can Meeks conclude from these passages as follows :

> Furthermore, while the biblical text is used in "The Sacrifices of Abel and Cain" to show that Moses' translation was the return of the perfect soul to the One who Is, Philo's other descriptions of Moses' assumption clearly depict the apotheosis of a divine *man*, not the return of an incarnate deity as Goodenough suggests. The distinction is important; while Philo does vacillate in his portrait of Moses, now elevating him virtually to a "second god" again restricting him to the sphere of the human, the vacillation remains with the compass of the θεῖος ἀνήρ.[86]

At his enthronement Moses is not only named god but also king. He was king of all the people who departed with him from Egypt, king of a nation destined to be consecrated above all others (*De vita Mosis* 1.147ff).[87] But he is king also over the whole world :

> And so, as he abjured the accumulation of lucre, and the wealth whose influence is mighty among men, God rewarded him by giving him instead

---

[82] Text and tr. F.H. Colson, LCL (Cambridge 1966) 6. 356-59.

[83] LCL (1968) 2. 98-101. Philo's version of Exod 7:1 is δίδωμι γάρ σε θεὸν φαραώ.

[84] Cf. also *De poster. C.* 28; *De gig.* 47ff; *Quod deus immut.* 23; *De conf.* 30f; *Q. Exod* 2, 40.

[85] LCL (1968) 2. 309.

[86] Meeks, *The Prophet-King,* 105. Goodenough refers to the incarnation of Moses in his *An Introduction to Philo Judaeus,* 2d ed. (Oxford 1962) 145.

[87] "The appointed leader of all these was Moses, invested with this office and kingship" LCL (1966) 6. 353; cf. Ezekiel Tr above.

the greatest and most perfect wealth. That is the wealth of the whole earth and sea and rivers, and of all the other elements and the combinations which they form. For, since God judged him worthy to appear as a partner of his own possessions, He gave into his hands the whole world as a portion well fitted for his heir. Therefore, each element obeyed him as its master, changed its natural properties and submitted to his command.[88]

As the basis for this gift of kingship to Moses, Philo offers three reasons, which Meeks has appropriately termed the haggadic, the philosophical and the mystic.[89] The haggadic reason consists in the fact that Moses was destined to receive the kingship of Egypt and yet willingly renounced it for the sake of God's people. Therefore, he was appropriately granted by God the kingship over them (*De vita Mosis* 1.148-49). Secondly, as the philosophical reason, Moses was appointed king "on account of his goodness and his nobility of conduct and the universal benevolence which he never failed to show."[90] Thirdly, he was appointed king as the paradigm of all those who achieve the mystic ascent and vision.[91]

In this respect, the tradition concerning the ascent of the seer is particularly significant. Like the apocalyptic seer, Moses ascends to heaven, but his vision here in *De vita Mosis* 1.158f is not of the throne of God and what is upon the earth and under the earth. Rather, Moses entered into the darkness where God was, "into the unseen, invisible, incorporeal and archetypal essence of existing things"; and thus he "beheld what is hidden from the sight of mortal nature." It is important to notice the dualism that is expressed in this passage. The divine realm is the realm of the essential over against which the earthly is merely "child's play."[92] However, although he considers the earthly of less value, Philo is not anti-cosmic as the gnostics. For him God is still the creator of the universe (*De vita Mosis* 1.212f).

The form which expresses this ascent and enthronement is no longer the dream-vision as in Dan 7 and Ezekiel Tr. The narrative description, which Philo employs for this scene, is due no doubt to the genre within

---

[88] *De vita Mosis* 1.155-56; LCL (1966) 6. 356-57.

[89] Meeks, *The Prophet-King*, 108 ff.

[90] *De vita Mosis* 1.148; LCL (1966) 6. 353.

[91] *De vita Mosis* 1.158-59; LCL (1966) 6. 356-59. Cf. Meeks, *The Prophet-King*, 111; Goodenough, *By Light, Light*, 205 ff.

[92] *De vita Mosis* 1.190: "Such, too, is the nature of the mind of those who have tasted of holiness. Such a mind has learned to gaze and soar upwards, and, as it ever ranges the heights and searches into divine beauties, it makes a mock of earthly things, counting them to be but child's-play, and those to be truly matters of earnest care." LCL (1966) 6. 375.

which he is writing, the treatise. Perhaps, it is due also to the desire to stress the reality of Moses' own ascent and mystic vision as the paradigm for others.

While Philo discussed Moses as king in his first book of the *De vita Mosis*, in the second book he treats the other offices which are proper to Moses, namely, legislator, high priest and prophet. His editorial comments—such as, "And of them it may be justly said, what is often said of the virtues, that to have one is to have all" (*De vita Mosis* 2.7)[93]—indicate that for Philo the enthronement of Moses as god and king is equally his installation in these other offices. As Goodenough has shown, Philo draws upon the Hellenistic notion of the king as the "living law"[94] in his portrayal of Moses as legislator. For our purposes, it is of interest merely to note in addition the distinction which Philo makes within the Law given through Moses :

> They (the sacred books) consist of two parts : one the historical, the other concerned with commands and prohibitions, and of this we will speak later, after first treating fully what comes first in order. One division of the historical deals with the creation of the world, the other with particular persons, and this partly with the punishment of the impious, partly with the honouring of the just.[95]

Again from the ideology of Hellenistic kingship, Moses is portrayed not only as king but also as high priest.[96] From Jewish tradition then Moses is portrayed as a prophet (cf. Deut 18:15-22 and 34:10).[97] For our purposes, again, the distinction, which Philo introduces into the oracles given through Moses, are of interest :

> Now I am fully aware that all things written in the sacred books are oracles delivered through Moses; but I will confine myself to those which are more especially his, with the following preliminary remarks. Of the divine utterances, some are spoken by God in His own Person with His prophet for interpreter (ἑρμηνεύς), in some the revelation comes through question and answer, and others are spoken by Moses in his own person, when possessed by God and carried away out of himself. The first kind are absolutely and entirely signs of the divine excellences, graciousness and

---

[93] LCL (1966) 6. 453-55.

[94] νόμος ἔμψυχος, cf. E. R. Goodenough, "The Political Philosophy of Hellenistic Kingship," *Yale Classical Studies* I (1928) 55-102; idem, *By Light, Light*, 196f.

[95] *De vita Mosis* 2.46-47; LCL (1966) 6. 470-71.

[96] Cf. Goodenough, *By Light, Light*, 190; Meeks, *The Prophet-King*, 113-15.

[97] Meeks, *The Prophet-King*, 130, notes perceptively that the ideology of Hellenistic kingship does not provide a parallel or basis for associating the king with a) prophecy or b) heavenly enthronement.

beneficence, by which He incites all men to noble conduct, and particularly the nation of His worshippers, for whom He opens up the road which leads to happiness. In the second kind we find a combination and partnership: the prophet asks questions of God about matters on which he has been seeking knowledge, and God replies and instructs him. The third kind are assigned to the lawgiver himself: God has given to him of His own power of foreknowledge and by this he will reveal future events. Now, the first kind must be left out of discussion. They are too great to be lauded by human lips; scarcely indeed could heaven and the world and the whole existing universe worthily sing their praises. Besides, they are delivered through an interpreter (ἑρμηνεύς), and interpretation (ἑρμηνεία) and prophecy are not the same thing.[98]

In his further presentation Philo characterizes the question-and-answer oracles as mixed (μικτὴν ἔχοντες δύναμιν).[99] Then, after various examples in which Moses foretold future events (2.246 ff), Philo concludes with a reference to the oracles prophesied by Moses before his death (e.g. Deut 33-34) some of which have already taken place and others of which are awaited.[100]

If we reflect then upon the function of the scene of the ascent, vision, and enthronement of Moses in the light of Philo's total presentation of Moses, it becomes clear that this scene serves to validate that Moses is the paradigm of the mystic who ascends for the vision of God.[101] More important for our purposes, it serves to authenticate that Moses is the divinely selected founder of God's chosen nation and people and that the books which he has written (De vita Mosis 1.4; 2.11), the Pentateuch,[102] are the divinely inspired sacred scriptures, even though there are distinctions as to the exact relationship of the divine to the various parts of these books.

---

[98] De vita Mosis 2.188-91; LCL (1966) 6. 543.

[99] De vita Mosis 2.192; LCL (1966) 6. 544-45.

[100] De vita Mosis 2.288-91; LCL (1966) 6. 593 ff.

[101] Cf. Meeks, "Moses as God and King," 369. Meeks is reluctant here to give complete assent to Goodenough's view in By Light, Light, 205 ff, concerning an organized, Jewish, cultic mystery with Philonic ideas; cf. also A. D. Nock, "The Question of Jewish Mysteries," Essays on Religion and the Ancient World, 1. 459-68; originally published as a review of By Light, Light in Gnomon 13 (1937) 156-65. However, Goodenough in his later reflections quite rightly stresses that by a Jewish mystery he means not distinct rites or initiations to which even Jews had to be especially admitted but rather a set of teachings which would re-interpret the normal Jewish festivals and consider them as leading the "initiate" out of matter into the eternal (cf. An Introduction to Philo Judaeus, 154f).

[102] For Philo, the Pentateuch is particularly the divinely revealed document; although the prophets and writings were also inspired, they were of less value. Cf. Goodenough, By Light, Light, 77f; and H. A. Wolfson, Philo (Cambridge 1947) 1. 140.

For our comparison with the Sabaoth account we shall find it important to note that in this portrayal of Moses in Philo the two traditions of the ascent of the seer and heavenly enthronement are conflated, that the mortal figure who ascends receives the name god and the title king, that he sees what is not apprehensible by reason, i.e. the invisible, and that this ascent and vision function to validate the Pentateuch. Further, we note that Moses functions as a judge (*De vita Mosis* 2.214-18), although not while he is ascended.

As in 1 Enoch, Ezekiel Tr and Philo, so the Sabaoth account —but now as a part of a myth of origins within a revelation discourse— conflates these two traditions. We have already discussed the tradition of the apocalyptic seer with respect to the Sabaoth account. Concerning the tradition of heavenly enthronement we note first of all that Sabaoth ascends. However, due to the influence of the apocalyptic seer tradition, the term is ⲧⲱⲣⲡ ⲉϩⲣⲁⲓ/ἁρπάζειν rather than עלה/ ἀναβαίνειν as, for example, in Ps 46(47):6. Sabaoth's enthronement —in the sense of installation in power rather than physically sitting upon a throne—is most clear in that he is placed in charge of the seventh heaven. The giving of a name to him in this context may also be part of his enthronement, as we shall discuss below. As in ancient Near Eastern myth and in Exod 15, the reference to the making of the symbol of authority occurs next. Although in these older materials one finds as this symbol either the temple or the throne, the identification of throne and chariot in Israelite tradition enables this change here simply to a chariot. We shall also see below that the separation into right and left and the immediate calling of right as life and the becoming of the left as a type of unrighteousness, can be considered as the beginning of or manifestation of Sabaoth's rule. Thereby, Sabaoth is installed as king of the seventh heaven and all the heavens below as well as of all those on earth who are represented by him; the gnostics, meanwhile, remain as those not subject to his rule but rather belong to the "kingless race."

As we return to the text from this lengthy discussion of the traditions involved in the Sabaoth account, we note that since Sabaoth is placed in charge of the seventh heaven the late Jewish and early rabbinic tradition of a plurality of heavens, more commonly seven,[103] is thus

---

[103] E.g. T. Levi 2f and Apoc Mosis 35; cf. H. L. Strack and P. Billerbeck, *Kommentar zum Neuen Testament aus Talmud und Midrasch* (Munich 1969) 3. 531-33; H. Traub and G. von Rad, οὐρανός, *TDNT* 5 (1967) 511f.

modified into an ogdoadic structure, which reserves the eighth heaven for the high god. This particular motif of the Ogdoad as opposed to the Hebdomad, is widespread in Gnosticism and probably derives from astrological speculation.[104]

Sabaoth is in charge of the seventh heaven but below the cosmic veil, which separates the infinite aeons from the lower aeons (94[142]. 9-12). This motif of the cosmic veil derives ultimately from the veil before the inner tent of the desert shrine (e.g. Exod 26:33) and then later from the veil before the Holy of Holies of the Jerusalem Temple (2 Chr 3:14). In interestamental Judaism, this earthly veil was transposed into the cosmic veil, which separates heaven and earth and also has upon it the images of the universe (cf. especially Josephus *War* 5.212-14, 19; *Ant.* 3.180-81 and Philo *De vita Mosis* 2.74; *Q. Exod.* 90f). This motif of the cosmic veil is not clearly expressed in the NT. Thus when found in Christian gnostic documents, this motif provides a lucid example of the debt of Gnosticism to a Judaism that is not mediated to it through the NT.[105]

Since Sabaoth is just below the cosmic veil, he is now described as between "Above" and "Below." From an astrological point of view, this realm of the universe would correspond to the realm of the fixed stars, which is above the seven planetary spheres.[106] Whether or not Nagel is correct in assuming τὰ ἄνω and τὰ κάτω as behind the Coptic,[107] it is only in intertestamental Judaism that one finds the phrase used absolutely rather than as in the LXX ἐν τῷ οὐρανῷ ἄνω καὶ ἐν τῇ γῇ κάτω (e.g. Exod 20:4; cf. Isa 8:21). Philo, for example, uses the phrase absolutely in *Quod det. pot. insid. soleat* 85.[108] Similarly,

---

[104] R. Reitzenstein, *Poimandres* (Leipzig 1904) 53f; J. Kroll, *Die Lehren des Hermes Trismegistos* (Münster i. W. 1914) 304-10; and F.J. Doelger, "Zur Symbolik des altchristlichen Taufhauses," *AntuChrist* 4 (1934) 172f and 181, who concludes to Pythagorean influence; F. Cumont, *AntuChrist* 5 (1936) 293f.

[105] G. MacRae, *Some Elements of Jewish Apocalyptic*, 30-114. In the Synoptics (Mark 15:38 par.) the veil is spiritualized to represent the Old Covenant and in Heb (6:19f; 9:1-14; 10:19f) the veil is allegorized to refer to the death of Christ. There is a possibility that the author of Hebrews also had in mind the heavenly veil in his allegory. However, the motif is not presented so clearly that it could have functioned as the source of gnostic imagery. For the OT veil, cf. also F.M. Cross, Jr., "The Priestly Tabernacle," *The Biblical Archaeologist Reader*, ed. G.E. Wright and D.N. Freedman (New York 1961) 201-28.

[106] Bullard, *The Hypostasis of the Archons*, 103. Note also that τὸ μέσον in Test Abr 12 (Rec. A) represents the realm for the soul that is neither totally good nor totally evil.

[107] Nagel, *Das Wesen der Archonten*, 79.

[108] Ed. Cohn-Wendland 1. 277: εἰς τὸ ἄνω προαγαγών.

in the NT τὰ ἄνω and τὰ κάτω are contrasted in John 8:23 (ὑμεῖς ἐκ τῶν κάτω ἐστέ, ἐγὼ ἐκ τῶν ἄνω εἰμί).[109] In this gnostic text, however, the contrast is no longer between heaven and earth as in the OT, or between the Father and the world as in John (8:23, 26), but between the infinite aeons and the seven heavens of chaos (96 [144].10-11).

After installation, Sabaoth is given a name as part of his enthronement. In the OT reception of a new name was probably part of the ceremony of enthronement for the king of Israel.[110] However, this aspect of enthronement was not mirrored in the psalms concerning the enthronement of Yahweh (e.g. Ps 47) nor in the later scenes of heavenly enthronement in apocalyptic (e.g. the Son of Man in Dan 7 or 1 Enoch 71) but is present in Philo's portrayal of the enthronement of Moses (De vita Mosis 1.158). It appears appropriate here in NatArch, as in Phil 2:9, that the name is given after the ascent (cf. OnOrgWld 104[152].9f). Yet, it cannot be argued that NatArch has influenced or been influenced by Phil 2:9, since there is no equivalence in the terminology used for the bestowing of the name.[111]

In this case, the name given is, of course, drawn from the God of the OT. However, it appears here in the odd formulation, "the God of the Forces, Sabaoth," rather than the expected "Lord of the Forces."[112] We shall see that this odd formulation is not by accident. Rather, the customary formula is altered purposely in order that the "God of the Forces" might indicate a second, lower God beneath the high God worshipped by the Gnostics.

The explicative ϫⲉ is then added and provides an opportunity to indicate the appropriateness of the name. Sabaoth is "the God of the Forces," since he is spatially above them. These forces are not as in the OT the angelic host of heaven, which Yahweh has created (Isa 40:26), or the heavenly army, which accompanies him in war

---

[109] Cf. Col. 3:1, 2 for τὰ ἄνω.

[110] G. von Rad, "Das judäische Königsritual," Gesammelte Studien zum Alten Testament (Munich 1958) 208ff. Note that the term used here in the Coptic ⲙⲟⲩⲧⲉ can translate καλεῖν, ἐπικαλεῖν, φωνεῖν, ὀνομάζειν (Crum, 192b) and that the major example pointed to by von Rad uses καλεῖν (Isa 9:5b καὶ καλεῖται τὸ ὄνομα αὐτοῦ), although in the formula καλεῖν τὸ ὄνομα. In the NT, cf. Phil 2:9 where the formula is ἐχαρίσατο αὐτῷ τὸ ὄνομα.

[111] Cf. preceding footnote.

[112] Frequent, of course, in the OT is the liturgical address κύριε, ὁ θεὸς τῶν δυνά-μεων (e.g. Ps 58[59]:6). However, only in one instance is the κύριε omitted, Ps 79(80):14 ὁ θεὸς τῶν δυνάμεων ἐπίστρεψον δή. Similarly, at Qumran in one instance the phrase appears as אלהי צבא[ו]ת (1 QSb 4:25); cf. also 2 Enoch 52:1, Rec. A.

(Judg 5:14).[113] The forces in this case are the demonic offspring of Ialdabaoth in the remaining six heavens and also in the nether world. In accord with the gnostic devaluation of the world, these regions together—rather than merely the nether world—are entitled chaos.[114] This motif of one being "above the forces" is found also in the NT in the portrayal of Christ (Eph 1:20f. ὑπεράνω πάσης ... δυνάμεως; cf. Rom 8:38; 1 Cor 15:24; 1 Pet 3:22) and thus cannot be used to establish the independence of the Sabaoth account from the NT.[115]

The pericope closes as the author adds again that it was Wisdom who installed Sabaoth. Thereby, his secondary importance is reinforced.

3. Creation of the Throne/Chariot of Sabaoth 95(143).26-28

26 ϩΟΤΙ ΔΕ ΑΝΑΕΙ ϢⲰΠΕ ΑϤΤΑΜΙΟ ΝΑϤ	Now (δέ) when (ὅτι) these events had come to pass, he made himself
27 ⲚΟΥΝΟ6 ⲚϩΑΡΜΑ ⲚⲬΕΡΟΥΒΙΝ ΕϤΟ Ⲛ	a huge four-faced (πρόσωπον) chariot (ἅρμα)
28 ϤΤΟΟΥ ⲘΠΡΟⲤⲰΠΟⲚ	of cherubim

The following pericope presents the creation of a chariot by Sabaoth and for himself. "Now when these events had come to pass" serves as a simple connective clause.[116] This chariot is described by the adjective, four-faced, which derives from Ezek 1:6, 10 and 10:14, and by the formulaic expression, the chariot of Cherubim, which expression does not occur in Ezek 1 and 10 but does refer to the vision in these chapters.[117] It should be noted that the presentation of Yahweh

---

[113] Cross, *Canaanite Myth and Hebrew Epic: Essays*, 68-71. The term "host of heaven" can also mean in the OT the heavenly bodies, i.e. sun, moon, stars (2 Kgs 17:16; 21:3, 5; 23:4f; Ps 33:6; Isa 34:4; Dan 8:10). In intertestamental material δυνάμεις can refer to a class of angels (e.g. T Levi 3:3; 3 Bar 1:8).

[114] Cf. 95(143).11ff, which makes clear that the gnostic author's world view in dependence upon Greek and Greek-speaking Jewish traditions conceives of Tartarus as the lowest, punitive place and the Abyss as the entire underworld (cf. Bauer, ad. loc.). Chaos, which also denotes the nether abyss in Greek tradition (cf. Liddell-Scott, 1976) but which appears rarely in Greek-speaking Jewish literature (not in this meaning in the LXX and only twice in Philo, *De aeter. mundi* 17f) is now applied by the gnostic to the whole world below the eighth aeon. In the NT, the term chaos does not appear.

[115] One should note, as Grundmann has observed, that the idea of Satan in the NT is not associated with the term δύναμις; W. Grundmann, δύναμαι, δύναμις κτλ., *TDNT* 2 (1964) 308, n. 80.

[116] The reading should be "when" (ὅτε) rather than "*because* (ὅτι) these events had come to pass," since the causal relationship is inappropriate. See Layton in "The Hypostasis of the Archons," (1974) 419, ad loc.

[117] Ezek 43:3 ἡ ὅρασις τοῦ ἅρμα οὗ εἶδον, κατὰ τὴν ὅρασιν ἣν εἶδον ἐπὶ τοῦ ποταμοῦ τοῦ χοβάρ. 1 Chr 28:18 τὸ παράδειγμα τοῦ ἅρματος τῶν χερουβιν. Sir 49:8 Ιεζεκιηλ ὃς εἶδεν ὅρασιν δόξης ἣν ὑπέδειξεν αὐτῷ ἐπὶ ἅρματος χερουβιν. Cf. Apoc Mos 22:3; Test Abr 9, 10 (Rec. A).

upon the chariot of Cherubim in Ezekiel is a specifically Israelite feature in contrast with Near Eastern mythology.[118] In the Canaanite background El was pictured as sitting upon his throne, the throne of Cherubim, in the midst of the divine assembly.[119] It was Baal then who was portrayed as riding upon the war chariot, the deified clouds, toward the holy war.[120] In the vision of Ezekiel the presentation of the chariot is most influenced by Baal language. Baal's war chariot predominates but it has been combined with El's throne of Cherubim. Just as El epithets influenced the understanding of Yahweh in the early period, so the later resurgence of Baal material influenced the combination of these motifs of El's throne of Cherubim and Baal's war chariot and their application to Yahweh in the sixth century proto-apocalyptic of Ezek 1 and 10.[121] Yahweh was thus presented as warrior and king. This association of throne and chariot was maintained in Judaism, as is attested by 4Q S1 40.24.3 ("the structure of the chariot throne")[122] and Apoc Abr 18 ("a chariot with fiery wheels ... over the wheels was a throne").[123] This gnostic document preserves the

---

[118] I am indebted to Professor Cross for this basic insight, which was given in an oral communication.

[119] M. H. Pope, *El in the Ugaritic Texts* (VTSup 2; Leiden 1955) 45-46.

[120] A. Kapelrud, *Baal in the Ugaritic Texts* (Copenhagen 1952) 93-94; U. Oldenburg, *The Conflict Between El and Ba'al in Canaanite Religion* (NumenSup, Altera Series 3; Leiden 1969) 75-76.

[121] For the ninth century resurgence of Baal material, cf. Cross, *Canaanite Myth and Hebrew Epic: Essays*, 190-94. On the Cherubim and the throne of Cherubim, cf. also W. F. Albright, "What Were the Cherubim?" *The Biblical Archaeologist Reader*, ed. G. E. Wright and D. N. Freedman (New York 1961) 95-97.

[122] J. Strugnell, "The Angelic Liturgy at Qumran, 4Q Serek Šîrôt 'ôlat Haššabat," *International Organization for the Study of the Old Testament. 3d Congress, Oxford 1959, Congress Volume* (VTSup 7; Leiden 1960) 335-37.

[123] Box, *The Apocalypse of Abraham*, 62; cf. 1 Enoch 14:18. Professor M. Smith has graciously called my attention to the magical papyri, gems, and amulets in regard to this portrayal of Sabaoth. Within the magical papyri, Sabaoth appears frequently as a deity (some 82 occurrences) and is often invoked, but there is no presentation of Sabaoth with a chariot of Cherubim. Within the gems and amulets, there is indeed a gem in the British Museum (BM 56044) with a human figure driving a chariot, which is drawn by two serpents. Above the figure one finds inscribed Iao, and on the bevel there is written Abrasax. On the reverse of a bloodstone representing the Sun and the Moon in their chariots (BM 56147) one finds the inscription: Iao, Sabaoth, Abrasax, The Existent One, Lord, protect me. Further, in a gem published by King there is the solar deity, who is cock-headed and anguipede and who drives the chariot by four horses; underneath there is inscribed Sabao(th). While it is possible that magical traditions have influenced the presentation of Sabaoth in NatArch, it is difficult to prove since such motifs as the four-faces and the myriads of angels in combination with the chariot of Cherubim are not found on the gems or amulets but rather in apocalyptic traditions and thus point to influence from there and since in the related OnOrgWld

same feature in that Sabaoth, an El title, is associated not with a throne but with a chariot, the chariot of Cherubim.

Usually in the OT the motif that Yahweh sits upon his throne is part of the enthronement, after he has ascended—e.g. Ps 47:8. However, as we pointed out earlier, in ancient Near Eastern mythology and in Exod 15:17 the motif is rather that a temple or abode is built for the deity, again as part of the enthronement. The fact that Sabaoth makes the chariot (as Yahweh makes his abode in Exod 15:17), that the chariot is for himself, and that the chariot functions as the throne in Israelite and Jewish literature, indicates to us that Sabaoth is thereby being enthroned in this pericope.

The Cherubim are not here considered as a separate class of angels as in 1 Enoch 61:10 ("the Cherubim, Seraphim and Ofannim"; cf. 71:7). To this expression, the chariot of Cherubim, is then added the adjective "huge." This phrase is not found in the OT but in 1 Enoch 14:10, 16 the adjective "large" or "huge" is applied to the two houses within which the throne-chariot is kept.

This motif of the chariot of Cherubim has not influenced and cannot be derived from the NT, since there is no mention in the NT of the chariot of the Lord. Only the "throne" is presented (e.g. Rev 4:6f). Similarly, the term Cherubim occurs only once in the NT but in the description of the Holy of Holies (Heb 9:5). Lastly, although the four creatures are presented in Rev 4:7, it is striking that only one is said to have a πρόσωπον, the man; the others are merely said to be "like unto."[124]

4. *Creation of the Angels* 95(143).28-31

MN ϨNΑΓΓΕΛΟC	and infinitely many angels (ἄγγελοι),
29 ΕΝΑϢϢΟΥ ΕΜN̄ΤΟΥ ΗΠΕ ΕΤΡΟΥΡ̄ϨΥ	to act as ministers (ὑπηρετεῖν),
30 ΠΗΡΕΤΕΙ ΑΥϢ ϨΜΨΑΛΤΗΡΙΟΝ ΜN̄ ϨN	and also harps (ψαλτήριον)
31 ΚΙΘΑΡΑ	and lyres (κιθάρα)

Iao and Sabaoth are considered as two distinct rulers and there is no reference to Abrasax. Cf. K. Preisendanz and A. Henrichs, eds., *Papyri Graecae Magicae I-II* (2. Aufl.; Stuttgart 1973-74); C. W. King, *Antique Gems and Rings* (London 1872) 2.46 and pl. VIII, 1; H. B. Walters, *Catalogue of the Engraved Gems and Cameos, Greek, Etruscan and Roman in the British Museum* (London 1926) 148 and # 1308; C. Bonner, *Studies in Magical Amulets* (Ann Arbor 1950) 29-32, 127-36, 172; E. R. Goodenough, *Jewish Symbols in the Greco-Roman Period* (Bollingen Series 37; New York 1953) 2.259-61 and vol. 3, # 1116, 1127.

[124] E.g. 4:7 τὸ ζῷον τὸ πρῶτον ὅμοιον λέοντι whereas in Ezek 1:6, 10 and 10:14 it is clearly τέσσαρα πρόσωπα.

Angels are also fashioned and described as "many" and "infinite." If ⲈⲘⲚⲦⲞⲨ ⲎⲠⲈ translates ἀναρίθμητος as is probable,[125] then it is noteworthy that this expression does not occur in the LXX or Philo or the NT in connection with angels but seems to derive from Jewish apocalyptic.[126]

The text draws upon the tradition whereby angels are presented as accompanying the chariot-throne (e.g. Apoc Moses 22) and portrays the function of the angels as to minister. If ὑπηρετεῖν was in the Greek original, then it is significant that ὑπηρετεῖν plays almost no role in the LXX or the NT. It does not occur as the term for the angelic service of God. Only with Philo are angels spoken of as God's ὑπηρέται.[127] Instead, the term for "the ministering angels" seems to have been λειτουργεῖν (e.g. T. Levi 3:5),[128] a term which in later Greek translations of the OT can be · rendered as ὑπηρετεῖν (e.g. Num 4:23 Sym). Thus, again, the terminology used in NatArch appears to derive from late Judaism rather than the OT or NT.

Created with the angels are also harps and lyres as the instruments for them. Although these instruments are frequently mentioned together in the LXX, they are not there associated with angels.[129] In the NT the κίθαρα are associated with the angels (Rev 5:8; 14:2).

5. *The Instruction of Sabaoth* 95(143).31-34

ⲀⲨⲰ ⲀⲦⲤⲞⲫⲒⲀ ϬⲒ ⲦⲈⲤϢⲈⲈⲣⲈ Ⲛ̄	And Wisdom (σοφία) took her daughter
32 ⲌⲰⲎ ⲀⲤⲦⲣⲈⲤ₂ⲘⲞⲞⲤ ₂Ⲓ ⲞⲨⲚⲀⲘ Ⲙ̄ⲘⲞϥ	Life (ζωή) and had her sit upon his right
33 ⲈⲦⲣⲈⲤⲦⲀⲘⲞϥ ⲀⲚⲈⲦϢⲞⲞⲠ [₂][Ⲛ̄] ⲦⲘⲀ₂	to teach him about the things
34 ϢⲘⲞⲨⲚⲈ	that exist in the Eighth (heaven).

In resumption of line 25 the text presents Wisdom as taking her daughter Life and seating her in the position of honor, the right hand. Her task is specifically to teach Sabaoth. Here Life replaces the

---

[125] Heb 11:12, Sah., has ⲈⲦⲈⲘⲚ̄Ⲧϥ ⲎⲠⲈ for ἀναρίθμητος. Crum, 527b gives ἀναρίθμητος for ⲀⲦⲎⲠⲈ but does not list the expression ⲈⲘⲚ̄ⲦⲀϥ-ⲎⲠⲈ.

[126] Cf. 1 Enoch 40:1 "And after that I saw thousands of thousands, and ten thousand times ten thousand, I saw a multitude beyond number" (Charles, *The Book of Enoch*; 1912; 77); 4 Ezra 6:3 "numberless armies of angels" (Charles, *APOT* 2. 574; cf. also 2 Bar 21:6; 59:11. For the biblical background of this motif, one may consult the positive formulation in Isa 40:26: "Lift up your eyes on high and see: who created these? He who brings out their host by number, calling them all by name; by the greatness of his might, and because he is so strong in power not one is missing." This reference was pointed out to me by Professor Cross in private communication.

[127] E.g. *De poster. C.* 92; *De mutat. nom.* 87; *Quod Deus immut.* 158. Cf. K. H. Rengstorf, ὑπηρέτης, ὑπηρετέω, *TDNT* 8 (1962) 534ff.

[128] Charles, *The Greek Versions of the Testaments of the Twelve Patriarchs*, 34.

[129] Gen 4:21; Job 21:12; Ps 56(57):8; Ps 80(81):2; etc.

angelus interpres found in apocalyptic literature in such a context (e.g. Uriel in 1 Enoch 19:1; Michael in Test Abr 10, Rec. A). It is indicative of the important role of Wisdom in the myth that it is she who does the placing. Further, it is significant that she places her daughter Life as the instructoress rather than an angel to represent righteousness, as in Test Abr 12 (Rec. A). As Böhlig has pointed out, the basis of the identification between Life and instructoress lies in a Semitic word-play. The name of Eve (חַוָּה), which is related etymologically in Gen 3:20 to the word meaning "live" (חָיָה), has been associated with the Aramaic word of the same sound meaning "instruct" (חִוָּא). Eve's name then is translated as *zoē* in the LXX, which in turn is here translated as Life.[130]

The significance of this "teaching about the things that exist in the Eighth" is signalled when one contrasts it with the mode and content of revelation to the apocalyptic seer. The main revelation for the apocalyptic seer is, of course, the vision of the divine throne and the Godhead upon it (e.g. 1 Enoch 14; 2 Enoch 20-22). Secondly, nothing remains hidden to the seer in heaven or in the cosmos; all the secrets of the universe are shown or laid bare to him (e.g. 1 Enoch 14-37; 2 Enoch 24-33), which revelation may later be communicated in special books (e.g. 1 Enoch 104:11-13; 2 Enoch 40:1-8; 54:1; 68:1-3). Here in this document the gnostic dualism makes its presence felt. Entrance into the divine world is not offered to Sabaoth since he is one born ultimately from evil matter. He must remain below the veil. Thus a vision as well as interpretation of a vision of the divine world are impossible; instead, Sabaoth receives instruction concerning the Eighth, the realm of imperishability (94[142].5). On the other hand, in this revelation to Sabaoth there is no mention of the secrets of the lower world. The total concern here is with the divine realm.

This pericope has neither influenced nor been derived from the NT. To be sure, Christ is there seated at the right hand of the Father (e.g. Mark 14:62 par; Acts 2:34). However, no one is placed at this right to instruct him nor, of course, is there mention of an Eighth in the NT.

---

[130] The Semitic word-play is carried further to associate the serpent and the instructor; cf. Böhlig, *Die koptisch-gnostische Schrift ohne Titel*, 73-74. Also B. Pearson, "Jewish Haggadic Traditions in *The Testimony of Truth* from Nag Hammadi (CG IX, 3)," *Ex Orbe Religionum: Studia Geo Widengren oblata*, ed. J. Bergman, K. Drynjeff and H. Ringgren (Leiden 1973) 1. 463-64.

6. *The Separation into Right and Left* 95 (143).34-96(144).3

ⲁⲩⲱ ⲡⲓⲁⲅⲅⲉⲗⲟ[ⲥ ⲛ̄ⲧⲉ ⲧⲟ]ⲣ	And the angel (ἄγγελος) [of] wrath (ὀργή)
35 ⲅⲏ ⲁⲥⲕⲁⲁϥ ϩⲓ ϩⲃⲟⲩⲣ ⲙ̄ⲙⲟϥ [ⲭⲓⲙ ⲫⲟ]	she placed upon his left. [Since]
36 ⲟⲩ ⲉⲧⲙ̄ⲙⲁⲩ ⲁⲩⲙⲟⲩⲧⲉ ⲁ ⲧ̣[ⲉϥⲟⲩⲛⲁⲙ]	that day, [his right] has been called
1 ϫⲉ ⲍⲱⲏ ⲁⲩⲱ ⲧ̣ϩⲃⲟ̣[ⲩ]ⲣ̣ ⲁⲥϣⲱⲡⲉ ⲛ̄ ⲧⲩⲡⲟⲥ	'Life (ζωή); and the left has come to represen (τύπος)
2 ⲛ̄ ⲧⲁⲁⲓⲕⲓⲁ ⲛ̄ ⲧⲙⲛ̄ⲧⲁⲩⲑⲉⲛⲧⲏⲥ ⟨ⲉⲧ⟩ ⲙ̄ⲡⲥⲁ ⲛ	the unrighteousness (ἀδικία) of the realm of abso lute power
3 ⲧⲡⲉ. ⲛ̄ⲧⲁⲩϣⲱⲡⲉ ϩⲁ ⲧⲟⲩⲉϩⲏ	above. It was before your time that they came int being.

In this pericope concerning the separation into right and left, the final elements in the ascent and vision of the apocalyptic seer and in the enthronement scene have been conflated. First of all, in the description of the chariot/throne in late Jewish apocalyptic, a final element is the portrayal of angels on the right and left. No doubt this motif has its origin in the OT presentation of Yahweh as seated upon his throne with the host of heaven on his right and left (1 Kgs 22:19//2 Chr 18:18; the tester who comes before the Lord should also be noted in this passage). That this picture was still vivid in late apocalyptic is shown in Adam and Eve 25:3 : "And many thousands of angels were on the right and left of that chariot." [131] In the OT the distinction between right and left can also indicate positive and negative value, as in Eccl 10:2 ("A wise man's heart inclines him toward the right, but a fool's heart toward the left"). [132] Within late apocalyptic and particularly in association with the vision of the divine throne/chariot, this distinction and its valence was also kept. Thus in Apoc Abr, after Abraham has received his vision of the divine throne/chariot (c. 17-18), he sees mankind divided into multitudes of people on the right side and on the left (c. 21 f). Here the right side represents Israel and the left side represents the heathen—some of whom are to be saved and some damned :

> And I saw there a great multitude—men and women and children half of them of the right side of the picture and half of them on the left side of the picture... These which are on the left side are the multitude of the peoples which have formerly been in existence and which are after thee destined,

---

[131] Text Meyer, *Vita Adae et Evae*, 229; translation Charles, *APOT* 2. 140. Cf. also Adam and Eve 21:1 and the probable restoration in 1QM 9:14ff, although the throne is not present here.

[132] Cf. Ezek 4:4. Philo in *Quis rer. div. heres sit* 209 (Cohn-Wendland 3. 48) gives a list of opposites interesting for our context here : ζωὴ θάνατος, νόσος ὑγεία, λευκὸν μέλαν, δέξια εὐώνυμα, δικαιοσύνη ἀδικία, φρόνησις ἀφρόνησις.

some for judgment and restoration, and others for vengeance and destruction at the end of the world. But these which are on the right side of the picture—they are the people set apart for me of the peoples with Azazel. These are they whom I have ordained to be born of thee and to be called My People.[133]

In Apoc Abr the whole history of mankind is then told from this perspective of the division into right and left (c. 21-29).

Similarly in Test Abr, another piece of late apocalyptic literature, this distinction and its valence is presented as a final element in the description of the throne. In this case, the throne is the one upon which Abel sits :

Between the gates there stood a fearsome throne which looked like awesome crystal, flashing lightning like fire. And upon it was seated a wondrous man, looking like the sun, like a son of God. Before him there stood a crystalline table, all of gold and byssus. Upon the table lay a book six cubits thick and ten cubits broad. On its right and on its left stood two angels holding parchment and ink and a pen. Before the table sat a luminous angel, holding a scale in his hand. On his left hand there sat a fiery angel altogether merciless and severe, holding a trumpet in his hand, holding within it all-consuming fire for the testing of the sinners.

And the wondrous man who sat upon the throne was himself judging and sentencing the souls. The two angels of the right and of the left were recording. The one on the right was recording the righteous deeds, the one of the left the sins, and the one who was before the table who was holding the scale was weighing the souls, and the fiery angel who was holding in the fire was testing the souls.

Then Abraham asked the Archistrategos Michael, "What are these things that we see?"

And the Archistrategos said, "These things that you see, O holy Abraham, are judgment and recompense."

And behold, the angel who was holding the soul in his hand brought it before the judge and the judge said to one of the angels who were attending him, "Open this book for me and find me the sins of this soul."

And he opened the book and he found that its sins and righteous deeds were equally balanced, and he delivered it neither to the tormentors nor to those who were saved, but set it in the middle.[134]

Secondly and with respect to heavenly enthronement, as Mowinckel states it, a final element in the enthronement scene is the description of "the state of things, which will now come about, or in an ideal sense has already come about ... his (Yahweh's) enemies are going to be struck with awe, whereas his people shall rejoice in his righteous

---

[133] Box, *The Apocalypse of Abraham*, 67-69.
[134] Test Abr 12 Rec. A; Stone, *The Testament of Abraham*, 28-31.

and luck-bringing rule." [135] That this element persisted in the enthronement tradition may be seen in Ps 47:8f ("God reigns over the nations;
God sits on his holy throne. The princes of the people gather as the
people of the God of Abraham"), Dan 7:14b ("his dominion is an
everlasting dominion, which shall not pass away, and his kingdom
one that shall not be destroyed") and 1 Enoch 71:16 ("And all shall
walk in *thy* ways since righteousness never forsaketh *thee*: With *thee*
will be their dwelling-places, and with *thee* their heritage, and they
shall not be separated from *thee* for ever and ever"). [136] The final
element in the enthronement scene could also be that Yahweh comes
to judge (e.g. Ps 96:13).

In this pericope, then, we shall now see in detail that the motifs
concerning the distinction between right and left as part of the description of the throne/chariot and the beginning of rule by the enthroned
have been conflated and reworked to suit gnostic purposes.

Since Life's role at the right of Sabaoth has already been expressed,
the Angel of Wrath—as Layton has restored the text—is then simply
placed at the left. Sabaoth's right hand (in a probable restoration) is
then given a name. Consistent with the myth, the name is Life, which
results in this unusual contrast between ζωή and ἀδικία. From Jewish
literature and from the NT one would customarily expect the contrast
between δικαιοσύνη and ἀδικία or even between ἀλήθεια and ἀδικία. [137]
In the Wisdom tradition, when Wisdom leaves the world, then unrighteousness abounds (1 Enoch 42:3; 4 Ezra 5:10). Here Wisdom
can also be identified with life (*Zoē*, Prov 8:35) but life is not
hypostatized. Thus the Wisdom tradition is not the direct source of
this contrast. Rather, the contrast here between Life and unrighteousness is probably a gnostic creation and the result of the hypostatization
of Life and her role as instructoress of Sabaoth. [138]

The left is then said to represent the unrighteousness or to be a
type of injustice, a type not in the sense of a hermeneutical term or

---

[135] S. Mowinckel, *The Psalms in Israel's Worship* (Oxford 1962) 1. 184.

[136] Charles, *The Book of Enoch* (1912) 145. Once again I have followed the text
with *thy* and *thee* rather than the emendation of Charles to the third person.

[137] Cf. G. Schrenk, ἀδικία, *TDNT* 1 (1964) 153ff; in the NT cf. John 7:18; Rom
3:5; 2 Thess 2:10; etc.

[138] One could consider it from the other point of view, namely that the expected
contrast would be between life and death (Deut 30:15) or life and punishment (Matt
25:46). The change from one of these terms to ἀδικία could perhaps then be seen
as related to the "rulers of unrighteousness" (93[141].1 and 7). However, this seems
less likely since the interest of the author is focused upon Life and would more easily
represent his own contribution than "unrighteousness."

heavenly original but in the sense of an image, a copy. It appears odd at first that the angel, who punished Ialdabaoth and therefore served the forces of good and is now associated with Life and the rehabilitated Sabaoth, should be considered negatively in association with ἀδικία. But note the change! *The* left rather than Sabaoth's left, i.e. the angel, has become the image of unrighteousness. Sabaoth's left is not *called* unrighteousness. Secondly, this association becomes understandable in the light of the angel of punishment in later apocalyptic; he too stands at the left of the chariot (e.g. Test Abr 12, Rec. A). In other words, Sabaoth and his angel are not unrighteous and thus Sabaoth's left cannot be *called* unrighteous. Rather, one aspect of Sabaoth's rule is to punish unrighteousness through this angel; Sabaoth is, in effect, a righteous deity with a righteous angel. "The left" then becomes not a heavenly prototype but a copy, an image, of that original unrighteousness perpetrated by Ialdabaoth.

That the blasphemy of Ialdabaoth should be termed ἀδικία is appropriate, since in the LXX it can represent unrighteousness in the sense of lying or untruthfulness (e.g. Ps 51[52]:5; 118[119]:69).[139] As we have already mentioned, in the Wisdom tradition when Wisdom withdraws from the world, the world is said to be left in unrighteousness. Further, in Jewish apocalyptic, the whole period preceding the Messianic revelation can be summed up as a time of unrighteousness (e.g. 4 Ezra 4:51ff; 1 Enoch 48:7; 91:5ff). For the gnostic the interest lies in showing that the unrighteousness of the world is bound up with pre-historic events, with the tyranny of Ialdabaoth. That tyranny took place above, not in the sense of within the pleromatic world but merely above the Abyss (cf. 95[143].10-13) and in the presence of Wisdom and Life as well as Sabaoth.

As his translation shows, Layton has correctly seen that the final line of this section, line 3, is a sentence in the second tense rather than a relative clause. With this final sentence, "it was before your time that they came into being," the angel Eleleth concludes one section of the myth of origins and resumes speaking directly to Norea. Thereby the dramatic setting of the dialogue between Eleleth and Norea is sustained and carried forth—cf. 93(141).4, 11, 18; 96(144).15, 19.

Again this pericope cannot be said to have influenced or to have been derived from the NT. To be sure, Christ appears enthroned in

---

[139] Cf. G. Schrenk, ἀδικία, *TDNT* 1 (1964) 153f.

the NT and separates the sheep from the goats, the former on the right and the latter on the left (Matt 25:33-46). The just sheep then are said to receive "eternal life" while the goats receive eternal punisment. However, the context is entirely different there. In the NT the scene is the coming of the Son of Man and therefore the final judgment, whereas in NatArch it is the pre-cosmic period and the establishment of the structures of the universe. Further, the motif concerning a heavenly figure or angel standing on the right and left of the Son of Man is missing. It seems more likely that both the NT and NatArch derive from a common Jewish background than that they are mutually related.

The sections of the Sabaoth account when exegeted show clearly that the material of the Sabaoth account derives from Judaism. The terminology and the motifs can be explained as drawn from the literature of Judaism. The pattern followed here is the same as that pertaining to the apocalyptic seer in Judaism : ascent, vision (here : making) of the chariot, instruction or revelation, separation into right and left. Thus one is justified in concluding that the pericope uses the Jewish tradition of the ascent and vision of the throne/chariot by the apocalyptic seer. Similarly, the pattern and thus the Jewish tradition of heavenly enthronement are in evidence here : ascent, enthronement, and the beginning of rule.

Although the material used in the Sabaoth account derives from Judaism, we shall argue subsequently on the basis of its function that the Sabaoth account is a Christian composition. However, the Sabaoth account itself has not been influenced by the NT. The Jewish traditions used in this account have not been mediated by or through the NT to the Christian circles responsible for the Sabaoth account. There is no evidence that the ascent of Paul (2 Cor 12:2ff) or John (Rev 4:1ff) has influenced this account. Secondly, although the tradition of enthronement is applied to Christ in the NT, there is no indication that the NT has influenced the Sabaoth account. In the NT Christ's enthronement is associated with his parousia (1 Cor 15:23ff; Mark 14:61f; Matt 25:31ff) or with his resurrection/ascension (e.g. Phil 2:6-11; Rom 8:34; Col 3:1; Eph 1:20; Acts 2:33f; John 12:32) and not with the creation of the world.[140] Further, the determinative

---

[140] In Col 1:15ff Christ's rule over all things is presented in the context of creation but on the basis of his being the image of God and his mediation in creation rather than his enthronement. Then in v. 18 he is portrayed as "first among all" on the basis of his resurrection.

motifs that are applied to Sabaoth are not in the NT applied to Christ. Repentance by Christ is not part of his enthronement. Nor is he "snatched up"; rather he ascends (ἀναβαίνειν e.g. John 20:17), is taken up (ἀναλαμβάνειν 1 Tim 3:16) or is exalted (ὑψοῦν e.g. Phil 2:9; Acts 2:33f; John 8:28). Nor is Christ placed in charge (καθίστημι) of the heavens; rather he sits at the right hand of the Father (κάθημαι e.g. Acts 2:34; Col 3:1). Nor is he given the name "God of the Forces"; rather he is called Lord (Phil 2:11). He is not given Life as his instructoress nor is he instructed concerning the Ogdoad. Lastly, as we have seen, a number of the minor motifs found in the Sabaoth account are not present in the NT. These motifs are as follows: matter as mother, loathing (σικχαίνειν), seven heavens, the heavenly veil, chaos, the Cherubim-chariot which is four-faced, infinitely many angels, angels who minister (ὑηρετεῖν), the harps of angels, a heavenly or angelic figure on the right and the left sides of the enthroned person, and the contrast between life and injustice.

These Jewish traditions concerning the ascent of the apocalyptic seer and heavenly enthronement have also been redacted in several ways by their re-use in the Sabaoth account of this document. First of all, the context has been changed. The ascent and the enthronement are placed within the account of the creation of the world. Secondly, the traditions are redacted in that the pattern is altered. The pericope concerning the repentance of Sabaoth is added as a preliminary to his ascent. Thirdly, the understanding of the world is different in the reuse of these traditions. Anti-cosmic dualism is clearly involved in the view that the world arose from the fall of Wisdom. Lastly, also strikingly new is the antipathy to the God of the OT that is expressed in the demotion of him on the one hand to the evil Demiurge Ialda-baoth and on the other hand to his repentant son Sabaoth.

B. FUNCTION

Concerning the function of the Sabaoth account in this document one should note first that the Sabaoth account is part of the pre-cosmic myth and second that the concern of the document is with the realm of imperishability and the origin, structure and ultimate fate of the entire cosmos. Within that framework then the reality of the rulers, among whom is Sabaoth, is presented.

The exact function of the Sabaoth account is not explicitly stated. In the further questions of Norea to Eleleth, after the Wisdom myth has been recounted, there is no added reference to Sabaoth. He does not appear to act as intercessor, mediator or revealer.

We propose that the Sabaoth account functions in a manner similar to the passages concerning Moses in Ezekiel Tr and Philo. Here, however, the account serves to authenticate not the prophet who composed but the God who revealed himself in the books of the OT. The books are validated as containing revelation about the realm of the Eighth because of the instruction of Life, even though the God who revealed himself was not from the Eighth. Secondly, the God of the OT is shown to be the one who rules this world and to be not completely evil, even though he is the offspring of an evil father Ialdabaoth. Thirdly, the Sabaoth account serves to evaluate theologically the Jewish people as belonging to this repentant ruler Sabaoth. In order then to support this interpretation of the function of the Sabaoth account, it will be necessary to consider some related gnostic literature and to observe the theological issues debated therein.

First of all, however, it must be said that the Nag Hammadi tractates have rendered suspect the clear differentiation of the gnostics into sects on the basis of distinct doctrines by the Church Fathers. Rather the documents contain within themselves teachings attributed to different sects [141] and thereby indicate that the mythologoumena were widely shared among the various branches of Gnosticism. Publication of the entire corpus from Nag Hammadi and further analysis will be necessary before a new classification is possible.

In the meantime, F. Wisse has provided an acceptable working definition of at least one sect, the Sethians, [142] within the branch of Syro-Egyptian Gnosticism. He derives his criterion from Epiphanius' presentation (*Pan.* 39) and characterizes their teaching as containing two basic elements : the evil origin of the world and of the non-gnostics and the heavenly origin of the race of Seth. These basic teachings

---

[141] For example, the ApocryJn in its four versions (BG 8502; CG II, 1; III, 1; IV, 1) surpasses the bounds of the Barbelognostics when this sect is identified on the basis of Iren. *Adv. haer.* 1.29. Cf. Wisse, "The Nag Hammadi Library and the Heresiologists," 205-23.

[142] F. Wisse, "The Sethians and the Nag Hammadi Library," *The Society of Biblical Literature*, One Hundred Eighth Annual Meeting, Seminar Papers, ed. Lane C. McGaughy, (SBL 1972) 2. 601-07. He correctly dismisses the account in Hippolytus (*Ref.* 5.19-22) as an adequate criterion for defining the Sethians. The very document which Hippolytus refers to as the source of their teachings, "The Paraphrase of Seth," is probably mistakenly named by him and should rather be entitled as "The Paraphrase of Shem" as CG VII, 1.

can then be expressed with a variety of mythologoumena by the different gnostic authors.

NatArch as a whole and the Sabaoth account in particular, if they cannot be characterized as stemming from the Sethians, at least belong to the circle of those gnostics who share common traditions with the Sethians. Thus, in order to present the function of the Sabaoth account within the document, we shall first consider the Sethian document, ApocAd (CG V, 5) and then the report in Iren. *Adv. haer.* 1.30, concerning unnamed gnostics, who nevertheless share some features with the Sethians, before considering NatArch itself. In considering these accounts we shall pay particular attention to their teaching concerning the God of Israel, the revelation in Israel's sacred books, and the people of Israel.

ApocAd[143] in its basic literary form is a testament,[144] in which Adam instructs his son Seth concerning the revelation which he has received. The evil Demiurge according to this revelation will try to destroy the race of gnostics through a flood and then through fire and brimstone. In each case, however, they will be saved, and in a third event an Illuminator will come to redeem men.

The text is definitely Sethian and has been accepted as such by scholars.[145] Discussion of the document, however, has led to divergence of opinion on two issues : first, whether the document presents an example of non-Christian Gnosticism[146] and second, whether the document is early.[147]

---

[143] A. Böhlig and P. Labib, *Koptisch-gnostische Apokalypsen aus Codex V von Nag Hammadi im koptischen Museum zu Alt-Kairo* (Wissenschaftliche Zeitschrift der Martin-Luther-Universität; Halle-Wittenberg 1963) 86-117.

[144] Cf. P. Perkins, "Apocalyptic Schematization in the Apocalypse of Adam and the Gospel of the Egyptians," *The Society of Biblical Literature*, One Hundred Eighth Annual Meeting, Seminar Papers, ed. Lane C. McGaughy (SBL 1972) 2. 591-95.

[145] Cf. Böhlig-Labib, *Koptisch-gnostische Apokalypsen aus Codex V*, 86f; Wisse, "The Sethians and the Nag Hammadi Library," 606.

[146] Böhlig in his introduction to the edition (*Koptisch-gnostische Apokalypsen aus Codex V*, 90ff) and subsequently has expressed the view that ApocAd is not a Christian document : i.e. A. Böhlig, "Die Adamapokalypse aus Codex V von Nag Hammadi als Zeugnis jüdisch-iranischer Gnosis," *OriensChrist.* 48 (1964) 44-49; and A. Böhlig, "Jüdisches und iranisches in der Adam-apokalypse des Codex V von Nag Hammadi," *Mysterion und Wahrheit* (Arbeiten zur Geschichte des späteren Judentums und des Urchristentums Band 6; Leiden 1967) 149-61. His views have received support from K. Rudolph in his review of the Böhlig-Labib edition in *TLZ* 90 (1965) 359-62; from G. MacRae in his articles "The Coptic Gnostic Apocalypse of Adam," *HeyJ* 6 (1965) 27-35 and "The Apocalypse of Adam Reconsidered," *The Society of Biblical Literature*, One Hundred Eighth Annual Meeting, Seminar Papers, ed. Lane C. McGaughy, (SBL 1972) 573-80; and from Luise Schottroff, "Animae naturaliter salvandae : Zum Problem

Our concern is particularly with the latter issue : whether the document is early. It is more probable that ApocAd is early since its speculation upon the gnostic hierarchy of beings is less elaborate, it stays mainly within the narrative framework, it does not try to explain everything,[148] and its schematization is close to that of apocalyptic material.[149] When taken together these indications point to an early date of ApocAd. Hopefully, our consideration of the Sabaoth account will also reinforce that conclusion.

Before examining the ApocAd, we should first discuss the relationship

---

der himmlischen Herkunft des Gnostikers," *Christentum und Gnosis*, hrsg. W. Eltester (BZNW 37; Berlin 1969) 65-97.

On the contrary, in their reviews of the Böhlig-Labib edition, the following have argued for a Christian provenience of the tractate : J. Daniélou, in *RSR* 54 (1966) 285-93; A. Orbe in *Greg* 46 (1965) 169-72; and H.-M. Schenke in *OLZ* 61 (1966) 32-34. W. Beltz in his Habilitationsschrift *Die Adam-Apokalypse aus Codex V von Nag Hammadi : Jüdische Bausteine in gnostischen Systemen* (Humboldt-Universität; Berlin 1970) has also defended the Christian derivation of the tractate in its present form.

Since the tractate GrPow (CG VI, 4) has also shown that in a literary setting of predictive prophecy a document can be Christian without there being explicit acknowledgement, the issue at present revolves around whether in ApocAd there are "explicit Christian allusions or veiled ones that are specifically Christian" (MacRae, "The Apocalypse of Adam Reconsidered," 575) and also whether the cluster of alleged allusions is possible in a non-Christian document : e.g. the Illuminator who is punished in his flesh (77.16-18), his name is taken upon the water (83.5f; cf. 77.19), the Holy Spirit (77.17f), water of life in a baptismal context (84.7f). It seems that final judgment upon this issue will only be possible when all of the gnostic documents are available and when each of these alleged allusions has been studied in terms of its function within the documents and of its place within the development of Gnosticism.

[147] Böhlig (*Koptisch-gnostische Apokalypsen aus Codex V*, 95), Kasser, (R. Kasser, "Textes Gnostiques : Remarques A Propos des Éditions Récentes du Livre Secret de Jean, et des Apocalypses de Paul, Jacques, et Adam," *Le Muséon* 78 [1965] 91), MacRae ("The Apocalypse of Adam," 576), Perkins ("Apocalyptic Schematization in the Apocalypse of Adam," 591ff) and Rudolph (in his review of the Böhlig-Labib edition, 361) have all stressed the early nature of the document. Schenke (in his review of the Böhlig-Labib edition, 32), Beltz (Die *Adam-Apokalypse aus Codex V von Nag Hammadi*, 220-22) and Schottroff ("Animae naturaliter salvandae," 82), however, have argued that it is late. Beltz, in particular, has set forth the arguments for this position and claimed that ApocAd is contemporaneous with the acknowledgedly late GEgypt, since the obscure elements in ApocAd can be clarified by the fuller GEgypt. However, it is equally possible that GEgypt is a later development of material in ApocAd. He has secondly argued for a late date because of Manichaean material, which he finds in 82.4-83.4. However, again this material could just as well be pre-Manichaean material, which was taken over by the Manichaeans rather than vice versa. For our purposes, it is worth noting that this alleged Manichaean material occurs in the excursus on the fourteen sayings concerning the Illuminator, which are probably a later addition to the basic document. Thus, even if Beltz were correct, the *Grundschrift*, in which we are interested, could still be early.

[148] Cf. MacRae, "The Apocalypse of Adam Reconsidered," 576.

[149] Cf. Perkins, "Apocalyptic Schematization in the Apocalypse of Adam," 591ff.

between ApocAd and NatArch. There is no question of literary dependence here, but both tractates do share common gnostic traditions. For example, in names both tractates definitely call the evil Demiurge Saklas (ApocAd 74.3, 7; NatArch 95[143].7) and probably relate Seth to the gnostics (ApocAd 85.24; NatArch probably 91[139].31).[150] Secondly, both tractates share common mythologoumena. Adam and Eve are androgynous at first and possess the divine element (ApocAd 64.6-12; NatArch 89[137].3-11). The separation of Eve from Adam causes the loss of the divine element (ApocAd 64.20-30; NatArch 89[137].3-11). Eve, as the spiritual woman, teaches Adam (ApocAd 64.12f; NatArch 89[137].11-22).

For our comparison with NatArch it is important to note the views of ApocAd on God—both the supreme God and the lower ruler. The supreme God is entitled God; God, the Eternal; the God of Truth; or the living God.[151] On the other hand, the lower ruler, who is drawn from the deity of the OT, is also termed a God and receives the names : God; the God who made us; the Lord, the God who made us; God, the Ruler of the Aeons; God the Almighty (*Pantokratōr*); Saklas, their God; the God of the Aeons; and the God of the Powers.[152]

The lower God functions as the Demiurge of man (66.17-21) and probably implicitly also as the Demiurge of the world. In creating man the Demiurge has given him a spirit of life to make him a living soul (66.21-23; cf. Gen 2:7). However, ApocAd makes clear that this soul perishes and that there is another spirit from above, which brings eternal life (cf. 76.15-27; 77.7-15; 84.1-3).

At the flood, it is the same God, the lower God, who both destroys all flesh and yet quiets his anger and unexplainedly spares Noah (69.2-17; 70.6-15).

---

[150] Cf. the restoration of the lacuna here by Layton in "The Hypostasis of the Archons," (1974) 409.

[151] God (ⲡⲛⲟⲩⲧⲉ): 72.14; 82.21; 83.13, 21; God, the Eternal (ⲡⲛⲟⲩⲧⲉ ⲡⲓϣⲁ ⲉⲛⲉϩ): 64.13f; 76.22; 85.15; the God of Truth (ⲡⲛⲟⲩⲧⲉ ⲛⲧⲉ ⲧⲙⲉ): 65.13; and the living God (ⲡⲛⲟⲩⲧⲉ ⲉⲧⲟⲛϩ): 84.9f; and possibly also the God of the Aeons (ⲡⲛⲟⲩⲧⲉ ⲛⲧⲉ ⲛⲛⲉⲱⲛ): 85.4f, unless the text is emended here to avoid attributing to the supreme God this title which also applies to the lower God and seems to connote the aeons of the evil creation.

[152] God (ⲡⲛⲟⲩⲧⲉ): 64.7; [66.28]; 70.6, 16; 71.16; 78.15; 81.16; the God who made us (ⲡⲛⲟⲩⲧⲉ ⲉⲧⲁϥⲧⲁⲙⲓⲟⲛ): 64.17; 65.17f, 31f; 66.20f, 25f; the Lord, the God who made us (ⲡϫⲟⲉⲓⲥ ⲡⲛⲟⲩⲧⲉ ⲉⲧⲁϥⲧⲁⲙⲓⲟⲛ): 66.14f; God, the Ruler of the Aeons (ⲡⲛⲟⲩⲧⲉ ⲡⲁⲣⲭⲱⲛ ⲛⲧⲉ ⲛⲉⲱⲛ) 64.20f; God the Almighty (ⲡⲛⲟⲩⲧⲉ ⲡⲡⲁⲛⲧⲟⲕⲣⲁⲧⲱⲣ) 69.[4], 7; 72.25; 73.9; Saklas, their God (ⲥⲁⲕⲗⲁ ⲡⲉⲩⲛⲟⲩⲧⲉ) 74.3f, 7 (without the phrase "their God"); the God of the Aeons (ⲡⲛⲟⲩⲧⲉ ⲛⲧⲉ ⲛⲓⲉⲱⲛ) 74.26f; and the God of the Powers (77.4).

After the flood Noah then divides the entire earth, in accord with
Gen 9:18f, among his sons Shem, Ham, and Japhet, who are to serve
the Pantokrator in fear and slavery (72.15-25). From the seed of
Ham and Japhet some 400,000 men enter the land of the true gnostics
and dwell with them (73.15-20). When the remaining seed of Ham and
Japhet reproach the lower God for this event, he is entitled Saklas.
On the other hand, the descendants of Noah through Shem have done
the entire will of the lower God (74.17-21),[153] who in this context is
named the Pantokrator (72.25; 73.9). There is only the one lower God,
however, who is presented under these different titles (cf. 74.3-21
where Saklas is identified as the deity of Ham, Japhet, and also "of
the son of Noah", i.e. Shem). It seems probable that the division of
the peoples of the world into the descendants of Shem, Ham and Japhet
and the particular dedication of the descendants of Shem to the lower
God as the Pantokrator indicate that Shem represents the Jews and
Ham and Japhet the Gentiles (cf. Gen 10f; Jub 7-8; I QM 2:13-14).[154]
The coming of the Illuminator then is to save the souls of those
from among the seed of Noah and the sons of Ham and Japhet,
who have thought the gnosis of the eternal God in their heart and
received a spirit from one of the eternal angels (76.8-27).[155]

Finally, it is important for our comparison with NatArch to note
how this knowledge is transmitted. It was not placed in a book nor
written down (85.5f) but rather angelic beings have brought these
words to a rock on a high mountain (85.7-11).[156] These words of
imperishability and truth have then not been recognized by all generations of men (85.8-13); but they are the revelation, which Adam gave

---

[153] The son of Noah here probably refers to Shem, cf. Beltz, *Die Adam-Apokalypse
aus Codex V*, 111.

[154] Cf. Beltz, *Die Adam-Apokalypse aux Codex V*, 99-102.

[155] It is probably no accident that the return of the gnostic men to the earth is
not mentioned after their second delivery from fire (75.9-76.7). Rather, the emphasis
in the tractate is upon the possibility of the remaining descendants of Shem, Ham and
Japhet to receive gnosis and the spirit. Does this indicate a propagandistic purpose for
the work?

[156] ApocAd here uses the Jewish tradition that the revelation to Seth was engraved
upon a stele to withstand the flood; cf. Jos. *Ant.* 1.68-70; Adam and Eve 50:1. Although
the terms in Josephus are (στήλη/stele) and in Adam and Eve (tabulae/tablets), the
terms πέτρα/rock are equally acceptable in this context : e.g. Jub 8:3 the rock upon
which the teaching of the Watchers was engraved. Cf. Perkins, "Apocalyptic Schematization in the Apocalypse of Adam," 593 and n. 23. The denial by Beltz of this
interpretation presses too far the phrase "not written." Is the sense not that the words
were not written in a book but inscribed upon a rock? Otherwise, the reference to a
rock is meaningless. Cf. Beltz, *Die Adam-Apokalypse aus Codex V*, 192.

to Seth and which Seth gave to his seed, and the hidden knowledge of Adam which is the holy baptism of those who know the eternal gnosis (85.19-31). This hidden tradition of words then is the source of gnosis. It stands apart from the Law and the Prophets, and the whole question of the role of the Law and the Prophets is bypassed.

We shall contend in our discussion of Sabaoth in NatArch that these views were later developed further. When the issue of the value of the Law and the Prophets in addition to gnostic revelation was raised, the materials were at hand for a solution. The two different names, Pantokrator (-Sabaoth)[157] and Saklas, were applied to two different rulers; and the former came to represent the God of the Jews, who was considered as not entirely evil and who saved his own people at the flood. Although he was not entirely evil, this God of the Jews could still not impart the spiritual principle from above which gives eternal life.

The second account to consider is Iren. *Adv. haer.* 1.30, before we consider directly the Sabaoth account in NatArch. As Bullard pointed out frequently in his commentary, Irenaeus' account here of the doctrine of an unnamed sect is also closely related to NatArch. The sect to which this teaching belongs has been generally accepted as the Ophites on the basis of the prominence of the serpent within the account and the descriptions of Hippolytus (*Ref.* 5.6) and Theodoret (*Haereticarum fabularum compendium* 1.14; ed. PG 83. 363-68), who identifies the Ophites with the Sethians. If the Ophites do not belong to the Sethians proper, they at least certainly share common traditions with them. For example, although the role of Seth is not greatly emphasized, yet those who have the particle of light ultimately derive from him.[158]

---

[157] The Hebrew *YHWH s^eba'ôt* is translated in the LXX in various ways: as *kyrios sabaôth* throughout Isa and occasionally elsewhere; as *kyrios tōn dynameōn* in 1-4 Kgs, Ps, Amos, Zech and Jer; as *pantokratōr* or *kyrios pantokratōr* in various places in 2 and 3 Kgs, 1 Chr, Hos, Amos, Mic, Nah, Hab, Zeph, Zech, Mal, Jer. Sabaoth is also maintained in transliteration in Sib Or 1.304, 316; 2.239; 2 Enoch 21:1; 52:1 as well as in the magical papyri and the curse tablets. Cf. C. H. Dodd, *The Bible and the Greeks* (London 1935) 16-19; Bousset, *Die Religion des Judentums*, 312, n. 2; MacRae, *Some Elements of Jewish Apocalyptic*, 130; Bauer, *Wörterbuch, sub voce*. It is doubtful whether Dodd's suggestion (17) is necessarily correct, i.e. that the translation into *kyrios sabaôth*, as if the two nouns were in apposition, gave rise to the treatment of Sabaoth as a proper name within the gnostic writings and magical papyri, since the other divine names from the OT are also treated individually as proper names (cf. Iao, Adoneus; Iren. *Adv. haer.* 1.30).

[158] In this respect F. Wisse's exclusion of Iren. *Adv. haer.* 1.30, from the Sethians may need to be modified; cf. Wisse, "The Sethians and the Nag Hammadi Library," 606. In Irenaeus it is the *humectatio luminis*, which has fallen from above (30.2; ed.

In particular Iren. *Adv. haer.* 1.30 shares with NatArch the stress on Wisdom as the one from whom this world derives (30.2; ed. Harvey 1. 228f), the figure of Ialdabaoth (30.4; ed. Harvey 1. 230) and the sons whom he has generated (30.3f; ed. Harvey 1. 229f). In addition Irenaeus here also has the mythologoumena that Eve has a power which leaves her (30.6; ed. Harvey 1. 233), that the mother comes in the serpent (30.7; ed. Harvey 1. 234), and also that the serpent is Wisdom and the wisest of animals (30.14; ed. Harvey 1. 241).

For our purposes again it is important to note the teaching within this account concerning God. In addition to the supreme God who is called the First Man (30.1; ed. Harvey 1. 227), the lower deity Ialdabaoth also claims to be God (30.5; ed. Harvey 1. 232) and demands to be worshipped as such (30.10; ed. Harvey 1. 237). He resides in the seventh heaven, with his sons in the six heavens underneath. Together they rule both heavenly and earthly things (30.4; ed. Harvey 1. 230f). He too breathes a spirit of life into Adam, which in this case serves to deprive Ialdabaoth of his power and to transfer it to Adam. Samael (who is also named Michael) then is the serpent offspring of Ialdabaoth who is cast down by him into this world. There Samael generated six sons in imitation of his father's hebdomad, who together with him form the demons that afflict mankind (30.8; ed. Harvey 1. 235).

At the flood it is Ialdabaoth who seeks to destroy mankind while Wisdom saves those who are around Noah because of the light within them (30.10; ed. Harvey 1. 237). Who exactly is responsible for saving Noah is left unsaid, but probably Ialdabaoth is to be understood. After the flood Ialdabaoth chooses for himself Abraham and his seed, leads his descendants out of Egypt, gives them the Law and makes them Jews (30.10; ed. Harvey 1. 237). Ultimately then Christ comes to bring back the particle of light to the perfect Aeon (30.11ff; ed. Harvey 1. 238-40).

Harvey 1. 228) and ultimately needs to be reintegrated in the incorruptible Aeon (30.14; ed. Harvey 1. 241). By the creation of Adam and Eve this *humectatio luminis* was transferred from Ialdabaoth to Adam to Eve and then back to Prunicos (30.5f; ed. Harvey 1. 232f). After they were driven out of Paradise, Adam and Eve received an *odor suavitatis humectationis luminis* in order to be reminded of their own (30.8f; Harvey 1. 235f). After the birth of Cain and Abel, it is through the providence of Prunicos that Seth and Norea are born, from whom come the rest of men (30.9; ed. Harvey 1. 236). From their descendants many became subject to the lower hebdomad, but Prunicos saved her own, namely, those of the *humectatio luminis*. At the flood Wisdom saved those who were around Noah in the ark because of the light within them (30.9f; ed. Harvey 236f). Then it is this light to which Christ is sent (30.11f; ed. Harvey 1. 238).

Unlike ApocAd the problematic of how this knowledge reaches one is resolved differently. A hidden, oral tradition, completely independent of the Law and the Prophets is not introduced. To be sure, the Law and the Prophets are attributed to Ialdabaoth and his rulers:

> Each of these receives his own herald for the purpose of glorifying and proclaiming God; so that, when the rest hear these praises, they too may serve those who are announced as gods by the prophets.
> Moreover, they distribute the prophets in the following manner: Moses, and Joshua the son of Nun, and Amos, and Habakkuk, belonged to Ialdabaoth; Samuel, and Nathan, and Jonah, and Micah, to Iao; Elijah, Joel, and Zechariah, to Sabaoth; Isaiah, Ezekiel, Jeremiah, and Daniel, to Adonai; Tobias and Haggai to Eloi; Michaiah and Nahum to Oreus; Esdras and Zephaniah to Astranphaeus.[159]

Nevertheless, this account considers that true knowledge still comes through Moses and the prophets because Wisdom also spoke through them without them realizing it. Thereby she was able to communicate something about the First Man, i.e. the Supreme God, and to prophesy concerning Christ:

> Each one of these, then, glorifies his own father and God, and they maintain that Sophia herself has also spoken many things through them regarding the first Anthropos (man) ... The (other) powers being terrified by these things, and marvelling at the novelty of those things which were announced by the prophets.[160]

Wisdom was even able to act through Ialdabaoth without his realizing it in order to prepare for the descent of Christ.[161]

> Prunicus brought it about by means of Ialdabaoth (who knew not what he did), that emissions of two men took place, the one from the barren Elizabeth, and the other from the Virgin Mary.

If we return then to the first section of Iren. *Adv. haer.* 1.30, we can see examples of the knowledge concerning the First Man which can be drawn from the Law and the Prophets and which was significant for gnostic mythology. The first light is incorruptible (cf. Gen 1:3f). That light is called the First Man, but there is also a Second Man (cf. Gen 1:26), who came from him. The Holy Spirit, the first woman,

---

[159] Iren. *Adv. haer.* 1.30.10; ed. Harvey I. 237; tr. The *Ante-Nicene Fathers* (reprint Grand Rapids 1956) I. 356f.

[160] Iren. *Adv. haer.* 1.30.10f; ed. Harvey I. 237f; tr. *The Ante-Nicene Fathers*, I. 357. As Harvey notes in his edition, the phrase *et incorruptibili Aeone* is only attested in the Clermont manuscript and is probably a later addition; 238, n. 1. Thus the translator has consigned the phrase to a footnote; cf. 357, n. 2.

[161] Iren. *Adv. haer.* 1.30.11; ed. Harvey I. 238; tr. *The Ante-Nicene Fathers*, I. 357.

is above chaos. From the union of the First Man and the Second Man with her the Third Male, Christ, issued forth (cf. Gen 1:2). She is also called the mother of the living (cf. Gen 3:20).

From this background the material in NatArch becomes much clearer. Here too there is, of course, the Supreme God, e.g. the Father of Truth 86(134).21. The lower God Ialdabaoth (94[142].21f) also creates offspring for himself to fill each of the heavens below him 95(143).1-4.[162] He is named Saklas as well as Ialdabaoth 95(143).7f. Further, he is identified as Samael 94(142).25f and thus the tradition associated with Samael, that he is a fallen heavenly being who is the leader of the demonic forces, is applied to Ialdabaoth as well. Therefore, Ialdabaoth is cast down to Tartaros below the abyss (95[143]. 10-13), where he begets further offspring (96[144].4-10). Within the myth then place is provided for Sabaoth to assume the role of Ialdabaoth, to reign over the seventh heaven, and thereby to function as an intermediate deity. There he is given Life and is named the God of the Forces (95[143].19-23 and 31-34).

The role of Sabaoth is not restricted merely to the revelation of Eleleth; rather he functions as well in the Noah story (92[140].4-21). Contrary to ApocAd and Iren. *Adv. haer.* 1.30, NatArch distinguishes between the deity who seeks to destroy all men and the deity who seeks to save Noah. It is Sabaoth, here entitled the Ruler of the Forces, who protects Noah, and Ialdabaoth as the Great One, who along with the other rulers causes the flood.[163] Norea as the representative of

---

[162] It is an indication of how carefully the myth is constructed that Ialdabaoth here creates seven sons and in Iren. *Adv. haer.* 1.30, creates only six. In Iren. Ialdabaoth remains in the seventh heaven; thus he and his six sons form the Hebdomad. In NatArch, since Ialdabaoth is cast out of the heavens, seven sons must be created in order to retain the Hebdomad. Cf. also OnOrgWld 101(149).24-102(150).2 and 106 (154).19-27.

[163] It is clear that the Ruler of the Forces is equal to the God of the Forces, i.e. Sabaoth, for two reasons. First, only in these two instances is the term "Forces" (δύναμις) used in a title and thus the two titles should be referred to the same person. Secondly, the narrative demands a distinction between the leader of the rulers and the Ruler of the Forces. In the narrative all the rulers plan to cause the flood and to destroy all flesh (92[140].4-8). However, the Ruler of the Forces is against this plan (92[140].8-14), insofar as he wants to protect Noah. Later, however, when the rulers come to Norea, there is no indication of division among them (92[140].19-21). Rather their great One is among them and united with them. As 86[134].27-31 shows, their Great One is none other than Ialdabaoth, who alone claimed to be the one God (cf. 94[142].21-26; 95[143].5-8). Although Bullard in his commentary alludes to the title of Sabaoth, he fails to draw out fully the implications and rests with the assumption that the Ruler of the Forces equals the Demiurge, i.e. Ialdabaoth (cf. *The Hypostasis of the Archons*, 94). Cf. the commentary of Layton in "The Hypostasis of the Archons, (1975) ad loc.

the race of the gnostics is then associated with the heavenly angel
Eleleth (92[140].32 ff).

Concerning revelation it is said that when the True Man comes,
he will teach the saved about everything (96[144].33-97[145].4), which
knowledge will make them immortal 96[144].25-27). In the meantime,
Norea has received a revelation from Eleleth but Sabaoth has also
received instruction from Life concerning the Eighth, although he is
below the veil in the seventh heaven (95[143].19-22 and 31-34).

It seems clear that the same problem is vexing the author of NatArch
as vexed the author behind Iren. *Adv. haer.* 1.30, namely, how to
account for the aspects of the Law and the Prophets which were
acceptable to the gnostics and which taught them, when the texts were
correctly interpreted, something about the pleromatic realm. Iren. *Adv.
hear.* 1.30, had solved the problem by having Wisdom speak through
the unknowing Ialdabaoth. NatArch has answered the same problem
but with a different solution in that the God of the Law and the
Prophets is another God than the evil Demiurge. To be sure, he is
descended from the Demiurge and a God of fear (95[143].13-15) and
yet not entirely evil since he has repented. His elevation to the seventh
heaven and instruction then concerning the things of the Eighth make
it possible for him to communicate this information to Moses and
the Prophets, although he himself is fated never to enter the Eighth.
Surely an appropriate tradition—the ascent of the visionary to the
chariot and throne of God—has been drawn upon to solve this problem
concerning the revelation contained in the books of Israel.

Insofar as Sabaoth saves Noah and is responsible for the revelation
in the Law and the Prophets, he is the God of the Jews and they are his
special people. That this assessment need not be a mere evaluation of
the past people of the OT but could also involve an evaluation of
contemporaneous Jewish people is shown by Origen's *Contra Celsum*,
in which Origen makes frequent reference to his discussions and debates
with Jews on the meaning of scripture.[164] In contrast the true gnostics
belong to the Father of the All 96(144).11-12 and 19-20.

In his commentary, Bullard has suggested that Sabaoth represents
the situation of one group among the three possible types of men,
namely, the psychics. He considers this passage from a Valentinian
background with its three categories of pneumatic, psychic, and hylic
men.[165] We shall see that Sabaoth in OnOrgWld does indeed represent

---

[164] Cf. *C. Cel.* 1.45; 2.28; 4.2; tr. H. Chadwick (rev. ed.; Cambridge, England
1965).

[165] Bullard, *The Hypostasis of the Archons*, 110.

the psychics. There the immortal Light-Man resides in the middle and represents the pneumatics (112[160].10-22); Sabaoth dwells in the seventh heaven and signifies the psychics (104[152].20f); and Ialdabaoth and his offspring abide in the other six heavens and typify the choics or hylics (106[154].19-27 and 122[170].6-9). However, in NatArch the anthropology is less clearly organized and systematized. Further, in NatArch it is the psyche that is said to come from above, from the Imperishable Light, rather than the pneuma (96[144].21f). To be sure, then, the spirit of truth will come and live within the soul and thus make the soul immortal (96[144].22-26). The elements for the separation of men into these three anthropological categories are all present, but they are not systematized as in OnOrgWld or in Valentinianism. The only separation that we find is the separation into those who have true knowledge, those represented by Sabaoth, i.e. the Jewish people, and those represented by the rulers.

It is also appropriate to his purpose that the gnostic author has drawn upon the tradition of enthronement in portraying the role of Sabaoth. Sabaoth has been placed in charge of the seventh heaven and implicitly in charge of all below. In effect, he has been installed as king—although without the title. Thereby, the people of Israel are subject to him as their king as well as the remaining peoples and rulers. For the gnostic author, unlike Moses' enthronement in Ezekiel Tr or Philo, which established him as the divinely appointed ruler of the world and the leader of the divinely founded people, the enthrone-ment of Sabaoth establishes his rule as part of the evil world and thus indicates the inferiority of him and his subjects to the true gnostics. Although Sabaoth has repented, he is still an offspring of Ialdabaoth, who remains below the veil.

This notion that the ruler below the Pleroma is a king is a familiar one in gnostic literature. In the TriProt (CG XIII, 2: 43.15-17) at the time of completion and at the time of the coming of the destroyer, the powers are disturbed and their "king" is afraid (cf. also 41.11ff).[166] Heracleon also considers the Demiurge in the Valentinian system as a king in Frag. 40 :

> Heracleon seems to say that the "royal officer" (v. 46) was the Demiurge, "for he himself ruled like a king (βασιλεύειν) over those under him. Because his domain is small and transitory he was called a royal officer," he says,

---

[166] Cf. also ApocryJn BG 8502 41.12-15 in which Ialdabaoth appoints seven kings over the world and five over the underworld.

"like a petty princeling who is set over a small kingdom by the universal king."[167]

Further, in Iren. *Adv. haer.* 1.30.4-5, Ialdabaoth and his descendants sit in order. Therefore Ialdabaoth is at the top, in the seventh heaven. Together they are said to "rule" heavenly and earthly things, a verb which is appropriate to royal dignity (*regere*).

In contrast, the author of NatArch states that the gnostics are those anointed with the anointing of eternal life from the "undominated race" (97[145].2-5). The gnostics are themselves from the Above, from the Imperishable Light (96[144].21-22). As here, so also in SJC BG 92.4-7, 10-11; 108.11-15 (cf. parallel in Eug III, 3), the "undominated race" are the pleromatic, divine beings. This negative motif emphasizes their radical freedom from entrapment in the evil rule of the world. By their origin and anointing, then, the gnostics are also radically free from the evil rule of this world.

There is a possibility that this negative motif implies its opposite, the positive motif, i.e. that the pleromatic beings are kings themselves and that the true gnostics are also the "undominated race." Thus in OnOrgWld 122(170).6-8 it is stated that there are three men and their races: the pneumatic of the aeon, the psychic and the earthly. After discussing the sending of the innocent spirits into the world (124[172]. 5—125[173].3), the author turns to the true gnostics and states:

Therefore (ὥστε) there are four
kinds (γένος). Three belong
to the kings of the Eighth. But (δέ) the fourth
kind (γένος) is a perfect (τέλειον) *kingless* one, which is
above them all. For these will go
into the holy place (τόπος) of their father
and will be at ease in rest (ἀνάπαυσις)
with their eternal, unspeakable glory
and with an unceasing joy. But (δέ) they are
kings among the mortal (θνητόν) as (ὡς) immortal.[168]

---

[167] Text W. Völker, *Quellen zur Geschichte der christlichen Gnosis* (Sammlung Ausgewählter Kirchen- und Dogmengeschichtlicher Quellenschriften 5; Tübingen 1932) 80; translation W. Förster, *Gnosis: A Selection of Gnostic Texts*, tr. R. McL. Wilson (Oxford 1972) 1. 177.

[168] OnOrgWld 125(173).3-12; Böhlig, *Die koptisch-gnostische Schrift ohne Titel*, 100-03. Cf. 127(175).4-14. The motif that the gnostics become kings is found in other circles of Gnosticism: e.g. ApocryJas 3.25-27; 10.1-5; GTh Saying 2, 81; ThCont 145.14; DialSav 138.11-15. While the highest God may not be named a king in gnostic documents, note that he or his spirit is termed a μοναρχία in ApocryJn BG 22.18, since no one rules (ἄρχειν) over him. See also the Naassenes and the reference to being a king and kingless in Hipp. *Ref.* 5.8.2, 18, 30 (ed. Wendland; GCS 26; 89-94).

However, it is possible that this positive aspect of the motif is a later development, when it is applied to gnostics while they are in the world. In either case, the claim is made for the radical freedom of the gnostic from the evil rule of this world.

There are also practical, political implications in this view. Although the *archai*, *exousiai* and *archontes* are demonic powers, the terms also carry political references in late antiquity. It is difficult not to see in them and in the gnostic view a rejection of the legitimacy of the governmental system in which the gnostic lived, i.e. the Roman Empire.[169] This rejection, however, would not imply a revolutionary drive to overthrow the government but rather to expose the false appearance and to establish the gnostics as an elite beyond the political system, as those who alone know the way to salvation.[170]

C. CONFIRMATION OF THE FUNCTION AND THE DATE

We have proposed above that the name of Sabaoth has been chosen for this ruler of the seventh heaven in order specifically to represent

---

[169] In his article, H. G. Kippenberg ("Versuch einer soziologischen Verortung des antiken Gnostizismus," *Numen* 17[1950] 211-31) has proposed this view and noted that there is no explicit reference to the political power of the Roman Empire in the gnostic document (225). Since the evil ruler of the world is often portrayed as the God of the OT in gnostic documents, however, did Gnosticism begin as a rejection of the Jewish God and Jewish hegemony by people in the Syria-Palestine area, as Bousset has suggested in *Hauptprobleme* 321-25, which rejection then would have been secondarily applied to Roman rule when the Romans became the ruling power? However, this question must be considered in conjunction with the possibility that this negative portrayal of the God of the OT arose out of increasing pessimism towards the world and his creation or out of reaction to his unfavorable traits (e.g. envy) rather than as a reaction to his unjust rule.

[170] Kippenberg, "Versuch einer soziologischen Verortung," 231. Cf. also the discussion in Origen *C. Cel.* 8.68 (tr. Chadwick 504-05). Celsus, the pagan, maintains that all should uphold that there be one king, the one who has received the power from "the son of crafty Kronos," i.e. Zeus. Origen, the orthodox Christian, agrees that there should be one king but denies that he is appointed by "the son of crafty Kronos," since—as Origen relates—the Greek myths say that he drove his father from rule and cast him into Tartarus. Rather, the king is to be the one appointed "by God who governs all things and knows what he is doing in the matter of the appointment of kings." If he were to join in the discussion, the answer of the gnostic author of NatArch would seem to be that there is to be one king, the one appointed by Sabaoth, whose father was cast into Tartarus, but that he and his appointee belong to the evil realm of the world and have no ultimate authority over the gnostics. For the identification of Ialdabaoth-Kronos-Saturn, see *C. Cel.* 6.31 and Bousset, *Hauptprobleme* 351-55. Sabaoth and Adonai are identified with Zeus by Celsus, but Origen denies that identification in *C. Cel.* 5.45 and 6.39. It deserves further study to see if the identification Sabaoth (or Adonai)-Zeus-Jupiter is found in the gnostic documents themselves and to see how vital the discussion of the divine right of kings was in the time of Gnosticism's existence.

the God of the Jews. A consideration of the Gnostikoi, the Archontics, and the Severians—all sects related to the Sethians—makes this evident and also confirms our hypothesis that the basic theological issue involved in the Sabaoth account is the revelation contained in the books of Israel.

Concerning the Gnostikoi, Epiphanius states (*Pan.* 25-26)[171] that this sect derives from the deacon Nicolas (*Pan.* 25.1.1); he claims to have encountered personally the sect as a young man and at that time to have read their books (*Pan.* 26.17.4-18.2). The presence of the mythological figures Barbelo (*Pan.* 25.2.2), Ialdabaoth (*Pan.* 25.2.2) and Prunikos (*Pan.* 25.3.2) indeed relates this sect to the Sethians. Their books further associate them with the Sethians. For example, some books are written in the name of Seth; there are *Apocalypses of Adam* (*Pan.* 26.8.1); there is a *Gospel of Eve* in which Eve received the food of knowledge through the revelations of the serpent (*Pan.* 26.2.6). Further, they have a book called *Norea*, the figure who is the wife of Noah and burned the ark three times, because she was refused admittance (*Pan.* 26.1.3-9). The list of rulers is also of interest to us, since Epiphanius reports a dispute concerning the occupants of the last two heavens (*Pan.* 26.10.2-3; cf. 25.2.2):

> Now some of them say that Ialdabaoth is in the sixth heaven, but others say Elilaeus. Now they propose that there is another, seventh, heaven in which, they say, Sabaoth is; now others say, "No! But Ialdabaoth is in the seventh."[172]

They also had a problem with the OT, although they continued to use it as a source of revelation since they found therein some words from the spirit of truth. Epiphanius expresses their problem in these words (*Pan.* 26.6.1-2):

> Now they use both Old and New Testament but they renounce the one who spoke in the OT. And whenever they find a word able to have a sense inimical to them, they say that this is spoken by the worldly spirit. But if any passage is able to be formed into the likeness of their desire —not as the word says but as their deluded mind says—they change this into their own desire and say that it was spoken by the spirit of truth.[173]

---

[171] Ed. Holl (GCS 25.1) 267-300.

[172] Ed. Holl (GCS 25.1) 287; translation mine. In contrast with NatArch, one notes that the myth related here by Epiphanius contains the figure Barbelo and the reference to the need to gather the power from bodies in order to return it to the above. On the other hand, this myth of Epiphanius contains no reference to Sabaoth's repentance, ascent and enthronement in the seventh heaven.

[173] Ed. Holl (GCS 25.1) 282-83; translation mine.

In their resolution of the problem, however, these Gnostikoi maintained that the God of the OT was entirely evil. In particular, in *Pan.* 26.10.6 (cf. also 10.7-11) it is Sabaoth who is portrayed as the evil Demiurge and also as the God of the Jews :

> Now some say that Sabaoth has the form of an ass; others say that of a pig. Therefore—he says—he commanded the Jews not to eat pork. And they say that he is the maker of heaven and earth, and of the heavens after him and of his own angels.[174]

In considering this report of Epiphanius, one should first note that it is late and compilatory, i.e. reflecting a number of views within the sect. Secondly, it is based upon the distant recollections of Epiphanius. Thirdly, the dispute concerning the occupants of the sixth and seventh heaven probably involves something deeper than just a name. It seems quite probable that this account of Epiphanius, with its dispute over the position of Ialdabaoth and Sabaoth echoes attempts to associate the evil Demiurge of the world more clearly with the God of the OT, with the God of the Jews. Since his name appears within the pages of the LXX, Sabaoth could be more easily taken as the God of the OT and of the Jews than the enigmatic figure and name of Ialdabaoth. The reference to the spirit of truth as the author of acceptable portions of the Law and the Prophets is then an alternate view of solving the problem than that of NatArch, which view, however, is similar to that of Iren. *Adv. haer.* 1.30.

Similarly the Archontics consider Sabaoth as the God of the Jews. As Puech has suggested, the Archontics probably did not fashion a separate sect.[175] At most the Archontics was the Palestinian name for Egyptian gnostics who were related to the Sethians. In our main source for the Archontics, Epiph. *Pan.* 40,[176] it is stated that Sabaoth is the ruler of the seventh heaven who acts the part of the tyrant over the other rulers (*Pan.* 40.2.6), who gave the Law (*Pan.* 40.2.8) and who is thus the God of the Jews. He is also, however, the God of the Christians, who are not gnostics since baptism and the mysteries are associated with his name :

> They consider as anathema the baptismal font, even if some among them have previously been taken and baptized. They reject the sharing and goodness of the mysteries as being alien and done in the name of Sabaoth.

---

[174] Ed. Holl (GCS 25.1) 287-88; translation mine.
[175] H.-Ch. Puech, "Archontiker," RAC I (1950) 635.
[176] Ed. Holl (GCS 31.2; Leipzig 1922) 80-90.

For, in accord with some of the other sects, they want him to be in the seventh heaven where he is a tyrant and has authority over the others... But they say that if this (soul) is in gnosis and flees the baptism of the church and the name of Sabaoth who gave the Law, it ascends through each heaven.[177]

Since the Law was associated with Sabaoth and thus evil, these gnostics found their revelation in another source. Like ApocAd, this revelation derives from Seth, who was brought up on high by the power above and his ministering angels. When he returned to earth, Seth then served the true God and made many revelations, which have been preserved in Books (*Pan.* 40.7.2ff).[178]

Lastly, the little known Severians, who are also associated with the Sethians, identify the chief evil ruler as Sabaoth or Ialdabaoth (Epiph. *Pan.* 45.1.4).[179] Epiphanius reports that they use apocryphal books but that they also use canonical books, which they search out to interpret in their own distinctive way. Obviously then they found some value in the OT but it is not clear as to how they explained the presence of revelation in the OT. In the abbreviated report of Epiphanius there is then no explicit statement that Sabaoth is the God of the Jews.

To help us confirm further the function and also to determine the date of the Sabaoth account in NatArch, we turn our attention now to the Marcionites and Valentinians. The problem of the OT and the God of the OT was raised in a particularly acute fashion in the second century by Marcion. For him the sacred books of the Jews were to be rejected and replaced by a modified Lukan Gospel, a Pauline corpus, and his own Antitheses, which presented the good God who is unknowable, separate from the world and yet revealed in Christ.[180] The God who is portrayed in the sacred books of Israel, on the other hand, is a second principle, the creator of the world, who is righteous (*dikaios*) but not good.[181] The revelation contained

---

[177] Epiph. *Pan.* 40.2.6 and 8. Ed. Holl (GCS 31.2) 82-83; translation mine.

[178] Ed. Holl (GCS 31.2) 87-88.

[179] Ed. Holl (GCS 31.2) 199.

[180] Justin *Apol.* 1.26 and 58; Iren. *Adv. haer.* 1.27.2-3. A. von Harnack in his classic monograph *Marcion: Das Evangelium vom fremden Gott,* 2. Aufl. (Darmstadt 1960) discusses the teachings of Marcion in pages 93-152.

[181] Harnack (*Marcion,* 30*-39*) is correct in insisting that Marcion used the distinction between the two Gods, one *agathos* and one *dikaios,* and that this usage has been transferred to Cerdo by the heresiologists, who also consider him the teacher of Marcion (Iren, *Adv. haer.* 1.27.1 and 3.4.2; ed. Harvey 1. 214-15 and 2. 17; Tertullian *Adv. Marc.* 1.2; ed. A. Kroymann, Pars 3; CSEL 47; Vienna 1906; 292-93). Cerdo,

in these books is then considered by Marcion to be true in itself but
related only to this righteous God and his world; there is nothing
in these books concerning the good God. Even the prophecies about
the Messiah can be considered as true by Marcion, but they again
refer only to the Jewish Messiah and not to Christ, who reveals the
good God.[182] As the Creator, the God of these sacred books is the
God of all men, but in particular he has chosen the Jewish people and
through them desires to be known to all men.[183] The world, however,
over which he rules is evil since the matter from which it is formed is
inherently evil.[184]

Among the disciples of Marcion there are two of particular interest,
Megethius and Apelles, because of their treatment of the righteous
God and the Jewish people. Megethius alters the teaching of Marcion
in one respect. He proposes instead of two principles a three principle
system : namely, a good God, a righteous God and an evil God.
To these Gods he then refers the Christians, Jews, and pagans. Although
the pagans are related to the evil God, yet—as Harnack has observed—
the main interest of Megethius was in the pagans rather than the
Jews since the redeemer came to free men from this evil God.[185]

Apelles, the disciple who broke with his master and founded his
own sect, further altered the teaching of Marcion. For him there was
only one God. The righteous creator was merely an angel, and the
one who spoke to Moses was a further fiery, fallen angel. Similar
to Megethius, Apelles refers these three heavenly beings to the divisions
of mankind : Christians, pagans and Jews. However, in this case the
Jews occupy the lowest place, and their sacred books are in turn further
devalued as lies and fables.[186]

The Valentinians,[187] who drew upon and further developed vulgar,

---

on the other hand, would have distinguished between a good and an evil God as is
stated by Epiphanius in *Pan*. 41.1 (ed. Holl; GCS 31.2; 90-92) and by Filastrius in
Diversarum hereseon liber 44 (ed. F. Heylen; CCSL 9.207-324; Turnhout 1957; 235-36).

[182] Tert. *Adv. Marc*. 3.6; ed. Kroymann, Pars 3 (CSEL 47) 383-86. Cf. Harnack,
Marcion, 113-18.

[183] Tert. *Adv. Marc*. 4.6, 33; ed. Kroymann, Pars 3 (CSEL 47) 432-33 and 529-32.

[184] Clem. Alex. *Stromateis* 3.3.12; ed. O. Staehlin, Bd. 2 (GCS 15; Leipzig 1906)
200-01.

[185] Adamantius *Dial*. 1.1-3; ed. W. H. van de Sande Bakhuyzen (GCS 4; Leipzig
1901) 2-7. Cf. Harnack, *Marcion*, 165-67; 56*-63*; 181; 344*-47*.

[186] Rhodon in Euseb, *Hist. eccl*. 5.13.2-7 (ed. E. Schwartz and T. Mommsen, Bd.
2.1; GCS 9.1; Leipzig 1903; 454-59) and in Hipp. *Ref*. 7.38.1-5 (ed. P. Wendland;
GCS 26; Leipzig 1916; 224-25). Cf. Harnack, *Marcion*, 194-96; 404*-20*.

[187] Our major sources for the Valentinians are the Fathers both in their direct
citations and in their indirect accounts of them. Among the direct citations are the

mythological Gnosticism,[188] share this same second century concern
about the God of Israel, the revelation in its sacred books, and the
people of the Jews. However, the Demiurge is not considered in Valentinianism to be hylic and therefore entirely evil. Rather he is psychic
and therefore capable of turning to the good. He is particularly
presented as a righteous God.[189] In contrast with NatArch, Valentinianism presents a righteous creator rather than a repentant ruler.

In reference to the sacred books of Israel the Valentinian attitude
to the Law is most clearly expressed in Ptolemy's *Letter to Flora*.
There he distinguishes those parts of the Law that are to be attributed
to God, to Moses or to the elders.[190] Only those parts attributed to God
are acceptable. He further divides the Law of God into three parts:
the pure, the mixed, and the typic or symbolic. Such parts as the Deca-
logue are pure but need to be perfected. Other mixed sections, such
as the law of talion—"an eye for an eye"—although righteous, were
given because of the weakness of the people and thus ended by the
Son. Finally, parts, such as the Sabbath or fasting, are ended according
to their visible or bodily fulfillment but retain a typic or symbolic
significance insofar as they indicate the pneumatic realm.[191] Thus the
entire Law is not rejected by Ptolemy. Some elements retain their

---

fragments from Valentinus, which are contained mainly in Clement's *Stromateis*; the
doctrinal letter in Epiphanius' *Pan.*; Ptolemy's *Letter to Flora*; fragments from Heracleon's *Commentary of John*; and fragments from Marcus as representatives of the
Italian school. The *Excerpta ex Theodoto* then are representative of the Oriental branch.
Irenaeus in *Adv. haer.* 1.1.1-8.4 and Hippolytus in *Ref.* 6.29.1-36.4 offer the indirect
accounts. The sources are conveniently gathered in Völker's *Quellen zur Geschichte der
Christlichen Gnosis*, 57-141. Scholarly discussion of the Nag Hammadi corpus has also
proposed GTr, GPh and OnRes as derived from Valentinianism. Cf. also Jonas, *Gnosis
und spätantiker Geist*, 1.362-75; and F.-M.-M. Sagnard, *La gnose valentinienne et le
témoignage de Saint Irénée* (Études de Philosophie Mediévale 36; Paris 1947).

[188] Cf. Jonas, *Gnosis und spätantiker Geist*, 1. 358ff; Wilson, *The Gnostic Problem*,
116ff; Sagnard, *La gnose valentinienne*, 446 and n. 1. Note also that in *Exc. Theod.* 54
and Iren. *Adv. haer.* 1.7.5 the Valentinians are said to teach that mankind is divided
into the descendants of Cain, Abel and Seth. It is Seth, who then represents the
pneumatics.

[189] Epiph. *Pan.* 33.3.5-7 (Völker, 87-88).

[190] Epiph. *Pan.* 33.4.14 (Völker 89). As a forerunner to these and the following
distinctions, cf. the distinctions that Philo introduces concerning the Law in his treatise
De vita Mosis 2.188ff: some oracles are from God, some are mixed, and some are
from Moses. In *De vita Mosis* 1.4, Philo states that he has gathered his information
concerning Moses from the sacred books and also from the "elders" (*presbyteroi*) of
the nation (LCL; Cambridge 1966; 6. 278f and 542ff). Cf. F. Fallon "The Law in Philo
and Ptolemy: A Note on the Letter to Flora," *VC* 30 (1976) 45-51.

[191] Epiph. *Pan.* 33.5.1-6.5 (Völker, 89-92).

value, although in need of perfection, while other parts maintain a typic value.

An even more positive evaluation of the sacred books of Israel is presented in the Valentinian discussion of the prophets. Irenaeus presents their view in the following passage :

> They maintain, moreover, that those souls which possess the seed of Achamoth are superior to the rest, and are more dearly loved by the Demiurge than others, while he knows not the true cause thereof, but imagines that they are what they are through his favour towards them. Wherefore, also, they say he distributed them to prophets, priests, and kings; and they declare that many things were spoken by this seed through the prophets, inasmuch as it was endowed with a transcendently lofty nature. The mother also, they say, spoke much about things above, and that through him and through the sons which were formed by him. Then, again, they divine the prophecies (into different classes) maintaining that one portion was uttered by the mother, a second by her seed, and a third by the Demiurge.[192]

Here one sees that the Valentinians again distinguish. Some prophecies are spoken by Wisdom through the Demiurge and through the souls fashioned by him. In these prophecies there is revelation concerning the realm above. Other prophecies are spoken by the spiritual seed, which comes from Wisdom. And lastly some prophecies are attributed to the Demiurge. Those prophecies from the Demiurge do not reveal the pleromatic realm since he is usually considered to be entirely ignorant of that realm.[193] Only when the Savior comes is he to be instructed in the things above.[194] Prophecies made by him concerning Christ are only prophecies concerning the psychic Christ and not the pleromatic Christ.[195] In one interesting variant, Wisdom is also said to have instructed the Demiurge previously about the Father and the mystery of the Aeons. However, he has kept this mystery to himself and revealed it to no one.[196]

---

[192] Iren. *Adv. haer.* 1.7.3 (Völker, 119); tr. *The Ante-Nicene Fathers* 1.325f.

[193] Iren, *Adv. haer.* 1.5.4 (Völker, 109-10); Hipp. *Ref.* 6.35.1 (Völker, 134).

[194] Iren. *Adv. haer.* 1.7.1-2, and 4 (Völker, 118-19). Thereby, the Demiurge ceases his blasphemy but also continues the economy of the cosmos, since it is necessary for the church and since he realizes that at the consummation he is to reach salvation in the place of the Middle. Cf. the similar conception of Basilides in Hipp. *Ref.* 7.26.1-7 (Völker, 53-54).

[195] Iren. *Adv. haer.* 1.7.1-2 (Völker, 118).

[196] Hipp. *Ref.* 6.36.2 (Völker, 135). The instruction of the Demiurge in this instance then does not function to provide him with information that he might further communicate concerning the pleroma through the Law and the Prophets. Rather it seems to emphasize his righteousness and his role in continuing the economy of the cosmos as in Iren. *Adv. haer.* 1.7.4 (Völker, 119).

In accord with this concern for the God of Israel and its sacred books, the Valentinians also manifest an interest in evaluating the people of the OT, the Jews. In their consideration of mankind as a whole, the Valentinians distinguish three categories: the hylic, those who are destined to destruction; the psychic, those who have free choice and can thus be either saved or destroyed; and the pneumatic, those who are saved by nature.[197] The pneumatics then are derived from Wisdom and are the gnostics. The psychics, on the other hand, come from the Demiurge and are the Jews[198] and also the orthodox Christians.[199] The hylics then are the pagans who are related to the Cosmocrator, the devil.[200]

In conclusion, then, the Sabaoth account in NatArch functions to show that the God of the OT, the ruler of the seventh heaven, is not entirely evil, that he was instructed in the realm above and therefore capable of making revelations concerning it, and that his people were the Jews who therefore were not perfect and thus could not enter the perfect realm.

In considering the date of NatArch, we should first note that the early tractate ApocAd shows no need to introduce a righteous God as the God of the OT. Secondly, the account in Iren. *Adv. haer.* 1.30, whose source must stem from prior to the middle of the second century and is closely related to NatArch, also shows no awareness of a righteous God in the OT. Thus one is led to suggest the middle of the second century as the *terminus post quem* for the Sabaoth account and NatArch.

Further, the influence of the Marcionites and the Valentinians, both of whom stressed the righteous God of the OT, was greatest in the second half of the second century. The issue of the value of the Law and the Prophets was also of central concern to the Marcionites and Valentinians of that time. The Marcionites, of course, rejected the Law and the Prophets while the Valentinians retained them and reinter-

---

[197] Iren. *Adv. haer.* 1.6.1 (Völker, 112). On the meaning of the expression "saved by nature," see the recent discussion of Schottroff, "Animae naturaliter salvandae," 83-97 and E. Pagels, *The Johannine Gospel in Gnostic Exegesis: Heracleon's Commentary on John* (SBLMS 17; Nashville 1973) 98-113. They agree that the usage of this expression by the Fathers reflects their polemical interest but disagree over the Valentinian interpretation and application of it.

[198] *Exc. Theod.* 37-38.2; F.-M.-M. Sagnard, *Extraits de Théodote* (SC 23; Paris 1948) 140-41. Heracleon, Frag. 20 (Völker, 73-74).

[199] Iren. *Adv. haer.* 1.6.2 (Völker, 115).

[200] Heracleon, Frag. 20 (Völker, 73-74).

preted them. For both heretical groups the Jewish people were associated with that righteous Demiurge. Again NatArch and its Sabaoth account with the same concerns fit most appropriately into this same time period, the latter half of the second century. However, this is not yet to say that Marcionite or Valentinian teaching has had direct influence upon NatArch. If that were so, one would expect the contrast between righteousness and unrighteousness rather than life and unrighteousness on the right and left of Sabaoth. Secondly, in neither Marcionite nor Valentinian teaching does the righteous Demiurge usually receive instruction concerning the upper realm. Thirdly, the proposed source of NatArch, the Revelation of Norea, as reflected in Epiph. *Pan.* 26.1.3-9, shows no awareness of a repentant, ascended and enthroned Sabaoth. We shall argue in reference to the Sabaoth account in OnOrgWld, on the other hand, that there is direct Valentinian influence in the document. Its date in the third century then will provide us with a *terminus ante quem* for NatArch and its Sabaoth account.

CHAPTER FOUR

THE SABAOTH ACCOUNT IN ONORGWLD

In OnOrgWld the Sabaoth account is also placed clearly within the cosmogony. The central theme for the treatise has been enunciated: that something did exist before chaos, namely, the light. From this came the shadow called darkness and also chaos (97[145].24ff; 98[146]. 26ff). From the darkness, in turn, came matter, the Demiurge and his archontic offspring, including Sabaoth. After the Demiurge's blasphemy, he is reprimanded by Faith. In contrast to NatArch, however, a new element is introduced. The Demiurge is wrong in his claim to be alone since an immortal Light-Man existed before him. He is to appear in their fashioning and tread upon the Demiurge (103[151].19-28). After saying this, Faith revealed her image in the water and then returned to the light (103[151].28-32). Then there follows the account of Sabaoth's repentance and enthronement in the seventh heaven. From his envy then came the demons (106[154].19ff). Later, that light does come from the Eighth, with the form of a man in it, and that angel is henceforth called the Light-Adam (108[156].2ff). After revealing himself upon the earth, the Light-Adam returns toward the light (111[159].29-112[160].1) but is unable to enter the Eighth because of the fault with which his light has been mixed. Therefore, he builds a great Aeon which is in a boundless region between the Eighth and chaos (112[160].10-22), i.e. the middle. The treatise continues then with its re-interpretation of Genesis, the sending of innocent spirits into the world, and the eschatological restitution.

A. Exegesis

The Sabaoth account (103[151].32-106[154].19) forms a distinct unit within OnOrgWld, to such an extent that Böhlig has suggested that it is an interpolation.[1] It is clearly a unit, since the focus of attention throughout is upon Sabaoth and his heavenly entourage, while previously in the treatise Ialdabaoth has been at the center. After the Sabaoth account, the Archigenetor again returns as the subject (106

---

[1] Böhlig, *Die koptisch-gnostische Schrift ohne Titel*, 49f.

[154].19). As we have already remarked while comparing the Sabaoth account with NatArch and OnOrgWld and as we shall see in more detail in the course of this exegesis, the unit incorporates further material than what is found in NatArch.

1) *The Repentance of Sabaoth* 103(151). 32-104(152).6

ⲥⲁⲃⲁⲱⲑ ⲇⲉ ⲡϣⲏⲣⲉ	But (δέ) Sabaoth, the offspring
33 ⲛ̄ⲓⲁⲗⲇⲁⲃⲁⲱⲑ ⲛ̄ⲧⲁⲣⲉϥⲥⲱⲧⲙ̄ [ⲛ̄]ⲧ	of Ialdabaoth, when he heard the
34 ⲥⲙⲏ ⲛ̄ⲧⲡⲓⲥⲧⲓⲥ ⲁϥϩⲩⲙⲛⲉⲓ ⲉⲣⲟ[ⲥ ⲁϥ]	voice of Faith (πίστις), praised (ὑμνεῖν) her. He
35 ⲕⲁⲧⲁⲅⲉⲓⲛⲱⲥⲕⲉ ⲙ̄ⲡⲉⲓⲱⲧ [ⲙⲛ̄ ⲧⲙⲁⲁⲩ]	condemned (καταγινώσκειν) the father and the mother
1 ⲉⲝⲛ̄ ⲡϣⲁϫⲉ ⲛ̄ⲧⲡⲓⲥⲧⲓⲥ [ⲁϥ]† ⲉⲟⲟⲩ ⲛⲁⲥ	on account of the word of Faith (πίστις). He glorified her
2 ϫⲉ ⲁⲥⲧⲁⲙⲟⲟⲩ ⲁⲡⲣⲱⲙⲉ̣ [ⲛ̄]ⲁ̣ⲑⲁⲛⲁⲧⲟⲥ	because she informed them of the immortal (ἀθάνατος) Man
3 ⲙⲛ̄ ⲡⲉϥⲟⲩⲟⲉⲓⲛ ⲧⲡⲓⲥⲧⲓⲥ ⲇⲉ ⲧⲥⲟⲫⲓⲁ ⲁⲥ	and his light. Then (δέ) Faith (πίστις) Wisdom (σοφία)
4 ⲥⲱⲧ ⲙ̄ⲡⲉⲥⲧⲏⲛⲃⲉ ⲉⲃⲟⲗ ⲁⲥⲡⲱϩⲧ ⲁϫⲱϥ	stretched forth her finger, and she poured forth upon him
5 ⲛ̄ⲟⲩⲟⲉⲓⲛ ⲉⲃⲟⲗ ϩⲙ̄ ⲡⲉⲥⲟⲩⲟⲉⲓⲛ ⲁⲩⲕⲁ	light from her light for a condemnation (κατάκριμα)
6 ⲧⲁⲕⲣⲓⲙⲁ ⲙ̄ⲡⲉϥⲉⲓⲱⲧ	of his father.

The particle δέ introduces the change in focus from the preceding account of the blasphemy of Ialdabaoth. As in NatArch, Sabaoth is identified as the offspring of Ialdabaoth (cf. 101[149].30) and the portrayal of him here is also influenced by three figures: the God of the OT, a leading angel and the apocalyptic visionary. Sabaoth hears the voice of Faith and praises her (cf. NatArch 95[143].17). There is no account of an angel who casts Ialdabaoth into Tartarus as in NatArch 95(143).10-13. The view of the author is thus more in accord with the usual apocalyptic notion that it is at the end of time that Ialdabaoth will be cast into the abyss (103[151].21 ff). Rather, the "voice of Faith" refers to the rebuke of the Demiurge by Faith in which she stated that an immortal Light-Man existed before Ialdabaoth and his offspring. He will reveal himself in their creation and tread upon them as they go into the abyss (103[151].20-24).

In this pericope, then, the change to "hearing the voice of Faith" from "seeing the strength of that angel" is a redactional touch of the author, since the immortal Light-Man is part of the author's own theology (cf. NatArch 94[142].23f for the voice from above). As we presented earlier, the basic theme of the author's theology is the contrast between light and darkness (e.g. 98[146].23-27); it pervades his treatise (e.g. 120[168]. 26-29). Related to this theme is the immortal

Light-Man, who descends from the Eighth and is called the Light-Adam (108[156].2-22). Because he cannot re-enter the light, on account of the fault mixed with his light, he builds a great Aeon in the middle (112[160].10-22) and is the type of the pneumatic men (122[170].6-9).

Faith is the figure Wisdom and can be called in this treatise either Faith alone or Faith-Wisdom (cf. 98[146].13f). As we remarked earlier, the use of Faith alone as a title seems to be a later development in contrast to the use of Wisdom alone or even Faith-Wisdom (NatArch 87[135].7f). In this document Wisdom alone could not be used here (as in NatArch 95[143].18), since that would designate a lower emanation (e.g. 102[150].26).

Faith had rebuked the Demiurge, revealed her image in the water and thus returned to the light (103[151].28-32). After hearing her voice, Sabaoth praises her and condemns the father and mother. As in NatArch 95(143).15-18, the father is probably to be identified as Ialdabaoth (101[149].23; 102[150].11ff) and the mother as matter or chaos (101[149].24). The redactor then adds that the specific reason for his action was "the word of Faith." This action comprises the repentance of Sabaoth, although the term μετάνοια does not occur in this pericope but only in 104(152).27.

The text then returns to Sabaoth's relation to Faith. Now he is said to glorify her. The reason given is that she instructed them about the immortal Man and his light. One would expect the singular object "him," referring to Sabaoth, in this context; but the plural refers back to the entire offspring of Ialdabaoth (103[151].21, 23). The content of the instruction is the immortal Man and his light.

While this figure of the immortal Light-Man is probably related to the *anthropos* figure in the male group of gnostic systems,[2] the presentation of the immortal Light-Man in this pericope and in the remainder of the treatise shows influence from the Wisdom tradition within Gnosticism. The immortal Light-Man fulfills a function performed by Wisdom in NatArch 94(142).23-33. There, after the blasphemy of the ruler and his challenge that anyone before him should appear, Wisdom sends forth her light, runs after it to chaos, and then returns to her light (*anachōrein*). In OnOrgWld 103(151).15-32 after the blasphemy, Faith rebukes the ruler and tells of the immortal Light-Man who will reveal himself. Then, without any motivation for so doing, Faith revealed her image in the water and thus returned to

---

[2] Jonas, *Gnosis und spätantiker Geist*, 1. 335-51.

her light (*anachōrein*). Later at 107(155).36ff the ruler utters the challenge that anyone before him should appear. In response to this, the light appears in which there is the form of a man, while there is no immediate concern with returning to the light. Since the motif concerning the descent of light in response to the blasphemy is applied consistently and coherently to Wisdom but not so to the Light-Man and since NatArch has been shown to represent the earlier stage of the Sabaoth account, it is clear that the motif is first applied to Wisdom and then is used to portray the descent of the immortal Light-Man.

Identification of this immortal Light-Man as the Light-Adam and as an angel helps to indicate some Jewish elements that probably contributed to the presentation of this figure. In rabbinic material there is speculation upon Adam as being a more than ordinary creature, a man of gigantic size.[3] Secondly, the angel Michael in particular is presented in late Jewish literature as a light-man. As we have already seen, Michael is the "Prince of Light" and the "Spirit of Truth" at Qumran. He is opposed to the "Prince of Darkness" and the "Spirit of Error" (1QS 3:13-25); and one of his roles is to lead the righteous into truth (1QS 4:2).[4] As the Light-Man in OnOrgWld 103(151).20-24 will punish the evil ruler, so Michael plays a leading role in punishing the fallen angels in 1 Enoch 10:11-16. Further, in Test Abr 7 (Rec. A) Michael is clearly the angel who appears like the light man :

> Isaac answered and began to say, "I saw, my lord, in this night, the sun and the moon above my head and it surrounded me with its rays and illuminated me. And while I saw these things thus and rejoiced, I saw the heaven opened and I saw a luminous man descending from heaven, shining more than seven suns. And this man of the sunlike form came and took the sun from my head and went back up into the heavens from which he had descended. Then I was very sad because he took the sun from me, and after a little time, while I was still mourning and distressed, I saw this man coming forth from heaven a second time, and he took the moon from me, from my head... The Archistrategos said, "Hear, O righteous Abraham! The sun which your child saw is you, his father, and the moon similarly is his mother Sarah. The luminous man who descended from heaven is he who is sent by God, who will take your righteous soul from you. Now know, most honored Abraham, that at this time you are going to leave the worldly life and depart to God.

---

[3] B.R. 8:1; 21:3; 24:2; Hag. 12a; PRE 11; as in L. Ginzberg, *The Legends of the Jews* (Philadelphia 1955) 1. 59 and 5. 79.

[4] Cf. Betz, *Der Paraklet*, 186-90.

Abraham said to the Archistrategos, "O strangest marvel of marvels! And for the rest, are you he who is going to take my soul from me?"

The Archistrategos said to him, "I am Michael the Archistrategos who stands before God." [5]

It is to be noted in this passage that Michael appears as the angel who is like a man, bears light, reveals the meaning of the vision, and will finally lead the soul to God. Michael's main role is not a martial one, i.e. to be leader of the heavenly hosts against evil forces. Further, it is to be noted that in Rec. B this light man is described as "a very large man, greatly shining from the heaven, like a light which is called father of light." [6] Box even suggests that in these words Michael is presented as the cosmic man. [7] The variant in Rec. B then shows a number of motifs that are striking in comparison with gnostic material:

> Do not weep because I have taken the light of your house, for it has been taken up from the toils to rest and from lowliness to height. They are taking him from the narrow place to the broad, they are taking him from darkness to light. [8]

In a remarkable passage in Joseph and Asenath (14:3-15:6), the angel Michael is again presented as a man, as light, as a revealer, and as one who instructs concerning the sacramental meal:

> And lo! hard by the morningstar the heaven was rent and a great and ineffable light appeared. And when she saw it Asenath fell upon her face upon the cinders, and straightway there came to her a man from heaven...
>
> And he (the man) said: "I am the chief captain of the Lord God and commander of all the host of the Most High: stand up and stand upon thy feet, that I may speak to thee my words." And she lifted up her face and saw, and lo! a man in all things like unto Joseph, in robe and wreath and royal staff, save that his face was as lightning, and his eyes as the light of the sun, and the hairs of his head as the flame of fire of a burning torch, and his hands and his feet like iron shining from fire ... be of good cheer, Asenath, the virgin and pure, for lo! thy name hath been written in the book of life and shall not be blotted out for ever; but from this day thou shalt eat the blessed bread of life and drink a cup filled with immortality and be anointed with the blessed unction of incorruption. Be of good cheer, Asenath, the virgin and pure, lo! the Lord God hath given thee today to Joseph for a bride, and he himself shall be thy bridegroom. [9]

---

[5] Stone, *The Testament of Abraham*, 14-17.

[6] Stone, *The Testament of Abraham*, 70-71.

[7] Box, *The Testament of Abraham*, 45, n. 2.

[8] Stone, *The Testament of Abraham*, 70-71.

[9] Ed. M. Philonenko, *Joseph et Aseneth* (SPB 13; Leiden 1968) 176-83; translation from E. W. Brooks, *Joseph and Asenath* (London 1918) 45-48.

Since Michael here appears as the archetype and guardian angel of Joseph[10] and since Joseph is portrayed as one powerful in wisdom and knowledge (4:9 δύνατος ἐν σοφίᾳ καὶ ἐπιστήμῃ), one can also consider Michael as filled with wisdom and knowledge. It seems clear then that in late Judaism Michael was widely identified as an angel of light and a man of light, who revealed to men.

It is probable, then, that such material concerning Wisdom, Adam, and Michael has influenced the presentation of this mythological figure, the immortal Light-Man.[11] However, in contrast to its Jewish background the material has been adapted. The motif of immortality is added to the description of the Light-Man. The context for his appearance is the creation of the world rather than the ascent of the soul at death or the rebirth of the soul, as with Michael. Lastly, the angelic Light-Man represents the pneumatic baptism and the pneumatic race (122[170].6-16). He is the type of a particular class of men, the pneumatics, below whom stand the psychic and choic men (122[170].6-9).

The figure of this immortal Light-Man is also free from influence of the NT. The term ἀθάνατος does not occur in the NT. Although Jesus is presented as the light of the world (e.g. John 1:4, 9; 3:19; 8:12), he appears as the Son of Man (John 3:13) rather than simply as Man, Light-Man, or immortal Man.

In response to Sabaoth's praise, Faith-Wisdom stretched out her finger (cf. NatArch 94[142].29 ff) and poured some light upon him. In the OT and the NT the idiomatic expression is "to stretch out the hand" rather than the finger (e.g. Gen 3:22 LXX and Matt 8:3 ἐκτείνειν τὴν χεῖρα).[12] This usage is continued through the intertestamental literature as well, e.g. CD 12:6 שלח את ידו.[13] However, the expression "to stretch out the finger" does occur in two passages of intertestamental literature: Jub 25:11 and 1QS 11:2, as well as in NatArch and here. Again we have a small motif drawn from inter-

---

[10] Philonenko, *Joseph et Aseneth*, 88.

[11] For a discussion of Hellenistic material which has influenced the presentation of the Light-Adam, see Tardieu, *Trois mythes gnostiques*, 85-99.

[12] ἐκτείνειν probably represents the Greek *Vorlage* for ϭⲱⲧ ⲉⲃⲟⲗ cf. Crum, 360a. In Philo neither the phrase to stretch out the finger nor the hand occurs. Cf. E. Fuchs, ἐκτείνω, *TDNT* 2 (1964) 460-63.

[13] E. Lohse, *Die Texte aus Qumran*, 2 Aufl. (Darmstadt 1971) 90f. שלח is the equivalent of ἐκτείνειν, e.g. Gen 3:22 (cf. K. H. Rengstorf, ἀποστέλλω, *TDNT* 1 [1964] 400, n. 13). Cf. also 1QSa 2:18, 20f; Apoc Mosis 37:4; Adam and Eve 48:1; Jos and Asenath 16:7, 10.

testamental Judaism, apocalyptic Judaism, rather than the OT or NT.[14] On the other hand, while the finger of God is also referred to in both the OT and the NT,[15] there is never an emission coming from it.[16]

The light, which represents the upper divine world (98[146].23ff; 126[174].35ff), is in a figurative sense poured upon him from her light. This motif of "pouring light" also derives from neither the OT nor the NT but from Judaism.[17] It is the light then which makes possible the condemnation of the father, a theme which runs throughout the work (cf. 117[165].28; 124[172].20).[18]

As in NatArch, so in OnOrgWld the repentance of Sabaoth, that is, his condemnation of chaos and praise of Faith, are a necessary preliminary to his enthronement.

2) *The Ascent and Enthronement of Sabaoth* 104(152).6-31

ca<baw>e 6e n̄ta	Moreover when Sabaoth
7 peqxi oyoein aqxi oynoб n̄ eϩογcia	received light, he received a great authority (ἐξουσία)
8 eϩογn enaynamic thpoy n̄πxaoc	among all of the forces (δύναμις) of Chaos (χάος).
9 xim πϩooy etm̄may aymoyte epoq xe	From that day, he was called

---

[14] Jub 25:11 "And thereupon she lifted up her face to heaven and extended the fingers of her hands (Charles, *APOT*, 2. 51; 1QS 11:2 שולחי איבצע). Perhaps the phrase echoes such a passage as Exod 8:17, 19, in which Aaron stretches out his hand with his staff and the Egyptian magicians exclaim to Pharaoh: "This is the finger of God." Cf. also that a variant translation in the LXX for שלח יד is ἐπιβάλλειν τὴν χεῖρα (e.g. Gen 22:12) and that in the NT one finds the phrase βάλλειν τὴν δάκτυλον (Mark 7:33; John 20:25, 27).

[15] Exod 8:19; 31:18; Deut 9:10; and Luke 11:20.

[16] In later Jewish material one finds this motif, e.g. 3 Enoch 40:3: "And in the moment that they do not utter the Holy in the right order, a consuming fire goes forth from the little finger of the Holy One, blessed be He ... and consumes them" (Odeberg, *3 Enoch* 126); and TB San. 38b, ed. L. Goldschmidt, *Der Babylonische Talmud* (Berlin 1904) 7. 156. However, it is not attested in the intertestamental period.

[17] ἐκχέειν ἐπί may well represent the Greek underlying πωϩτ eϩn cf. Crum, 284a. In the LXX and the NT ἐκχέειν ἐπί is used both literally for the pouring out of fluids and figuratively for spiritual gifts, e.g. Joel 2:28 (3:1) πνεῦμα; Lam 2:11 δόξα; Sir 39:28 ἰσχύς and Matt 9:17 οἶνος; Tit 3:6 πνεῦμα ἅγιον. But in neither the LXX nor the NT is φῶς "poured out." In Philo, however, the verb is used in connection with the rays of light, although not with the light alone—*De Abra.* 157 διττὴ δὲ φωτὸς φύσις ... ἑκάστου τῶν ἀστέρων αὐγὰς ἐκχέοντος (Cohn-Wendland, 4. 36). Also De *opif. mundi* 71, *De Abr.* 76. Cf. J. Behm, ἐκχέω ἐκχύν(ν)ω, *TDNT* 2 (1964) 467-69.

[18] Although NatArch uses καταγινώσκειν (95[143].16) and κατακρίνειν (89[137].29), OnOrgWld employs both καταγινώσκειν in 103(151).35 and 107(155).33; κατάγνωσις in 107(155).35f and 125(173).29; κατάκριμα here, κατάκρισις 124(172).20, and κατακρί-νειν elsewhere (110[158].28; 120[168].34; 125[173].13).

10 ⲡⲭⲟⲉⲓⲥ ⲛ̅ⲛ̅ϭⲟⲙ ⲁϥⲙⲉⲥⲧⲉ ⲡⲉϥⲉⲓⲱⲧ ⲡⲕⲁ	"the lord of the powers." He hated his father, the darkness,
11 ⲕⲉ ⲁⲅⲱ ⲧⲉϥⲙⲁⲁⲩ ⲡⲛⲟⲩⲛ ⲁϥⲥⲓⲭⲁⲛⲉ ⲁ	and his mother, the abyss. He loathed (σικχαίνειν)
12 ⲧⲉϥⲥⲱⲛⲉ ⲡⲙⲉⲉⲩⲉ ⲙ̅ⲡⲁⲣⲭⲓⲅⲉⲛⲏⲧⲱⲣ	his sister, the thought of the Archigenetor (ἀρχιγενέτωρ),
13 ⲡⲉⲧⲛ̅ⲛⲏⲩ ϩⲓ.ⲭⲛ̅ ⲙⲙⲟⲟⲩ ⲉⲧⲃⲉ	the one who moves to and fro over the water. Now (δέ) because
14 ⲡⲉϥⲟⲩⲟⲉⲓⲛ ⲇⲉ ⲁⲛⲉⲝⲟⲩⲥⲓⲁ ⲧⲏⲣⲟⲩ ⲕⲱϩ	of his light, all of the authorities (ἐξουσία) of
15 ⲉⲣⲟϥ ⲛ̅ⲧⲉ ⲡⲭⲁⲟⲥ ⲁⲅⲱ ⲛ̅ⲧⲁⲣⲟⲩϣⲧⲟⲣⲧⲣ̅	Chaos (χάος) were jealous of him. And when they were disturbed,
16 ⲁⲅⲉⲓⲣⲉ ⲛ̅ⲟⲩⲛⲟϭ ⲙ̅ⲡⲟⲗⲉⲙⲟⲥ ϩⲛ̅ ⲧⲥⲁϣ	they made a great war (πόλεμος) in the seven
17 ϥⲉ ⲙ̅ⲡⲉ ⲧⲟⲧⲉ ⲧⲡⲓⲥⲧⲓⲥ ⲧⲥⲟⲫⲓⲁ ⲛ̅ⲧⲁⲣⲉⲥ	heavens. Then (τότε) when Faith (πίστις) Wisdom (σοφία)
18 ⲛⲁⲩ ⲁⲡⲡⲟⲗⲉⲙⲟⲥ ⲁⲥⲭⲟⲟⲩ ⲛ̅ⲥⲁⲃⲁⲱⲑ	saw the war (πόλεμος), she sent to Sabaoth
19 ⲉⲃⲟⲗ ϩⲙ̅ ⲡⲉⲥⲟⲩⲟⲉⲓⲛ ⲛ̅ⲥⲁϣϥ ⲛ̅ⲁⲣⲭⲁⲅ	from her light seven archangels (ἀρχάγγελος).
20 ⲅⲉⲗⲟⲥ ⲁⲩⲧⲟⲣⲡϥ ⲉϩⲣⲁⲓ̈ ⲉⲧⲙⲁϩⲥⲁϣϥⲉ ⲙ̅	They snatched him up to the seventh
21 ⲡⲉ ⲁⲅⲱϩⲉ ⲉⲣⲁⲧⲟⲩ ϩⲓⲧⲉϥϩⲏ ϩⲱⲥ ⲇⲓⲁⲕⲟ	heaven; they stood before him as (ὡς) servant (διάκονος).
22 ⲛⲟⲥ ⲡⲁⲗⲓⲛ ⲁⲥⲭⲟⲟⲩ ⲛⲁϥ ⲛ̅ⲕⲉϣⲟⲙⲧ	Again (πάλιν), she sent to him another three
23 ⲛ̅ⲁⲣⲭⲁⲅⲅⲉⲗⲟⲥ ⲁⲥⲥⲙⲛ̅ ⲧⲙⲛ̅ⲧⲉⲣⲟ ⲛⲁϥ	archangels (ἀρχάγγελος). She established the kingdom for him
24 ⲛ̅ⲧⲡⲉ ⟨ⲛ⟩ⲟⲩⲟⲛ ⲛⲓⲙ ⲭⲉⲕⲁⲁⲥ ⲉϥⲛⲁϣⲱⲡⲉ	above every one in order that he might come to be
25 ⲙ̅ⲡⲥⲁ ⲛ̅ϩⲣⲉ ⲙ̅ⲡⲙⲛ̅ⲧⲥⲛⲟⲟⲩⲥ ⲛ̅ⲛⲟⲩⲧⲉ	above the twelve gods
26 ⲙ̅ⲡⲭⲁⲟⲥ ⲛ̅ⲧⲁⲣⲉⲥⲁⲃⲁⲱⲑ ⲇⲉ ⲭⲓ ⲡⲧⲟⲡⲟⲥ	of Chaos (χάος). But (δέ) when Sabaoth received the place (τόπος)
27 ⲛ̅ⲧⲁⲛⲁⲡⲁⲩⲥⲓⲥ ⲉⲡⲙⲁ ⲛ̅ⲧⲉϥⲙⲉⲧⲁⲛⲟⲓⲁ	of rest (ἀνάπαυσις) in exchange for his repentance (μετάνοια),
28 ⲉⲧⲓ ⲁⲧⲡⲓⲥⲧⲓⲥ ϯⲛⲁϥ ⲛ̅ⲧⲉⲥϣⲉⲉⲣⲉ ⲛ̅ⲍⲱⲏ	Faith (πίστις) moreover (ἔτι) gave him her daughter Life (ζωή),
29 ⲙⲛ̅ ⲛⲟⲩⲛⲟϭ ⲛ̅ⲉⲝⲟⲩⲥⲓⲁ ⲭⲉⲕⲁⲁⲥ ⲉⲥⲛⲁ	with a great authority (ἐξουσία) in order that she might
30 ⲧⲁⲙⲟϥ ⲁⲛⲉⲧϣⲟⲟⲡ ⲧⲏⲣⲟⲩ ϩⲛ̅ ⲧⲙⲁϩ	instruct him about all those in the
31 ϣⲙⲟⲩⲛⲉ	eighth (heaven).

Introduced by the particle "then" (ϭⲉ), this next section presents the ascent and enthronement of Sabaoth. In accord with his own theology, the redactor states (cf. NatArch 95[143].19-25) that it is the light, which Sabaoth receives, that is the source of his great authority over all the powers of chaos. In contrast with NatArch 95(143).19ff, Sabaoth is given a name before he is raised up to the seventh heaven. As we discussed earlier, NatArch retains the earlier tradition here, both because the name-giving appears more appropriate after the elevation (e.g. Phil 2:9) and because the redactor's hand is visible here in the motif of light. It is not Wisdom and Life who give the name here, as in NatArch 95(143).22f; rather, the impersonal "from that day he was called" is used (cf. OnOrgWld 106[154].14 and NatArch 95[143].35f). In accord with LXX usage, he is called "Lord of the Forces" rather than, as in NatArch, "God of the Forces." By this return to the expected nomenclature, the original function of Sabaoth has been obscured, i.e. to be a second, lower God and the God of the OT. This change is a further indication that the concern of the author of OnOrgWld is not with the problem of the God of the OT but rather with the different types of men.

For a third time this account turns to the condemnation of the lower world. Its repetitious nature and also its motif of light versus darkness mark this condemnation as deriving from the redactor. On this occasion the condemnation provides an opportunity for taking Sabaoth by means of an exegesis of Gen 1:2: σκότος ἦν ἐπάνω τῆς ἀβύσσου καὶ πνεῦμα θεοῦ ἐπεφέρετο ἐπάνω τοῦ ὕδατος. Sabaoth hated his father, identified now not as Ialdabaoth, but to fit the biblical text and the redactor's theology as darkness.[19] Also, he hated his mother, not matter (NatArch 95[143].16f) but the abyss (cf. NatArch 87[135].7; OnOrgWld 103[151].24).[20] In contrast with NatArch 95(143).17, an extra motif of "the sister" is introduced in order to parallel the biblical text; he loathed his sister, a strange epithet. As Böhlig has pointed out, the fact that Spirit is feminine in Semitic determines the epithet "sister".[21] Perhaps it is also derived from consideration of Wisdom, who can be called sister (Prov 7:4),[22] as identified with the Spirit (ApocryJohn BG 44.19ff).[23] The sister, then, is the thought not of the high God but of the Archigenetor, which appeared in a Spirit going back and forth upon the waters (cf. 100[148].29-101 [149].9).[24]

---

[19] ⲕⲁⲕⲉ can be a translation of σκότος Crum, 101b; and ⲛⲟⲩⲛ of ἄβυσσος Crum, 226b. The masculine ὁ σκότος and feminine ἡ ἄβυσσος would also lend themselves to the interpretation. We have not yet located this motif of the "father as darkness" elsewhere. In Philo, for example, the father is positive, e.g. νοῦς, λόγος, ἥλιος and thus never is portrayed as darkness. Cf. Leisegang's index to the Cohn-Wendland edition, 637.

[20] The motif of "the mother as the abyss" is not found in the LXX or the NT. There is only one passage in Philo, which indirectly refers to the mother as the abyss, De fuga et invent. 192f (Cohn-Wendland 3.151f).

[21] Böhlig, Die koptisch-gnostische Schrift ohne Titel, 51.

[22] Cf. A. Orbe, "Spiritus Dei ferebatur super aquas. Exegesis gnóstica de Gen. 1:2b," Greg 44 (1963) 691-730.

[23] Ed. Till (TU 60) 128-31.

[24] A. Orbe in "Spiritus Dei ferebatur super aquas," has helpfully pointed out that the transition from local to discursive movement is grounded in ἐπιφέρεσθαι and that contrary to the usual gnostic interpretation, the Spirit in this passage is that of the

The controlling motif for the following thought is the antipathy between light and darkness. Philo too in interpreting the same biblical text, Gen 1:2b, speaks about the war that arises when light invades darkness:

> Right too is his statement that "darkness was above the abyss' (Gen 1:2). For in a sense the air is over the void, inasmuch as it has spread over and completely filled the immensity and desolation of the void, of all that reaches from the zone of the moon to us. After the kindling of the intelligible light, which preceded the sun's creation, darkness its adversary withdrew: for God, in His perfect knowledge of their mutual contrariety and natural conflict, parted them one from another by a wall of separation. In order, therefore, to keep them from the discord arising from perpetual clash, to prevent *war* in place of peace prevailing and setting up disorder in an ordered universe, He not only separated *light* and *darkness*, but also placed in the intervening spaces boundary marks, by which he held back each of their extremities: for, had they been actual neighbours, they were sure to produce confusion by engaging with intense and never-ceasing rivalry in the struggle for mastery. As it was, their assault on one another was broken and kept back by barriers set up between them. These barriers are evening and dawn.[25]

Thus, because of the light which Sabaoth has received, all the powers of chaos envied him. It is not that they fought against Sabaoth but rather they envied him, a motif which probably derives from the cause of the fall of the angels. The source of their disturbance is the coming of light into the realm of darkness. However, again the war is not against the light or against Sabaoth but seems rather to be among the powers of chaos themselves. Thus the motif of the enmity between light and darkness is modified by another motif, namely, that of the mutual fighting among the offspring of the fallen angels as their punishment, e.g. 1 Enoch 10:9:

> "And to Gabriel said the Lord. 'Proceed against the bastards and the reprobates, and against the children of fornication: and destroy the children of fornication and the children of the Watchers from amongst men: and cause them to go forth: send them one against the other that they may destroy each other in battle: for length of days they shall not have."[26]

---

lower and not the high god (704f). But he overlooks the gnostic reinterpretation when he identifies the thought as the intentional creation of heaven and earth (705), since it is explicitly identified as the blasphemous thought that he alone existed in 100(148). 32-34.

[25] Philo, *De opif. mundi* 32-34; text Cohn-Wendland, 1. 10 and translation LCL (1962) 1. 24-27.

[26] Tr. Charles, *1 Enoch* (1912) 23f.

The same motif is represented as well in 1 Enoch 88:1-2. In this passage, then, the tradition is applied not to the offspring of the fallen angels but to the fallen angels themselves[27] and indicates that the powers of chaos are judged by the advent of the light. Further, the war takes place now not on earth but in the seven heavens.

Such an exegesis of Gen 1:2 cannot be found in the NT. Thus it is clear again that with this pericope the author is using exegetical material from Judaism rather than material just from the OT or from the NT. He has taken over this material and inserted it into his own treatise because it suited his own theology with its antipathy between light and darkness. The occasion is thus given for Faith-Wisdom to take Sabaoth up to the seventh heaven. When she sees the war in the seven heavens, she alone—there is no mention of Life as in NatArch 95 (143).19—sends from her light seven archangels. As is the case with the visionary in apocalyptic and with Sabaoth in NatArch, Sabaoth here is also "snatched up". He is brought by the arch-angels to the seventh heaven; but thereby Sabaoth is demoted in contrast to NatArch 95(143).19ff. In NatArch Sabaoth occupies the seventh heaven, which is the highest realm immediately below the veil. Here Sabaoth continues to occupy the seventh heaven, but there is a higher realm, the middle, between him and the veil. Since in OnOrgWld the immortal Light-Man rules over the middle (112[160].10-22) and since he typifies the pneumatics, Sabaoth then represents the psychics (cf. 122[170].6-9).

In contrast with this view, although he has not devoted a chapter to the Sabaoth myth, in scattered references Tardieu has considered Sabaoth as the type of the elect, the pneumatic, those who are definitely among the saved because of their repentance.[28] However, this does not seem likely for the following reasons. First, it would be rather odd to have as the representative of the saved one who is the son of Ialdabaoth and thus ultimately descended from evil matter. Second, one would expect knowledge rather than repentance to characterize the elect. Third, Tardieu has located Sabaoth in an intermediary place, a place of rest above the seven heavens and below the ogdoad.[29] Such a location would be appropriate, if Sabaoth represented the elect. However, as this pericope shows (cf. 104[152].29f), Sabaoth is in the seventh heaven, thus still within the realm of evil rule, and therefore

---

[27] Cf. Rev 12:7 where, however, the war is a war between Michael and the dragon rather than among the forces of the dragon.

[28] Tardieu, *Trois mythes gnostiques*, 118, 221, 230.

[29] Tardieu, *Trois mythes gnostiques*, 224.

a more appropriate representative of some other group than the elect. The place of Sabaoth is indeed termed a place of rest (104[152].26-27). But its identification as the seventh heaven indicates only that the notion of a place of rest has been reinterpreted rather than that Sabaoth is in the pleromatic realm or an intermediary place. Instead, it is the Light-Adam who is above Sabaoth, who occupies the intermediary place, and who represents the elect.

Next, in a phrase which derives from late Jewish apocalyptic, the seven archangels are said to "stand before him."[30] They stand before him as servants (διάκονοι).[31]

In the following sentences concerning the further archangels, the enthronement of Sabaoth is made clear. First, three other archangels are sent to Sabaoth. The exact reason for this number, however, is not evident; it may be a remnant of other calculations.[32] After sending these archangels to him, Faith established the kingdom for him, i.e. she installed him in kingly power or enthroned him, that he might be above the twelve gods of chaos. The twelve are the male and female deities of the six heavens underneath Sabaoth, among which deities Ialdabaoth is now found (106[154].19-27 and 107[155].14-17).[33] Comparison with 106(154).9-11, as well as the motif of the twelve gods of chaos, shows that this motif of Sabaoth's kingdom above the heavens of chaos probably stems from the author of OnOrgWld.

The seventh heaven is now identified as the place of rest, a motif which probably stems from the Wisdom tradition, in which Wisdom seeks a place of rest (Sir 24:7). For his repentance, i.e. his praise of Faith-Wisdom and condemnation of his father and mother, Sabaoth receives this place of rest.

Faith then gave her daughter Life with a great power to teach him about everything in the Eighth. As we discussed earlier, this is the first of two such pericopes in OnOrgWld on the instruction of Sabaoth. The name Faith alone and the phrase "with a great authority" (cf. 104[152].7 where "great authority" is associated with "the light")

---

[30] E.g. 1 Enoch 14:22; 39:12f; 4 Ezra 8:21; Test Sol 24. It is also found in the NT, e.g. Rev 8:2 καὶ εἶδον τοὺς ἑπτὰ ἀγγέλους οἱ ἐνώπιον τοῦ θεοῦ ἑστήκασιν. The Coptic ⲱⲣⲉ may translate the Greek ἱστάναι, cf. Crum, 537b.

[31] Cf. 2 Cor 11:14f οἱ διάκονοι αὐτοῦ (i.e. Satan).

[32] Cf. ApocryJn BG 39.10-19 and CG III, 1: 16.8-13 in which each authority under Ialdabaoth has seven angels and three powers or forces. In the BG version the number of the angels is then given as 360, although the exact manner of tabulation is not clear.

[33] Cf. also W. R. Schoedel, "Scripture and the Seventy-Two Heavens of the First Apocalypse of James," *NovT* 12 (1970) 126-27.

mark this pericope as redacted by the author. NatArch thus probably preserved the original position of the pericope in the account. By this earlier instruction of Sabaoth, the redactor provides for the source of Sabaoth's ability to create his throne, chariot and court (104 [152].31 ff). As the redactor in 106(154).6-9 states, Sabaoth is informed about the Eighth so that he might make likenesses thereof in his realm. By specifically redirecting Sabaoth's power and knowledge to this ability, the redactor again obscures the original function of Sabaoth. No longer is Sabaoth presented mainly as the God of the OT, who has received revelation concerning the Eighth and therefore can communicate some saving knowledge through the books of the OT. His knowledge enables him, rather, to create likenesses of those things above so that his kingdom might remain.

As in NatArch, so this pericope on the ascent and enthronement of Sabaoth betrays no influence upon or from the NT. Rather, further material from the heritage of intertestamental Judaism has been woven into the account without passing through the intermediary stage of the NT.

3) *Creation of the Throne/Chariot of Sabaoth* 104(152).31-105(153).16

ϩⲱⲥ ⲉⲩⲛ̄ⲧⲁϥ ⲇⲉ ⲛ̄ⲟⲩⲉⲝⲟⲩⲥⲓⲁ	Now (δέ) since he had an authority (ἐξουσία)
ⲁϥⲧⲁⲙⲓⲟ ⲛⲁϥ ⲛ̄ϣⲟⲣⲡ ⲛ̄ⲟⲩⲙⲁ ⲛ̄ϣⲱ	he fashioned for himself at first a dwelling-
ⲡⲉ ⲟⲩⲛⲟϭ ⲡⲉ ⲉϥⲧⲁⲉⲓⲏⲩ ⲉⲙⲁⲧⲉ ⲉϥⲟ ⲛ̄	place. It is great, very glorious;
[ⲥⲁϣ]ϥ̣ ⲛ̄ⲕⲱⲃ ⲡⲁⲣⲁ ⲛⲉⲧϣⲟⲟⲡ ⲧⲏⲣⲟⲩ	[seven] times more glorious than (παρά) all that are
[ϩⲛ̄ ⲧⲥ]ⲁ̣ϣϥⲉ ⲙ̄ⲡⲉ ⲙ̄ⲡⲙ̄ⲧⲟ ⲇⲉ ⲉⲃⲟⲗ	in the seventh heaven. Then (δέ) before
ⲙ̄ⲡⲉϥⲙⲁ ⲛ̄ϣⲱⲡⲉ ⲁϥⲧⲁⲙⲉⲓⲟ ⲛ̄ⲟⲩⲑⲣⲟ	his dwelling-place he fashioned
ⲛⲟⲥ ⲉⲩⲛⲟϭ ⲡⲉ ⲉϥϩⲓϫⲛ̄ ⲟⲩϩⲁⲣⲙⲁ ⲉϥⲟ	a great throne (θρόνος), which was upon a chariot (ἅρμα);
ⲛ̄ϥⲧⲟⲟⲩ ⲙ̄ⲡⲣⲟⲥⲱⲡⲟⲛ ⲉⲩⲙⲟⲩⲧⲉ ⲉⲣⲟϥ	it was four-faced (πρόσωπον) and called
ϫⲉ ⲭⲉⲣⲟⲩⲃⲓⲛ ⲡⲭⲉⲣⲟⲩⲃⲓⲛ ⲇⲉ ⲟⲩⲛ̄ⲧⲁϥ	Cherubin. Now (δέ) the Cherubin
ⲙ̄ⲙⲁⲩ ⲛ̄ϣⲙⲟⲩⲛⲉ ⲙ̄ⲙⲟⲣⲫⲏ ⲕⲁⲧⲁ ⲡϥ	has eight forms (μορφή) at each (κατά)
ⲧⲟⲩⲕⲟⲟϩ ϩⲙ̄ⲙⲟⲣⲫⲏ ⲙ̄ⲙⲟⲩⲉⲓ ⲁⲩⲱ ϩⲙ̄	of the four corners : lion forms (μορφή) and
ⲙⲟⲣⲫⲏ ⲙ̄ⲙⲁⲥⲉ ⲁⲩⲱ ϩⲙ̄ⲙⲟⲣⲫⲏ ⲣⲣⲱ	bull forms (μορφή) and human forms (μορφή)
ⲙⲉ ⲙⲛ̄ ϩⲙ̄ⲙⲟⲣⲫⲏ ⲛ̄ⲁⲉⲧⲟⲥ ϩⲱⲥⲧⲉ ⲙ̄ⲙⲟⲣ	and eagle (ἀετός) forms (μορφή) so that (ὥστε)
ⲫⲏ ⲧⲏⲣⲟⲩ ⲥⲉⲉⲓⲣⲉ ⲛ̄ⲥⲉⲧⲁϥⲧⲉ ⲙ̄ⲙⲟⲣⲫⲏ	all of the forms (μορφή) amount to sixty-four forms (μορφή)
ⲁⲩⲱ ⲥⲁϣϥ̄ ⲛ̄ⲁⲣⲭⲁⲅⲅⲉⲗⲟⲥ ⲉⲩⲁϩⲉⲣⲁⲧⲟⲩ	and seven archangels (ἀρχάγγελος) who stand
ϩⲓⲧⲉϥϩⲏ ⲛ̄ⲧⲟϥ ⲡⲉ ⲡⲙⲁϩϣⲙⲟⲩⲛ ⲉⲩⲛ̄	before him. It is he who is the eighth, since
ⲧⲁϥ ⲉⲝⲟⲩⲥⲓⲁ ⲙ̄ⲙⲟⲣⲫⲏ ⲧⲏⲣⲟⲩ ⲥⲉⲉⲓⲣⲉ	he has authority (ἐξουσία). All the forms (μορφή) amount to
ⲛ̄ϣⲃⲉⲥⲛⲟⲟⲩⲥ ⲉⲃⲟⲗ ⲅⲁⲣ ϩⲙ̄ ⲡⲉⲉⲓϩⲁⲣⲙⲁ	seventy-two for (γάρ) from this chariot (ἅρμα)
ⲁⲩϫⲓ ⲧⲩⲡⲟⲥ ⲛ̄ϭⲓ ⲡϣⲃⲉⲥⲛⲟⲟⲩⲥ ⲛ̄ⲛⲟⲩ	the seventy-two gods received a pattern (τύπος).
ⲧⲉ ⲁⲩϫⲓ ⲧⲩⲡⲟⲥ ⲁⲧⲣⲟⲩⲣ̄ⲁⲣⲭⲉⲓ ⲉϫⲛ̄ ⲧϫⲃⲉ	They received a pattern (τύπος) to rule (ἄρχειν) over
ⲥⲛⲟⲟⲩⲥ ⲛ̄ⲁⲥⲡⲉ ⲛ̄ⲛ̄ϩⲉⲑⲛⲟⲥ	the seventy-two languages of the nations (ἔθνος).

As in NatArch, the next step in the enthronement of Sabaoth is his fashioning of a chariot. However, here Sabaoth first makes a dwelling place and throne and then the chariot. Thus, the motif in ancient mythology of building a temple or sanctuary as part of the enthronement pattern is recalled (cf. Yahweh in Exod 15:17 and Ps 102[103].19); also here explicitly set forth is the specifically Israelite motif, which associates the throne of Cherubim and the chariot with one another.[34] The source of Sabaoth's creative ability is the authority brought to him by Life. The dwelling place, which he built for himself (line 32) with this authority, is then described as great and more glorious than anything in the seven heavens. Neither in the OT[35] nor in the NT, but rather in Judaism, does one find a description of the dwelling place. For example, in 1 Enoch 14 the dwelling place of God is also described as great (vv. 10, 15) and glorious (v. 16).

Next, he built a great throne (cf. 2 Enoch 22:2), strangely in front of the dwelling place.[36] The text does not state here explicitly that the throne is for Sabaoth himself nor that he sits upon it. Later, in 106(154).3f Sabaoth is said to sit upon "a" throne; however, there is no clear reference that it is "the" throne, which has previously been fashioned. Yet the context makes it evident that the throne is for Sabaoth himself. The dwelling place is for himself (104[152].32). The kingdom is established for him (104[152].23). He has the authority (105[153].12) over all the forms deriving from the chariot. Later, in 105(153).16-20 the Seraphim who are created upon the throne, glorify him. As we shall discuss later, the fact that in 106(154).3f Sabaoth sits on "a" throne, which is not explicitly identified as the throne he created, is due to the incorporation there of another piece of tradition by the redactor.

The throne is portrayed as on a chariot, which is described as in NatArch 95(143).26-28, i.e. it is four-faced and called Cherubin. The Cherubin then have eight forms in each of the four corners.[37] As Böhlig suggests, they are to be considered as male and female. There-

---

[34] Cf. supra 111-13.

[35] Cf. 1 Kgs 22:10, 19; 2 Chr 18:7, 18; Isa 6; Ezek 1 and 10; Dan 7:9ff.

[36] Cf. 1 Enoch 14:18 where the adverb "therein" is missing in one of the Greek manuscripts (Charles, 1 Enoch [1912] 34).

[37] Schmitz has remarked that there is no description of the divine throne in Hellenistic Judaism. However, 2 Enoch 22:2 contains the rudiments of such a description and thus indicates awareness of such a tradition. He is probably correct, however, in saying that Philo and Josephus avoid the idea of God's throne as too anthropomorphic. Cf. O. Schmitz, θρόνος, TDNT 3 (1965) 160-67.

fore, the sum of thirty-two can be doubled to reach sixty-four (line 9).[38] Further, as Böhlig also points out, the forms of lion, ox, man, and eagle are drawn from Ezek 1 and 10; and taken over in Christianity by Rev 4:7, which exhibits the same order as in OnOrgWld.[39] Together with the seven archangels and Sabaoth, the total of forms makes seventy-two, but Sabaoth has power over all the forms.

The text here draws upon the tradition, found in late Jewish apocalyptic literature, concerning the seventy angels in heaven, who are each over a particular nation. In the OT the figure seventy is significant in the seventy years of Jer 25:11; 29:10 and the seventy periods of Dan 9:24ff. The figure of seventy nations derives from Gen 10, while in the LXX it appears as seventy-two. In the intertestamental literature, then, this figure is applied to the heavenly leaders of the nations—in 1 Enoch 89 to the shepherds who punish Israel. These seventy angels who are over the gentile nations and also their languages (Targ Ps.-Jon Gen 11:8) are also considered as gods by their peoples in the late Hebrew T Napht 8:4-5 and 9:1, 2, 4:

> "For at that time the Lord, blessed be He, came down from His highest heavens, and brought down with him seventy ministering angels, Michael at their head. He commanded them to teach the seventy families which sprang from the loins of Noah seventy languages ... And on that day Michael took a message from the Lord, and said to the seventy nations, to each nation separately: 'You know the rebellion you undertook, and the treacherous confederacy into which you entered against the Lord of heaven and earth, and now choose today whom you will worship, and who shall be your intercessor in the height of heaven' ... and every nation chose its own angel."[40]

They are also considered as gods in the Ps.-Clem. *Rec.* 2.42, but here the angels are numbered as seventy-two:

> For every nation has an angel, to whom God has committed the government of that nation; and when one of these appears, although he be thought and called God by those over whom he presides, yet, being asked, he does not give such testimony to himself. For the Most High God, who alone holds the power of all things, has divided all the nations of the earth into seventy-two parts, and over these He hath appointed angels as

---

[38] Böhlig, *Die koptisch-gnostische Schrift ohne Titel*, 52.

[39] Cf. also Apoc Abr 18 where only the position of ox and man has been reversed in the order. Hag. 13b has cherub, man, lion, eagle.

[40] Charles, *APOT* 2. 363. In his discussion in *The Greek Versions of the Testaments of the Twelve Patriarchs*, 242-43, Charles characterizes the Hebrew testament as late; the manuscripts are from the 12th and 13th centuries.

princes. But to the one among the archangels who is greatest, was committed the government of those who, before all others, received the worship and knowledge of the Most High God.[41]

The role of Michael is to be noted as well in this material. At first in Jewish tradition, the view is expressed that there is no angel over Israel. God alone would be their ruler (Jub 15:31). But Michael is presented in 1 Enoch 20:5 as the angel over "the best part of mankind", namely, Israel (cf. T Dan 6:2). Michael also appears as the angel, who records the excesses of punishment by the seventy angelic shepherds in 1 Enoch 89:61.[42] Thus, it is understandable that in T Napht Michael is expressly stated as the leader of the seventy angels, who are over the nations.

In this gnostic text, then, once again the tradition appropriate to Michael is associated with that of Sabaoth. As in the traditions of the LXX and of those circles represented by Ps.-Clem. *Rec.*, seventy-two are counted; they are designated gods; and they are formed in order to rule over the seventy-two languages of the world.

The tradition is modified by the novel association of these deities with the chariot. They are formed from the chariot in order to rule over the seventy-two languages of the peoples.

Again, this pericope is drawn from Judaism rather than simply from the OT or from the NT. Neither in the OT nor in the NT is there a description of the dwelling place of God. The four-faced chariot of Cherubim cannot come from the NT, as we pointed out in the discussion of NatArch. Nor is there mention in the OT or NT of the seventy (seventy-two) angels over the nations.

4) *Creation of the Angels* 105(153).16-106(154).3

ϨΙΧΝ ΠΘΡΟ	Then (δέ) upon that throne (θρόνος)
17 ΝΟϹ ΔΕ ΕΤΜΜΑΥ ΑϤΤΑΜΙΕ ϨΝΚΕΑΓΓΕ	he also fashioned angels (ἄγγελος)
18 ΛΟϹ ΜΜΟΡΦΗ ΝΔΡΑΚΩΝ ΕΥΜΟΥΤΕ ΕΡΟ	in the form (μορφή) of a dragon (δράκων) wh were called
19 ΟΥ ΧΕ ϹΑΡΑΦΙΝ ΕΥϮ ΕΟΟΥ ΝΑϤ ΝΝΑΥ	Seraphin (and) who glorified him
20 ΝΙΜ ΜΝΝϹΩϹ ΑϤΤΑΜΙΟ ΝΟΥΕΚΚΛΗϹΙΑ	continually. Afterwards, he fashioned an angel (ἄγγελος)
21 ΝΑΓΓΕΛΟϹ ϨΝϢΟ ΜΝ ϨΝΤΒΑ ΕΜΝΤΟΥ	church (ἐκκλησία)—thousands and myriads, infin tely many—
22 ΗΠΕ ΕϹΤΝΤΟΝΤ ΕΤΕΚΚΛΗϹΙΑ ΕΤϨΝ	which was similar to the church (ἐκκλησία)

---

[41] Text in B. Rehm, *Die Pseudoklementinen : 2 Rekognitionen* (GCS 51; Berlin 1965) 76-77; tr. from *The Ante-Nicene Fathers* (reprint 1956) 8. 109.

[42] Cf. Charles, *1 Enoch* (1912) 201.

23 ΤΜΑϩϢΜΟΥΝΕ ΑΥШ ΟΥϢΡΠΜΜΙСЄ | that was in the Eighth and a first-born

24 ЄΥΜΟΥΤЄ ЄΡΟϥ ΧЄ ΠΙСΡΑΗΛ ЄΤЄ ΠΑЄΙ | called Israel, which is

25 ΠЄ ΠΡШΜЄ ЄΤΝΑΥ ЄΠΝΟΥΤЄ ΑΥШ ΚЄ | "the man who sees God" and

26 ΟΥΑ ΧЄ ΙΗС ΠЄΧС ЄϥΤΝΤШΝ ЄΠСШΤΗΡ | another, Jesus Christ, who was like the savior (σωτήρ)

27 ЄΤϩΙ ΠСΑ ΝΤΠЄ ΝΤΜΑϩϢΜΟΥΝЄ Єϥ | who was above in the Eighth. He

28 ϩΜΟΟС ϩΙ ΟΥΝΑΜ ΜΜΟϥ ϩΙΧΝ ΟΥΘΡΟ | sits at his right upon an

29 ΝΟС ЄϥΤΑЄΙΗΥ ϩΙ 6ΒΟΥΡ ΔЄ ΜΜΟϥ ЄС | excellent throne (θρόνος). And (δέ) on his left

30 ϩΜΟΟС Ν6Ι ΤΠΑΡΘЄΝΟС ΜΠΠΝΑ ЄΤΟΥ | the virgin (παρθένος) of the holy spirit (πνεῦμα) sits

31 ΑΑΒ ϩΙΧΝ ΟΥΘΡΟΝΟС ЄСϯ ЄΟΟΥ ΝΑϥ | upon a throne (θρόνος) glorifying him.

32 ΑΥШ СЄΑϩЄΡΑΤΟΥ ϩΙΤЄСЄϩΗ Ν6Ι ΤСΑ | And the seven virgins (παρθένος)

33 Ϣ⟨ϥ⟩Є ΜΠΑΡΘЄΝΟС ЄΥΜ ΜΑΑΒЄ Ν6Ι[Θ]Α | stand before her. In their hands are thirty lyres (κιθάρα)

34 ΡΑ ΝΤΟΟΤΟΥ ΜΝ ϩΜΨΑΛΤΗΡΙΟΝ [ΜΝ] | and harps (ψαλτήριον)

1 ϩΝСΑΛΠΙΓϪ ЄΥϯ ЄΟΟΥ ΝΑϥ ΑΥШ ΝСΤΡΑ | and trumpets (σάλπιγξ) glorifying him and

2 ΤЄΥΜΑ ΤΗΡΟΥ ΝΝΑΓΓЄΛΟС СЄϯ ЄΟΟΥ ΝΑϥ | all the hosts (στράτευμα) of angels (ἄγγελος) glorify him

3 ΑΥШ СЄСΜΟΥ ЄΡΟϥ | and praise him.

As in NatArch this next pericope relates the creation of the angels. Yet in contrast with NatArch, OnOrgWld adds at this point a reference to the angels who are called Seraphin. However, this reference is not clearly identifiable as the work of the redactor. Since Isa 6, Seraphim had also been connected with the throne.[43] Thus, Sabaoth here also fashioned them as angels upon the throne. The strange motif is then added that they are in the form of a dragon, which draws upon an idea found only in 1 and 2 Enoch.[44] They are then said to glorify him at every moment. Again, this material has neither influenced nor been transmitted by the NT since neither the motif of Seraphim nor that of their form as a dragon is found in the NT.

---

[43] Isa 6:2, 6; Apoc Moses 33:3; 1 Enoch 61:10; 71:7; 2 Enoch 29:3B and probably also in 2 Enoch 12:1 and 19:6. In this pericope the Cherubim are not clearly identified as a separate class of angels; they are still only presented as the bearers of the chariot. In contrast, 1 Enoch 71:7 lists Seraphin, Cherubin and adds Ophannin as classes of angels.

[44] 1 Enoch 20:7 in a context of the seven archangels and Cherubim states: "Gabriel, one of the holy angels, who is over Paradise and the serpents and the Cherubim"; 2 Enoch 12:1 states: "And I looked and saw other flying elements of the sun, whose name are Phoenixes and Chalkydri, marvellous and wonderful, with feet and tails in the form of a lion, and a crocodile's head... their wings are like those of angels." In the note on 2 Enoch 12:1 Forbes and Charles remark "Chalkydri, seemingly a transliteration of χαλκύδραι, brazen hydras or serpents. These are classified with the Cherubim in 1 Enoch 20:7, and so equal the Seraphim of Isa 6:2, 6. These then were perhaps conceived as winged dragons, as the analogy of the animal-like forms of the Cherubim in Ezek 1:5-11 would lead us to suppose" (Charles, *APOT*, 2. 201 and 436).

As in NatArch Sabaoth next fashions "infinitely many" angels. However, again in contrast, he fashions here in OnOrgWld "an angelic church."[45] The angels are described as thousands and myriads, a motif customary in Jewish apocalyptic since Daniel.[46] This angelic church is like the church in the Eighth, which suggests that more mythical elements concerning the inner life of the divine realm above the veil could also be adduced by the author, if he desired, beyond the bare statement that the aeon of truth is all light (98[146].23-26).[47]

The text then adds that Sabaoth fashioned a first-born, called Israel, a motif which is not found in NatArch. Certainly this motif of Israel as a first-born is familiar in Israelite times (Exod 4:22) and in Judaism (Sir 36:11; Jub 2:20; 4 Ezra 6:58). However, in neither was Israel considered as a preexistent entity. In the NT the motif of Israel as the first-born is not found; instead, the term first-born is applied to Christ (e.g. Rom 8:29). The further explanation of the name Israel as "the man who sees God" draws upon an exegetical tradition, which is not witnessed in the OT or NT but well attested in Philo.[48] Since Israel is a creation of Sabaoth, it is implicitly downgraded. Just as the realm of the Eighth is above Sabaoth, so those who belong to that realm are higher than Israel.

Similarly, within Valentinianism the Jews are considered as righteous and psychic, rather than pneumatic. They worship the Demiurge rather than the Father of Truth:

"The mountain represents the Devil or his world, since the Devil was *one* part of the whole of matter," says Heracleon, "but the world is the total mountain of evil, a deserted dwelling-place of beasts, to which all (who lived) before the law and all the Gentiles render worship. But

---

[45] I have not located this expression in biblical or intertestamental literature.

[46] Dan 7:10; cf. 1 Enoch 14:22; 60:1; 71:8; Rev 5:11. That ϣⲟ translates χίλιοι, see Crum 549b; that ⲧⲃⲁ translates μυρίας, see Crum 399a.

[47] Tardieu states that the place of rest where the first Adam sojourns is the land of election, which the Naassenes identify with the angelic church. He further states that the angelic church refers to the place of sojourn which Sabaoth created for himself. Then he concludes to a cosmological proximity between the angelic church as the place of rest of Sabaoth and the angelic church as the land of election in which the pneumatic Adam rests (*Trois mythes gnostiques*, 225). However, Tardieu misinterprets the passage. The Eighth in which the prototypical angelic church is found is the realm of light to which the pneumatic Adam could not return (112[160].10-14; cf. 124[172].5-13). Instead, the pneumatic Adam is in an aeon between the Eighth and the seven heavens below (112[160].13-22). Sabaoth then creates an angelic church in the seventh heaven in imitation of the church of the Eighth.

[48] E.g. *De poster. C.* 92; *De Abr.* 57-59; *Leg. Gaj.* 4; etc. As Böhlig remarks (*Die koptisch-gnostische Schrift ohne Titel*, 54), the Hebrew presupposed is אִישׁ רָאָה אֵל.

Jerusalem (represents) the creation or the creator whom the Jews worship." But, in the second place, he thinks that "the mountain is the creation which the Gentiles worship, but Jerusalem is the creator whom the Jews serve. You, then," he adds, "as the pneumatics will worship neither the creation nor the Demiurge, but the Father of truth."[49]

As we suggested earlier, the sentences concerning the creation of Jesus Christ are part of the redactor's contribution to OnOrgWld. These sentences are unnecessary to the context. With them the pericope is overloaded with its second right/left schema. Jesus Christ is then like the Savior in the Ogdoad and sits at the right hand as do Life (NatArch 95[143].32ff) and Sabaoth (OnOrgWld 106[154].11ff)—but on an excellent throne (cf. Matt 19:28; 25:31). On Sabaoth's left there sits the virgin of the Holy Spirit. Evidently, as Jesus Christ is the image of the Savior above, so the virgin of the Holy Spirit is the image of the Holy Spirit above. She likewise sits on a throne and praises Sabaoth.

It is strange that Jesus Christ sits at the right of Sabaoth. More expected in gnostic thought is that Christ descends upon the human Jesus (e.g. the unnamed gnostics in Iren. *Adv. haer.* 1.30.6 and Cerinthus in Iren. *Adv. haer.* 1.26.1; ed. Harvey l. 238 and 211). Thus Christ himself is considered as coming from the pleromatic realm rather than from some realm below the veil.[50]

However, within Valentinianism Christ is considered as the creation of the Demiurge, sits at his right, is the image of the savior in the

---

[49] Heracleon, Frag. 20; text in Völker, 73-74; tr. Förster, *Gnosis*, 171. Cf. also Frag. 13 (Völker, 69-70) and Hipp. *Ref.* 6.34.4-6 (Völker, 133). In her study, *The Johannine Gospel in Gnostic Exegesis*, Pagels argues that for Heracleon in his commentary on John the Jews represent consistently the psychic Christians and that Heracleon is not concerned with the actual members of the twelve tribes, the nation of Israel (67-68). While it is clear that "the Jews" are used by Heracleon to represent the psychic Christians, I consider this fragment to indicate that the matter is not an either/or but both/and. Just as Heracleon in this passage can judge theologically as hylic those who in a temporal sense were "before the Law" as well as their successors the pagans, so here he judges theologically the historical Jews as psychic. In other passages, then, "the Jews" can be taken to represent their successors, the non-gnostic Christians, who are also judged as psychic. Pagels seems implicitly to grant as much when she comments upon this passage, "When the savior says that Jerusalem is the topos where 'the Jews worship,' he refers *even* (emphasis mine; N.B. rather than only) to Christian worship that occurs on a psychic level" (89). This need not prove Heracleon inconsistent, since as Pagels points out (74-75), Heracleon can interpret terms on three levels. Just as the passover from the hylic level is the ancient festival of Israel and from the psychic level is a prefiguration of the passion and death of Jesus (74-75), so too I suggest that "the Jews" on different levels can indicate both the nation of Israel and the non-gnostic Christians.

[50] Cf. Epiph. *Pan.* 26.10.4 (ed. Holl; GCS 25.1; 287).

eighth heaven and represents the psychic. For example, *Exc. Theod.* 62.1 expresses the following in this regard :

> Now the psychic Christ sits on the right hand of the Creator, as David says, "Sit thou on my right hand" and so on. And he sits there until the end.[51]

Jesus, then, who is from the Pleroma and who is also called the savior, puts on Christ at his descent into the world :

> And when he came into Space Jesus found Christ, whom it was foretold that he would put on, whom the Prophets and the Law announced as an image of the Saviour.[52]

However, Jesus can also be said to sit at the right of the Demiurge after his earthly ministry. He waits there with the pneumatic seed until the consummation and their re-entry into the Pleroma :

> From thence Jesus was called and sat down with Space, that the spirits might remain and not rise before him, and that he might subdue Space and provide the seed with a passage into the Pleroma.[53]

Therefore, we suggest that the inclusion of Jesus Christ as seated at the right hand of Sabaoth in the Sabaoth account reflects Valentinain influence. The fact that the name of Jesus Christ rather than Christ alone can probably be explained as a fusion of the motifs of Christ before the earthly ministry and Jesus after it, as seated beside the Demiurge. As in Valentinianism then Jesus Christ is the creation of the Demiurge and also the image of the Savior in the eighth heaven (OnOrgWld 105[153].20-27). In Valentinianism too not only the Jews but also the orthodox Christians are considered as psychic and thus as belonging to the Demiurge.[54] In the same way here in OnOrgWld, the fact that Jesus Christ and the virgin of the Holy Spirit are considered as creations of Sabaoth would place Christians on the same level as Israel—namely, psychics.[55]

---

[51] Text and tr. in R. P. Casey, *The Excerpta ex Theodoto of Clement of Alexandria* (Studies and Documents 1; London 1934) 80-81. Cf. Iren. *Adv. haer.* 1.7.1-2 (Völker, 118).

[52] *Exc. Theod.* 59.2; Casey, *The Excerpta ex Theodoto*, 78-79. Cf. *Exc. Theod.* 23.2; Casey, *The Excerpta ex Theodoto*, 58-59.

[53] *Exc. Theod.* 38.3; Casey, *The Excerpta ex Theodoto*, 66-67. Casey has accepted the emendation of πράγματα to πνεύματα, as his translation indicates.

[54] Iren. *Adv. haer.* 1.6.2: "The psychic men have been instructed in psychic matters; they are strengthened by works and mere faith, and do not have perfect knowledge; and these, they teach, are we of the Church" (text Völker, 115; tr. Förster, *Gnosis*, 193).

[55] Cf. also SJC BG 123.11ff which distinguishes mankind as well among the categories : gnostic, Christian, hylic.

However, there is one difficulty with this solution. As we mentioned earlier, 117(165).28-118(166).2 is a summary statement which clearly belongs to the hand of the redactor. In these verses, then, the redactor distinguishes among the pneumatic Adam, the psychic Adam, and the choic Adam, whom he identifies as the man-of-law. Similarly, the author distinguishes three kinds of men and their races until the end of the world: the pneumatic of the Aeon, the psychic, and the choic (122[170].6-9). Since this "man-of-Law" clearly refers to the man of the Torah, the choic Adam and the choic race of men must encompass the Jews. It is difficult, then, or rather impossible to consider the Jews as both choic and psychic at the same time. Since the sentences concerning Jesus Christ are also clearly secondary and redactional in this context, we suggest that the reference to Sabaoth's creation of Israel was part of the redactor's inherited material, which he has not completely adapted to his own purposes. Thus, for the redactor, Sabaoth and the Christians are the ones who are truly psychic, whereas the Jews—as men of Law—are actually choic.

The redaction continues in the reference to the seven virgins, who stand before the Holy Spirit. That this sentence is also a redaction is clear since the παρθένοι stand before the παρθένος (hitesehē) but glorify Sabaoth (eutieoou naf). Secondly, the figure thirty is applied only to the lyres and not to the other instruments, and without explanation or evident connection. Also, if this sentence were part of the original, one would expect that the virgins would be the object of the verb ⲧⲁⲙⲓⲟ, which is stated consistently (104[152].32; 105[153].1, 17, 20). It is unclear why the virgins are said to have specifically thirty of the lyres. It is possibly an echo of the Valentinian idea that there are thirty aeons in the Pleroma, which are also signified by the thirty days of the month.[56]

Besides having thirty lyres, the virgins are said to have harps, as in NatArch 95(143).30f.[57] Trumpets, which are appropriate to a context of enthronement, are also added and said to render him glory.[58] The pericope closes as all the forces of angels glorify him. It seems likely that before this redaction the passage simply continued after ⲡⲣⲱⲙⲉ

---

[56] Cf. Iren. Adv. haer. 1.1.3 (ed. Harvey 1. 11) and 1.17.1 (ed. Harvey 1. 166-67); Hipp. Ref. 6.31.3 (Völker, 130).

[57] But in reverse order, i.e. zithers and psalteries.

[58] E.g. royal coronation 2 Sam 15:10; enthronement psalm Ps 47:5; eschatological end 4 Ezra 6:23. Cf. G. Friedrich, σάλπιγξ, TDNT 7 (1971) 71-88.

ϵⲧⲛⲁⲩ ϵⲡⲛⲟⲩⲧϵ with a reference to the lyres, harps, and trumpets and to the praise of Sabaoth.

Once again this section exhibits material that derives from neither OT nor NT but from Judaism and therefrom passes into Christian gnostic hands.

5) *The Instruction of Sabaoth* 106(154).3-11

ϵϥϩⲙⲟⲟⲥ ⲇϵ ϩⲓⲭⲛ̄ ⲟⲩ	But (δέ) he sits on a
4 ⲑⲣⲟⲛⲟⲥ ⟨ϩⲛ ⲟⲩ⟩ⲟⲩⲟϵⲓⲛ ⲛ̄ⲛⲟϭ ⲛ̄ⲕⲗⲟⲟⲗϵ ϵⲥⲥⲕϵ	throne (θρόνος) in a great cloud of light that con ceals (σκεπάζειν)
5 ⲡⲁⲥϵ ⲙ̄ⲙⲟϥ ⲁⲩⲱ ⲛϵⲙⲛ̄ ⲗⲁⲁⲩ ⲛⲙ̄ⲙⲁϥ	him. And there was no one with him
6 ϩⲛ̄ ⲧϵⲕⲗⲟⲟⲗϵ ϵⲓⲙⲏⲧⲓ ⲁⲧⲥⲟⲫⲓⲁ ⲧⲡⲓⲥⲧⲓⲥ	in the cloud except (εἰμήτι) Wisdom (σοφία) Faith (πίστις),
7 ϵⲥⲧⲥϵⲃⲟ ⲙ̄ⲙⲟϥ ⲁⲛϵⲧϣⲟⲟⲡ ⲧⲏⲣⲟⲩ ϩⲛ̄ ⲧⲙⲁϩ	teaching him about all those which exist in the
8 ϣⲙⲟⲩⲛϵ ϫϵⲕⲁⲁⲥ ϵⲩⲛⲁⲧⲁⲙϵⲓⲟ ⲛ̄ⲛⲧⲟⲛ	Eighth in order that there might be fashioned the likenesses
9 ⲧⲛ̄ ⲛ̄ⲛⲏ ϣⲓⲛⲁ ⲧⲙⲛ̄ⲧϵⲣⲟ ϵⲥⲛⲁⲙⲟⲩⲛ ϵⲃⲟⲗ	of those so that (ἵνα) the kingdom might remain
10 ⲛⲁϥ ϣⲁ ⲧⲥⲩⲛⲧϵⲗϵⲓⲁ ⲛ̄ⲙⲡⲏⲩϵ ⲙ̄ⲡⲭⲁⲟⲥ	for him until the consummation (συντέλεια) of the heavens of Chaos (χάος)
11 ⲙⲛ̄ ⲛⲟⲩⲇⲩⲛⲁⲙⲓⲥ	and their Forces (δύναμις).

As we presented earlier, this second account on the instruction of Sabaoth is another piece of tradition which has been incorporated into OnOrgWld. It is clearly another piece of tradition since it reduplicates a previous pericope, contradicts what precedes and follows, and uses the name Wisdom-Faith rather than Faith-Wisdom. However, this pericope has also clearly been incorporated by the author rather than inserted by a later interpolator, since the second purpose clause —"so that the kingdom might remain for him until the consummation (συντέλεια) of the heavens of Chaos and their Forces"—betrays the theological concern and the terminological usage of the author in the term συντέλεια.[59] Thus, at least this second purpose clause stems from the redactorial hand of the author.

---

[59] The term συντέλεια occurs frequently throughout the treatise. Most often the term occurs in the phrase "the consummation of the Aeon": cf. 110(158).13; 114 (162).24; 121(169).26f; 122(170).6, 33; 123(171).30; 125(173).32. However, the term also occurs alone (117[165].11; 123[171].19), in the phrase "the consummation of the world" (122[170].7f), in the phrase "the consummation of your works" (103[151].25) and only here at 106(154).10f in the phrase "the consummation of the heavens of Chaos and their powers."

Use of the term συντέλεια for the consummation of the world is found within Valentinianism, e.g. *Exc. Theod.* 63.1 (Casey, *The Excerpta ex Theodoto*, 82-83) and Iren. *Adv. haer.* 1.6.1 (Völker, 114). The term is also found in other strands of

In this piece of tradition Sabaoth is presented as sitting on a throne in a cloud of light, which covers him. He is alone except for the presence of Wisdom-Faith. Rather than simply an allusion to Exod 24:15ff, in which God is enclosed within a cloud of glory, the motif of a great cloud concealing Sabaoth is probably derived from late Jewish tradition, in which the theophanic cloud of Ps 18:11//2 Sam 22:12 and Ps 104:2 is associated with the heavenly veil.[60] For example, in Targ Job 26:9 God sits on His throne within the cloud of His glory, which covers Him as a veil.[61] He sits alone within it, and the cloud prevents the angels from seeing Him.

It is probable that this scene concerning the instruction of Sabaoth by Wisdom-Faith derives from Valentinian influence. Usually in Valentinianism, the Demiurge is considered to be ignorant of the realms above him until the coming of the Savior.[62] However, in one report concerning the Valentinians the Demiurge is said to have been previously instructed by Wisdom:

> For the Demiurge was instructed by Sophia to the effect that he is not God alone, as he imagined with no other existing apart from him; but taught by Sophia, he recognized the higher (deity); for he was instructed, initiated, and indoctrinated into the great mystery of the Father and of the aeons, and he disclosed it to no one.[63]

The incorporation of this pericope into OnOrgWld serves to stress the role of Wisdom in instructing Sabaoth. A double purpose clause then explains the importance of this teaching. First, it is that likenesses to these things might be made; and second, that the kingdom might remain for him until the end. Thus the incorporation of this piece of tradition by the author adds another reason as to why the teaching comes prior to the creation by Sabaoth: because Sabaoth has made likenesses of what exist in the Eighth, he has authority over all below him; his kingdom extends over all below. Thereby, the kingly role of Sabaoth is again explicitly emphasized.

Gnosticism, e.g. GEgypt CG III, 2: 61.1ff//IV, 2: 72.10ff and *Pistis Sophia* 86 (tr. C. Schmidt and W. Till, *Koptisch-gnostische Schriften* GCS 45, 3te Aufl.; Berlin 1962; 123). Thus, while the use of the term in this sense is not specifically Valentinian, its use throughout the document is appropriate if one can detect other specifically Valentinian influence and thus supportive of that other evidence.

[60] MacRae, *Some Elements of Jewish Apocalyptic*, 102f. Wisdom also dwells in a cloud in Sir 24:4.

[61] *Str-B*, 1. 976.

[62] E.g. Iren. *Adv. haer.* 1.5.4 (Völker, 109-10); 1.7.1-2 (Völker, 118); 1.7.4 (Völker, 119); Hipp. *Ref.* 6.35.1 (Völker, 134).

[63] Hipp. *Ref.* 6.36.2 (text Völker, 135; tr. Förster, *Gnosis*, 193).

6) *The Separation into Right and Left* 106(154).11-19

ΤΠΙCΤΙC ΔΕ ΤCΟΦΙΑ ⟨Δ⟩C	Now (δέ) Faith (πίστις) Wisdom (σοφία)
12 ΠΟΡΧϤ ΕΠΚΑΚΕ ΑCΜΟΥΤΕ ΕΡΟϤ ΕΟΥΝΑΜ	separated him from the darkness. She called him to her right,
13 ΜΜΟC ΠΑΡΧΙΓΕΝΕΤΩΡ ΔΕ ΑCΚΑΑϤ ϨΙ ϬΒΟΥΡ	but (δέ) the Archigenetor (ἀρχιγενέτωρ) she put on her left.
14 ΜΜΟC ΧΙΜ ΦΟΟΥ ΕΤΜΜΑΥ ΑΥΜΟΥΤΕ ΕΟΥ	From that day, right is called [the]
15 ΝΑΜ ΧΕ ⟨Τ⟩ΔΙΚΑΙΟCΥΝΗ ϬΒΟΥΡ ΔΕ ΑΥΜΟΥ	righteousness (δικαιοσύνη) but (δέ) left is called
16 ΤΕ ΕΡΟC ΧΕ ΤΑΔΙΚΙΑ ΕΤΒΕ ΠΑΕΙ ϬΕ ΑΥΧΙ	the unrighteousness (ἀδικία). Moreover because of this they all received
17 ΤΗΡΟΥ ΝΟΥΚΟCΜΟC ΝΤΕΚΚΛΗCΙΑ ΝΤΑΙΚΑΙ	a world (κόσμος) of the church (ἐκκλησία) of righteousness (δικαιοσύνη)
18 ΟCΥΝΗ ΜΝ ΤΑΔΙΚΙΑ⟨ΕC⟩ΑϨΕ Ε⟨Ϩ⟩ΡΑΪ ΕΧΝ	and unrighteousness (ἀδικία), since it stands over
ΟΥCΩΝΤ	a creation.
19 [ΤΗΡΟΥ]	

As in NatArch, this last pericope concerning separation into right and left conflates the final element of the ascent and vision of the throne/chariot by the apocalyptic seer—i.e. angels on right and left— and the final element of enthronement—i.e. the beginning of rule. As we also previously discussed, this pericope presents a later stage in the tradition than NatArch, since "darkness" and "righteousness" reflect the hand of the redactor and since the pericope contradicts the previous narrative of the ascent of Sabaoth.

The particle "now" introduces the pericope, and Faith-Wisdom is then said to separate Sabaoth from the darkness. In contrast to NatArch, Faith-Wisdom assumes the middle position rather than Sabaoth. Also in contrast to NatArch she calls Sabaoth to her right and Ialdabaoth to her left rather than Life and the angel. From that day the right is called righteousness and the left unrighteousness.[64] In NatArch, on the other hand, the contrast is between life and unrighteousness. The change then from NatArch to OnOrgWld serves to emphasize particularly the role of Faith-Wisdom and the contrast between righteousness and unrighteousness.

One finds a similar conception within Valentinian circles. For example, there it is Wisdom who creates the Demiurge and the Ruler of the World, who are respectively related to right and left.[65] The Demiurge in particular is considered as the God of righteousness while

---

[64] Tardieu errs in ascribing righteousness and thus the creation of Paradise to Faith-Wisdom. Rather, it is Sabaoth who is related to righteousness and thus probably to the creation of Paradise (*Trois mythes gnostiques*, 225).

[65] *Exc. Theod.* 33.3-34.1 and 47.2-3 (Casey, *The Excerpta ex Theodoto*, 64-65 and 70-73); Iren. *Adv. haer.* 1.5.1 (Völker, 106).

the Ruler of the World is unrighteous.[66] Then the right represents
the psychic and the left represents the hylic or choic.[67] To be sure,
however, one does not find within Valentinianism the scene in which
Wisdom is seated with the Demiurge and the Ruler of the World
beside her in one heaven. Rather, Wisdom occupies the middle; the
Demiurge resides in the seventh heaven; and the Ruler of the world
is in the cosmic realm.

Yet this pericope concerning the separation into right and left in
OnOrgWld shows Valentinian influence. Valentinian conceptions have
not been taken over directly. Rather this pericope of the Sabaoth
account as found in NatArch has been adapted in the light of Valentinian influence. Now Faith-Wisdom—as Wisdom in Valentinianism—
is placed in the position of prominence rather than Sabaoth. The
contrast becomes righteousness versus unrighteousness rather than life
versus unrighteousness; and Sabaoth represents the psychic type of
man (122[170].9).

The fact that Sabaoth is here contrasted with Ialdabaoth rather
than with an angel may also be partially explained by the tradition
concerning the divine Middot. Following Palestinian exegetical tradition, Philo had ascribed the aspect of God's ruling power to the title
κύριος and His goodness and creative power to the title θεός.[68] That
this tradition was known in Gnosticism is demonstrated by ApocryJn
BG 62.12ff:

> One (μέν) is righteous (δίκαιος), but (δέ) the other is unrighteous (ἄδικος).
> Eloim is the righteous (δίκαιος), Jave is the unrighteous (ἄδικος).[69]

In OnOrgWld, then, this same contrast is maintained between the
righteous and unrighteous (although here in the nominal rather than

---

[66] Ptolemy, *Letter to Flora* 3.5; 3.7; and 7.5 (Völker, 87f and 92).

[67] Iren. *Adv. haer.* 1.6.1 (Völker, 112).

[68] A. Marmorstein, *The Old Rabbinic Doctrine of God*; 1. *The Names and Attributes of God* (Oxford 1927) 43-53. As Marmorstein suggests, the latter reversal of rabbinic tradition so that Yahweh represents the merciful aspect and Elohim the judgmental may well represent an anti-gnostic reaction.

[69] Ed. Till (TU 60) 164-65. In the longer form of ApocryJn CG II, *1* : 24(72).20ff (ed. M. Krause and P. Labib, *Die drei Versionen des Apokryphon des Johannes im Koptischen Museum zu Alt-Kairo*; Abhandlungen des Deutschen Archäologischen Insti- tuts Kairo, Koptische Reihe 1; Wiesbaden 1962; 177f) the association of names is reversed so that Yahweh is righteous and Elohim unrighteous. This fact makes it difficult to assess whether the gnostics are following the earlier tradition of the middot represented by Philo or the later Rabbinic reversal. For our purposes, it is sufficient to note that this tradition was known by the gnostics. Cf. MacRae, *Some Elements of Jewish Apocalyptic*, 207ff.

adjectival form) and applied to the archontic names Sabaoth and Ialdabaoth rather than the two names of God.[70] Again, as in NatArch, the beginning of rule is shown in that the names are said to be used "from that day". Secondly, because of this separation into right and left, the world that exists below is then characterized as belonging to the church of righteousness and unrighteousness, since it stands over creation.

As in NatArch, so also here in OnOrgWld the Sabaoth account is derived from Jewish material, draws upon the tradition of the ascent and vision of the heavenly throne/chariot by the apocalyptic seer and upon the tradition of heavenly enthronement, and thus redacts these traditions by applying them to Sabaoth.

Specifically, apart from the small reference to Jesus Christ and the virgin of the Holy Spirit within the Sabaoth account (105[153].26-31), the account in OnOrgWld stems from Jewish material. There is no discernible influence of this account upon the NT nor is there influence from the NT portrayals of the enthronement of Christ upon this account. Thus the Jewish material has been mediated by Christians other than those whose writings appear in the canonical writings. As in NatArch the determinative motifs applied here to Sabaoth are not ascribed to Christ in the NT : e.g. Sabaoth's repentance, his being "snatched up" to the seventh heaven, his title specifically as Lord of the Forces, Life as his instructoress concerning the Eighth. Although Sabaoth does sit at the right hand (106[154].12f), this motif does not stem from NT influence but rather from the author's desire to contrast Sabaoth and Ialdabaoth, right and left. Lastly, a number of the minor motifs and traditions stem from Judaism. There are those that are also found in NatArch : seven heavens, the heavenly veil, the four-faced chariot of Cherubim, infinitely many angels, the harps of angels. In addition there occur here the following : the stretching

---

[70] Marmorstein in *The Old Rabbinic Doctrine of God*, 1. 50, has stated that these middot were used by the gnostics to contrast the Highest God and the God of the Jews (cf. Iren. *Adv. haer.* 2.35.3). This passage in OnOrgWld, however, would suggest that the contrast was between two rulers both of whom were below the Highest God. Further, in both versions of ApocryJn (cf. the preceding note) the righteous figure is placed over fire and wind and the unrighteous over water and earth, which would suggest that they are in some way comparable, related to the cosmos, and less than the remote Highest God. Thus, OnOrgWld would reflect the earlier use of this tradition in its application of the middot to both a positive and a negative ruler, who are rulers of the cosmos underneath the Highest God. ApocryJn, then, where the middot are related to Cain and Abel, would reflect a later stage in which the application of the tradition to different gods or rulers has lost its original significance.

out of the finger, the exegetical tradition relating light and darkness to Gen 1:2b, the description of the dwelling place of Sabaoth, the tradition of the seventy-two angels over the nations, the Seraphim as dragonlike, and Israel interpreted as "the man who sees God."[71]

B. FUNCTION

Professor Böhlig has perceptively noted that OnOrgWld 103(151).30 would be most appropriately followed by 107(155).17, if the Sabaoth account were missing. Therefore, he proposes that the Sabaoth account is an interpolation in the original treatise.[72] While we agree that the Sabaoth account is an identifiable unit of tradition, yet we consider it neither as a later interpolation into the text nor as a unit of tradition which has simply been inserted into the text. Rather, the Sabaoth account is a piece, which the author has redacted and integrated to serve a function in his treatise as a whole.

We have already shown that the author has redacted the Sabaoth account by means of his theology of the immortal Light-Man and the contrast between light and darkness (cf. 103[151].15-28 and 104 [152].2-11).[73] Secondly, the further references to Sabaoth throughout the treatise indicate that Sabaoth has been integrated into the system of the document. In 113(161).12f Wisdom-Life is said to be with Sabaoth; in 114(162).16f the souls of Sabaoth and his Christ are referred to; and also in 122(170).22f the sun and moon are considered as a witness to Sabaoth.

The function of the Sabaoth account in OnOrgWld then is related to the particular theology of OnOrgWld. As we have shown previously, the Sabaoth account in NatArch functions to answer the theological

---

[71] Bullard in *The Hypostasis of the Archons*, 111, suggested that the relationship of the Sabaoth account to Merkabah mysticism should be investigated by someone. I have done that. As the detailed analysis of the motifs in the Sabaoth account has shown, however, almost all of the motifs can be found in intertestamental Judaism. The few remaining motifs, such as the consuming fire which proceeds from the outstretched finger, can be found in Rabbinic Judaism as well as in Merkabah material. There is no isolatable motif that is particular to these gnostic accounts and to Merkabah material. Thus, the demonstrable relationship of these Sabaoth accounts and the Merkabah material consists only in that they are both derived from the same matrix, late Judaism. For an interesting study of the motifs of the throne and the chariot in Judaism and in Jewish esoteric, see J. Maier, *Vom Kultus zur Gnosis: Bundeslade, Gottesthron und Märkabah* (Kairos, Religionswissenschaftliche Studien 1; Salzburg 1964).

[72] Böhlig, *Die koptisch-gnostische Schrift ohne Titel*, 49f.

[73] Cf. supra 16-18 and also the commentary for further specific examples and argumentation.

problem concerning the God of the OT and the revelation contained
in the books of the OT. Here, however, in OnOrgWld the Sabaoth
account serves an anthropological rather than a theological function.
At the very beginning of the cosmogony, the author indicates a major
concern that he has—namely, men. For him the veil separates not
the above and the aeons below (as in NatArch 94[142].8-10) but men
and heaven (98[146].22f).[74] Within this theology, then, Sabaoth represents one class of men, the psychics. We shall contend that in his use
of the Sabaoth account the author has been influenced by Valentinianism. It is our view that the author has been subject to Valentinian influence and in the light of this influence has redacted the
Sabaoth account and composed his treatise. However, he has not
been bound by Valentinianism but developed further beyond it.

We have already argued within the commentary that there is evidence
of Valentinian influence in the Sabaoth account.[75] The creation of
Christ by Sabaoth to sit at his right hand, the instruction of Sabaoth
by Faith-Wisdom alone, and the presentation of Wisdom surrounded
by Sabaoth and Ialdabaoth, who represent righteousness and unrighteousness, are clear examples of Valentinian influence. Possibly the
reference to the thirty lyres (105[153].33f) is also a result of Valentinian
influence.

There is also evidence of Valentinian influence in the treatise as a
whole. First the pneumatic figure must reside in a middle realm between
the seventh heaven and the divine realm, until the consummation
of the Aeons (112[160].10-22). He cannot enter the divine realm until
then because of the stain with which his Light has been mixed
(127[175].1-5). So, too, in Valentinianism Wisdom as the pneumatic
figure resides ἐν τῇ μεσότητι until the consummation.[76] However,
the author of OnOrgWld has developed beyond Valentinianism in
that he has associated Faith-Wisdom with Sabaoth and introduced
another figure, the immortal Light-Man, as the resident of the realm
of the middle. Secondly, in OnOrgWld 125(173).4f the seven heavens
plus the middle are referred to as the Eighth. This designation is
somewhat strange in that elsewhere in the text the Eighth refers to

---

[74] The same redactional interest is seen in the serpent's response to Eve. Contrary
to the biblical account (Gen 3:5) and to NatArch (90[138].6-10), the difference for
OnOrgWld is not the difference between good and evil but between evil and good
men (118[166].34-119[167].6).

[75] Cf. supra 104-15.

[76] Iren. *Adv. haer.* 1.5.4. and 1.7.1 (Völker, 108ff and 117-18).

the divine realm (e.g. 112[160].12). Also in Valentinianism these lower realms are designated as the second or lower Ogdoad.[77] Thirdly, OnOrgWld 122(170).6-9 distinguishes three types of men : the pneumatic of the Aeon, the psychic and the earthly (πνευματικός, ψυχικός, χοϊκός). In Valentinianism as well there is a distinction among three classes of men. Usually the distinction is among πνευματικός, ψυχικός and ὑλικός (e.g. Iren. *Adv. haer.* 1.6.1).[78] However, the series πνευματικός, ψυχικός and χοϊκός is also attested in the account of Iren. *Adv. haer.* 1.6.1 and in Frag. 15 of Heracleon.[79]

Fourthly, the passage in OnOrgWld concerning the creation of Adam shows Valentinian influence. There is a strange, apparent contradiction in OnOrgWld in that at 115(163).1 the creation of the Archigenetor and his rulers is said to be ψυχικός and yet at 115(163).10f, 13f, 34 he is stated explicitly to have no ψυχή. If one compares the parallel passage in NatArch 87(135).23-88(136).16, there is no such contradiction. Within Valentinianism the psyche comes from the righteous ruler of the seventh heaven, the Demiurge; and those who possess the soul from the Demiurge, but not the Spirit from Wisdom, are ψυχικός.[80] On the other hand, those who merely receive matter from the world-ruler are ὑλικός. In OnOrgWld then the author has accepted his inherited material, in which the Archigenetor and his rulers fashioned a man that was ψυχικός, but altered it in that this creature is said to have no ψυχή.[81] As in Valentinianism, so within this document souls are said to belong to the righteous ruler of the seventh heaven, Sabaoth (ψυχή 114[162].16). It is also to be noted that Wisdom-Life, who is with Sabaoth (113[161].12f and 114[162].15f), is the one who sends Life-Eva to the earthly man and finally gives him a psyche (115[163].30-116[164].8). Thus it is clear that Valentinian influence has caused this apparent contradiction and provides its solution.[82]

---

[77] Iren, *Adv. haer.* 1.3.4 and 1.5.2. (Völker, 101 and 107) and Epiph. *Pan.* 31.6.1-2 (ed. Holl; GCS 25.1; 392-93).

[78] Völker, 112. Cf. *Exc. Theod.* 54.1-2 (Casey, *The Excerpta ex Theodoto*, 76-77) and Heracleon, Frag. 44 (Völker, 83).

[79] Völker, 112ff and 70.

[80] E.g. Iren. *Adv. haer.* 1.6.1 (Völker, 112f); Heracleon, Frag. 44 (Völker, 83).

[81] This conception may be possible on the basis of a distinction between an earthly, material soul and a soul of that intermediate stuff between spirit and matter. Cf. *Exc. Theod.* 50.1-51.1 (Casey, *The Excerpta ex Theodoto*, 72-75).

[82] Tardieu notes the parallel between the three lordships and the three races. Thus he relates the lordship of Sabaoth to the pneumatics, the lordship of the second Adam to the psychics, and the lordship of the *psychai* to the hylics. However, he misinterprets the function of Sabaoth who represents the psychics (see supra). He also fails

Fifthly, Valentinian influence can be detected in the reference to a fourth race of men. Again a seeming contradiction provides our starting point. OnOrgWld had consistently maintained that there were three races of men : the pneumatic, psychic and the choic (e.g. 122 [170].6-9). Then at 125(173).3f one finds the unexpected statement : "Therefore there are four kinds." The statement follows a discussion of the innocent spirits, i.e. the small blessed ones, and the angel who is manifest to them. Within Valentinianism Jesus as the fruit of the Pleroma can be entitled as Savior or Logos (e.g. Iren. *Adv. haer.* 1.2.6)[83] and also as Angel.[84] As the Angel of the Pleroma, Jesus has been granted all authority.[85] He has also created other angels, who surround him and who are the counterparts of the pneumatic seed in the world. These angels then pray for their counterparts in order that they may be reunited and re-enter the Pleroma.[86] This pneumatic seed is then identified as a τέκνον or νήπιον and as τὰ διαφέροντα σπέρματα.[87] At the consummation then the angelic counterpart and its pneumatic seed are to be reunited, as the Savior is with Wisdom, and enter into the nuptial chamber of the Pleroma.[88] Here too in OnOrgWld 124(172).12-15 there is an angel who is not powerless before the Father, who is manifest to the innocent spirits, who possesses the entire gnosis and who can give it. Clearly here OnOrgWld is drawing upon the Valentinian notion of Jesus as the Angel of the Pleroma.[89] The innocent spirits that are sent into the world are then identified as "your images"; they are the small, blessed ones

---

to see this apparent contradiction between being ψυχικός but not having a ψυχή. Since the ψυχή comes from Sabaoth, it seems more likely that the lordships of Sabaoth, of the second Adam and of the *psychai* all relate consistently to the psychics.

[83] Völker, 99.

[84] Ἄγγελος τοῦ πληρώματος *Exc. Theod.* 35.1 (Casey, *The Excerpta ex Theodoto*, 64-65); ὁ τῆς βουλῆς ἄγγελος *Exc. Theod.* 43.2 (Casey, *The Excerpta ex Theodoto*, 70-71).

[85] καὶ δόντος πᾶσαν τὴν ἐξουσίαν τοῦ πνεύματος, συναινέσαντος δὲ καὶ τοῦ πληρώματος ἐκπέμπεται "ὁ τῆς βουλῆς ἄγγελος." καὶ γίνεται κεφαλὴ τῶν ὅλων μετὰ τὸν Πατέρα *Exc. Theod.* 43.2 (Casey, *The Excerpta ex Theodoto*, 68-71).

[86] *Exc. Theod.* 35.1-4 (Casey, *The Excerpta ex Theodoto*, 64-67).

[87] *Exc. Theod.* 41.1-2 (Casey, *The Excerpta ex Theodoto*, 68-69); Iren. *Adv. haer.* 1.6.4 (Völker, 116). G. Quispel argues that τὰ διαφέροντα is a technical term of the Valentinians for the spiritual seed in *Ptolémée: Lettre à Flora* (Paris 1966) 36.

[88] *Exc. Theod.* 64 (Casey, *The Excerpta ex Theodoto*, 82-83).

[89] Böhlig has suggested an allusion to Matt 18:10, particularly on the basis of the mention of the guardian angel in OnOrgWld 124(172).12f—*Die koptisch-gnostische Schrift ohne Titel*, 100. However, the reference here is to *one* angel for all the innocent spirits rather than to a guardian angel for each individual person as in Matt 18:10.

(124[172].9-11). They have been fashioned by the Savior (124[172].33f); and they, rather than the seed, are the ones who are κατὰ διαφορά (124[172].26f). Here too OnOrgWld is drawing upon Valentinian notions but also developing them further. The author has increased in his system the classes of men from three to four. Thereby he has made use of the notion of angelic counterparts, sent them into the world, and considered them as the fourth race, which is perfect and thus above the pneumatics.[90] With this theologoumenon, the author is moving in the direction of Manichaeism, which also distinguishes the "elect" as more perfect than the catechumens or hearers.[91]

Lastly, OnOrgWld possibly shows Valentinian influence in its conception of the consummation. In Valentinianism after separation from the body the pneumatics reside in the middle with Wisdom, and the psychics reside in the seventh heaven with the Demiurge. The consummation occurs when all the pneumatic seed has been perfected (τελειοῦν). At the consummation, which is expressed by the term συντέλεια, the pneumatics along with Wisdom enter the Pleroma while the psychics and the Demiurge enter the realm just vacated, i.e. the middle.[92] In OnOrgWld the term used for the consummation is also συντέλεια (e.g. 125[173].32f), although the term is also used in other strands of Gnosticism and therefore not peculiarly Valentinian (e.g. GEgypt III, 2: 61.1ff/IV, 2: 72.10ff). Also here at the consummation the light returns to its root, the divine realm 127(175).4. Those who have entered the divine realm then are named the perfect (τέλειος cf. 127[175].5-10). Those who are not perfect then receive their glories in their aeons and in their immortal kingdoms (127[175].10-13). Implicitly then Sabaoth would remain in his kingdom (cf. 104[152].23 and 106[154].9) along with those associated with him.[93] In contrast, NatArch 97(145).5-21 presents a return to the light at the end but shows no concern for those who are less than perfect. The reference

---

[90] Tardieu suggests Pythagorean arithmology as the background for the notion of the fourth as the designation for the elect (*Trois mythes gnostiques*, 81, n. 236).

[91] Cf. H. J. Polotsky, "Manichaeismus," *PW*, Sup 6 (1935) 259, 262-64.

[92] *Exc. Theod.* 34.2 and 63.1 (Casey, *The Excerpta ex Theodoto*, 64-65 and 82-83); Iren. *Adv. haer.* 1.6.1 and 1.7.1 (Völker, 112 and 117f). Cf. the discussion of Pagels in *The Johannine Gospel in Gnostic Exegesis*, 94-97, who proposes that only those psychics who have not attained salvation remain in the middle.

[93] Tardieu suggests that the kings of history and the prophets are those who do not enter kinglessness but remain in immortal kingdoms (*Trois mythes gnostiques*, 82). However, there is no clear basis for this statement. 127(175).7 refers to the fulfilment of prophecy at the consummation; and the following verse seems to refer to the gnostics as kings rather than the kings of history (cf. 125[173].5-12).

to a heavenly marriage and to a movement of Sabaoth into the middle
are missing in OnOrgWld, and yet the treatise may reflect Valentinian
influence in its presentation of the return of the light at the συντέλεια
and of immortal kingdoms for the non-perfect.

Since the Sabaoth account has been integrated into the treatise as
a whole and since the account reflects Valentinian influence, it is
clear that Sabaoth represents the psychic class of men. Because the
perfect realm of the Eighth is light (98[146].23-26), the immortal Light-
Man represents the pneumatic type of men and resides in the middle
(112[160].10-22). Sabaoth is therefore placed below him in the seventh
heaven (104[152].20f). Ialdabaoth then and his offspring in the lower
heavens represent the choic type of men (106[154].24ff).

In this midrashic reflection upon Genesis, the author has also
presented three Adams—the pneumatic, the psychic and the choic.
In a clear systematization (117[165].28-35), which reflects the hand of
the author, it is said :

> Moreover the first Adam of the light
> is pneumatic (πνευματικός). He appeared
> On the first day. The second
> Adam is psychic (ψυχικός). He appeared
> on the fourth day, which
> is called 'Aphrodite'. The third
> Adam is earthly (χοϊκός),
> that is, 'the man of law' (-νόμος).[94]

In accord with this description of the three Adams, for the author
there are also three kinds of men and their races until the end of the
world : the pneumatic of the Aeon, the psychic and the earthly (122
[170].6-9). All souls are at first captured and enclosed in matter
(114[162].14-24; 117[165].24-26). It is gnosis, however, which makes
one aware of the true situation (119[167].12-15) and leads one, like
Sabaoth, to condemn the authorities (110[158].24-29; 113[161].7-9; 120
[168].29-35). Just as there are three men and their races, so there are
three phoenixes (the first is immortal, the second makes a thousand
years, and the third is destroyed) and also three baptisms (the first is
pneumatic, the second is fiery, the third is of water 122[170].6-16).
We have already discussed how the author has then altered this system
to introduce a fourth class of men, the perfect.

To whom then are the various classes of men ascribed? The reference
to the third, choic Adam as the man of the Law is clearly a reference

---

[94] Cf. Böhlig, *Die koptisch-gnostische Schrift ohne Titel*, 29f and 84f.

to the Jews.[95] Since the author, in incorporating the Sabaoth account, has added the reference to Jesus Christ as a creation of Sabaoth (105 [153].26), it is clear that the orthodox Christians are the psychics (cf. 114[162].16).[96] The gnostics then would be the pneumatics; and the elect among them are the perfect (124[172].32ff).

Corresponding to this anthropological function are ecclesiological and political consequences of this Sabaoth account. The Jews and Christians form a church of unrighteousness and righteousness to which the world is subject (105[153].20-21 and 106[154].16-18). The gnostics, however, form the true church (105[153].22-23 and 124[172].25-35). For the gnostic author of OnOrgWld, then, the heavenly enthronement of Sabaoth is a validation that Sabaoth is a divinely appointed ruler but a ruler only over the church of righteousness and unrighteousness and the world below him. Neither Sabaoth nor his church nor his rulers have any authority over the true gnostics. Thereby, this version of the Sabaoth account must have arisen when the gnostics no longer felt themselves welcome within or attracted to their Jewish or Christian brethren.

The further significance of this account in OnOrgWld, in contrast to NatArch, is that it shows the development within this stream of Gnosticism. The trend is from the simple to the more complex. Further mythical figures are introduced, i.e. the immortal Light-Man; further traditions are incorporated with the result that inner contradictions within the account are possible (e.g. 106[154].11-12 where Faith-Wisdom separates Sabaoth from the darkness, although he is already in the seventh heaven). From this single example, of course, one cannot generalize to the trend of all Gnosticism. However, further such studies in the Nag Hammadi corpus may serve either to verify or disprove such a general development.

The fact that the document as a whole is in the form of a treatise or tract should also not be overlooked. The conscious polemic against those who derive the world from chaos (97[145].24-29) with its allusion to Hesiod, the reference to the blessed in each country (124[172]. 25ff), and the form of a treatise or tract indicate a changed life-situation. No longer is the community merely an esoteric community. Rather, it is one conscious of a world-wide dispersion.

---

[95] For further pejorative references to the Law, cf. TestTr CG IX, *3*: 29.13-15 and 45.23-25; GMary BG 8502 8.22-9.4.

[96] Sabaoth is also said to have created Israel. Since the author himself considers the Jews as related to the choic rather than psychic class of men, probably the phrase concerning Israel was part of his pre-existing source (105[153].24).

Because this text is subsequent to NatArch, betrays Valentinian influence and shows a development beyond it, its date is probably in the first half of the third century. The treatise does not exhibit the wildly developed speculation of the end of the third century as witnessed in *Pistis Sophia*.

C. THE SABAOTH ACCOUNTS : REFLECTIONS THEREOF IN LATE GNOSTIC DOCUMENTS?

This same tradition concerning Sabaoth is found in another document from Nag Hammadi, GrSeth (CG VII, *2*), although in this document the name of ruler is Adonaios rather than Sabaoth. GrSeth is a revelation of Jesus Christ, the Son of Man (69.20-22), which particularly polemicizes on the one hand against the orthodox Christian church and stresses on the other hand the unity within the true church of the gnostics. The tractate polemicizes against the orthodox Christian church by attacking its doctrine of the death of Jesus Christ upon the cross and by considering it as the product of the rulers (49.26f; 60.13-61.28). For the true gnostic, in contrast, Jesus Christ did not truly die (55.15-56.13), but his revelation effects a unity between him and those who have accepted this knowledge (67.19-68.16).

The tractate itself is comparatively late. This is clear, first of all, because of its nature as a compilation. Although there is no indication that the document is Basilidean in itself, yet it has taken over the tradition of the substitution of Simon of Cyrene for Jesus upon the cross (56.4-13), which is attributed to Basilides (cf. Iren. *Adv. haer.* 1.24.4 and Epiph. *Pan.* 24.3.2-5). Secondly, it is clearly late because of the persecution by the orthodox Christian church (59.19-60.12).[97] Although there was polemical discussion between orthodox and gnostic, there is no evidence of persecution in the early stages of this confrontation. It should be further mentioned that it is impossible to locate this tractate within a particular gnostic sect.

Within the two parallel mythical cycles (49.10-54.14 and 54.14-59.19), which comprise the first part of the tractate and which treat of the heavenly origin of the revealer and his descent into the world, there appear the references to Adonaios (52.17-25 and 54.32-55.15).[98] In

---

[97] 59.22-26 : "... we were hated and persecuted, not only (οὐ μόνον) by those who are ignorant, but (ἀλλά) also by those who think that they are advancing (εὐπορεῖν) the name of Christ."

[98] In the following pages I am greatly indebted to the dissertation of J. Gibbons, *A Commentary on the Second Logos of the Great Seth* (Ph.D. diss., Yale University

the first, an allusion is presented to the earlier flight of Adonaios :

> And
> all those who have come down,
> who belong to the same race (γένος) as he
> who fled from the throne (θρόνος) (those of the race of Adonaios)
> flee to the Sophia (σοφία) of Elpis (ἐλπίς),
> since she had earlier given the sign
> concerning us and all the ones with me.[99]

In the second reference (54.32-55.15), a disturbance arises at the descent of the revealer, whom Adonaios knows because of Hope (Elpis) :

> And (δέ) there came about a disturbance
> and a battle surrounding
> the Seraphim and the Cherubim,
> since their glory will be dissolved;
> ... and confusion around
> Adonaios on both sides
> with their dwelling to the Cosmocrator (κοσμοκράτωρ)
> and him who said,
> 'Let us seize him!'; others
> again : 'The plan will certainly not materialize.'
> For (γάρ) Adonaios knows me
> because of Elpis (ἐλπίς)
> (And [δέ] I was
> in the mouth of lions) and

1972), for his analysis of the document as a whole and his examination of the relationship between Sabaoth and Adonaios.

[99]   ⲁⲩⲱ ⲱⲁⲩⲡⲱⲧ ⲛ̄ϭⲓ
ⲛⲁⲓ̈ ⲧⲏⲣⲟⲩ ⲉⲛⲧⲁⲩⲉⲓ ⲙⲛ̄ ⲡⲓ
ⲅⲉⲛⲟⲥ ⲉⲡⲉⲥⲏⲧ ⲉⲃⲟⲗ ϨⲘ̄ ⲡⲏ
ⲉⲛⲧⲁϥⲡⲱⲧ ⲉⲃⲟⲗ ϨⲘ̄ ⲡⲓⲑⲣⲟ
ⲛⲟⲥ ⲱⲁ ϯⲥⲟⲫⲓⲁ ⲛ̄ⲧⲉ ϯϨⲉⲗ
ⲡⲓⲥ ⲉⲁⲥⲣ̄ ⲱⲟⲣⲡ̄ ⲛ̄ϯⲙⲁⲉⲓⲛ ⲉ
ⲧⲃⲏⲏⲧⲛ̄ ⲙⲛ ⲛⲏ ⲧⲏⲣⲟⲩ ⲉⲧⲱⲟ
ⲟⲡ ⲛⲘ̄ⲙⲁⲉⲓ ⲛⲓ ⲉⲃⲟⲗ ϨⲘ̄ ⲡⲓⲅⲉ
ⲛⲟⲥ ⲛ̄ⲧⲉ ⲁⲇⲱⲛⲁⲓⲟⲥ

Text and tr. Gibbons, *A Commentary on GrSeth*, 103f. In his commentary (175-76) Gibbons rightly proposes two emendations in this passage. As he states, the text at present reads : "And they are fleeing, all those who have come down with the race, from him who had fled from the throne (θρόνος) to the Sophia of Elpis, since she had earlier given the sign concerning us and all those who are with me—those of the race (γένος) of Adonaios." He suggests that the Greek *Vorlage* must have been something like καὶ φεύγουσιν οἱ πάντες καταβάντες σὺν γένει (read : συγγενεῖς) τοῦ φύξαντος τοῦ θρόνου πρὸς τὴν σοφίαν τῆς ἐλπίδος ... οἱ τοῦ γένους Ἀδωναίου. Thus a misreading of σὺν γένει for an original συγγενεῖς by the translator and a mis-translation of τοῦ φύξαντος as the object of the verb φεύγουσιν rather than a genitive modifying συγγενεῖς produced the present faulty text.

the plan which they devised
about me to do away with
their Error (πλάνη) and their senselessness.
I did not succumb to them as
they had planned.[100]

It is clear from the names and motifs involved that these pericopes concerning Adonaios and his race reflect the same mythologoumenon as that found in NatArch and OnOrgWld concerning Sabaoth. To be sure, the name is changed to Adonaios, but as both GEgypt (CG III, 2: 57.13f) and ApocryJn (CG II, 1: 10(58).33f) state, Sabaoth is called or identified with Adonaios.[101] In an earlier incident, Adonaios is said to have "fled from the throne" (52.20). The "throne" is surely a metaphor for the Demiurge, Ialdabaoth (cf. ApocryJn CG II, 1: 10[58].14-19), from whom Sabaoth also turns. Further, just as Sabaoth is instructed by Life the daughter of Wisdom in NatArch

---

[100]   ΟΥϢΤΟΡΤ͞Ρ ΔΕ
Μ͞Ν ΟΥ† ΑϤϢϢΠΕ Μ͞ΠΚϢΤΕ
Ν͞ΝΙΣΑΡΑΦΙΝ Μ͞Ν ΝΙΧΕΡΟΥΒΙΝ
ΕϤΝΑΒϢΛ ΕΒΟΛ Ν͞ϬΙ ΠΟΥΕΟΟΥ
Μ͞Ν ΠΤϢ͞Ϩ ΕΤϢΟΟΠ Μ͞ΠΚϢ
ΤΕ Ν͞ΑΔϢΝΑΙΟΣ Μ͞ΠΙΣΑ Μ͞Ν
ΠΑΪ Μ͞Ν ΠΕΥΗΕΙ ϢΑ ΠΙΚΟΣΜΟ
ΚΡΑΤϢΡ Μ͞Ν ΠΗ ΕΝΕϤΧϢ Μ͞
ΜΟΣ ΧΕ ΜΑΡΝ͞ϬΙΤϤ Ϩ͞ΕΝΚΟ
ΟΥΕ ΟΝ ΧΕ ΝΕϤϢϢΠΕ Ν͞ϬΙ ΠΙ
ϢΟΧΝΕ˙ ΕϤΣΟΟΥΝ ΓΑΡ ΜΜΟΪ
Ν͞ϬΙ ΑΔϢΝΑΙΟΣ ΕΤΒΕ ΟΥϨΕΛ
ΠΙΣ˙ ΑΝΟΚ ΔΕ ΝΕΕΙϢΟΟΠ
Ϩ͞Ν ΡϢΟΥ Ν͞Ϩ̄ΕΝΜΟΥΕΙ ΑΥϢ
ΠΙϢΟΧΝΕ Ν͞ΤΑΥΣΟΟΥΝ Ν͞Ϩ
ΤϤ ΕΤΒΗΗΤ ΕΥΒϢΛ ΕΒΟΛ Ν͞ΤΕ
ΤΕΥΠΛΑΝΗ Μ͞Ν ΤΕΥΜΝΤΑΘΗΤ
Μ͞ΠΙ† ΕϨΟΥΝ ΕΧϢΟΥ Ν͞ΘΕ Ν͞
ΤΑΥϢΟΧΝΕ

Text and tr. Gibbons, *A Commentary on GrSeth*, 108f. As he suggests in his commentary (197), there must be a lacuna after the clause "since their glory will be dissolved," if we are to explain the following incomplete sentence. The scribe must have omitted a line, which contained the beginning of the following sentence, such as: "Some fled from the disturbance..."

[101] This identification of Sabaoth and Adonaios occurs only in the codex II version of ApocryJn and not in BG 8502, Codex III or Codex IV of Nag Hammadi. Since this identification of Sabaoth and Adonaios would be a later development in the simple listing of the archontic offspring of the Demiurge, it is another small indication that Codex II represents a later version of ApocryJn than BG 8502 and Codex III. Cf. Rudolph, "Gnosis und Gnostizismus, ein Forschungsbericht," *ThRu* 34 (1969) 143-47, for the present state of the discussion concerning the priority of the shorter or longer recension.

(e.g. 95[143].18 and by Wisdom-Life the daughter of Faith-Wisdom in OnOrgWld (e.g. 113[161].12f), so Adonaios is instructed by Wisdom of Hope (52.21) or Hope (55.7f). One can see the Christianization at work in the change from NatArch and OnOrgWld. Rather than Life, Hope is the daughter of Wisdom, whose name probably stems from Wisdom's action in 51.11-15, where she prepares men to receive the "life-giving word," which will come from the revealer in the future. Secondly, the instruction is no longer concerning the eighth heaven, but rather concerning the future revealer, who is later identified as Jesus Christ, the Son of Man (69.21f).

In these pericopes not only the reference to the earlier flight of Adonaios but also the description of the later revolt of the race of Adonaios is drawn from the same tradition as the Sabaoth account. Here too at the appearance of a heavenly figure (cf. the light in OnOrgWld 104[152].5) there is a disturbance (ωTOPT$\bar{p}$) in the cosmos and a battle (54.27-33; cf. OnOrgWld 104[152].15f).[102] There is an unexplained reference to the Seraphim and Cherubim in connection with Adonaios (54.34; cf. OnOrgWld 105[153].3f, 18f). There is the flight from the Demiurge and to Wisdom of Hope (52.20f). There is probably even a reflection of the division into right and left in the phrase that there was confusion around Adonaios "on both sides" (55.2; cf. NatArch 95[143].31ff and OnOrgWld 106[154].11ff).

In conclusion, then, one can say that the presentation of the earlier flight of Adonaios and the later revolt of the race of Adonaios in these pericopes is drawn from the same tradition as that of the Sabaoth account, even though the specific motifs of repentance and enthrone-ment in the seventh heaven are missing. Gibbons has noted and detailed this relationship as well,[103] and suggests that GrSeth is in-corporating this myth into its descent of the savior myth.[104] What is still puzzling, however, is the function of these pericopes within the document as a whole. There is no indication that Adonaios represents

---

[102] The term in GrSeth is † which translates μάχη, πάλη and πολεμικός in the phrase ϩοπλον ⲛⲧⲉ ⲡ† (cf. Crum, 395b); in OnOrgWld the term is πόλεμος.

[103] Gibbons, *A Commentary on GrSeth*, 175-80 and 196-200, to which I am happily indebted in the preceding.

[104] Gibbons, *A Commentary on GrSeth*, 198. Gibbons suggests that in both cycles (49.10-54.14 and 54.14-59.19) an original descent of the savior myth has been Christianized and that the Sabaoth or Adonaios account has also possibly been interpolated into this myth (189ff). Is it not more probable that the Wisdom myth plus Sabaoth account as we see it in NatArch and OnOrgWld has as a whole been Christianized and applied to the descent of the revealer/savior Christ?

an attempt to rescue a portion of the OT. The God of the OT is thoroughly evil and identified with Ialdabaoth (53.30-54.1), he is the chief ruler (64.18) and ruler of the seventh heaven (62.27-64.1) and implicitly also the creator (50.3f). The revelation in the Law and the Prophets is denigrated entirely, for the revealer can state that the leading OT figures were "laughingstocks" (62.27-64.1) and that those "from Adam to Moses and John the Baptist, none of them knew me nor my brothers" (63.33ff). The Law itself is also dismissed as something which did not know truth, as a doctrine of angels and a bitter slavery in its observance of certain foods (64.1-6). The race of Adonaios at least in the present document represents the angels surrounding him and thus not the people of the Law and the prophets.[105] The only function then that these pericopes serve is the Christological one. Adonaios and his race no longer serve a representative function in themselves; rather their purpose is merely to point to the revealer-savior, who is identified as Jesus Christ. It seems then that we have a piece of tradition which has lost its original mythical function and which is yet retained, since it can be slightly reworked and made to serve an external, Christological function. An indication of Adonaios' original function, to represent an intermediate deity and thereby to rescue a portion of the revelation contained in the Law and the Prophets, is still retained, however, in the motif that Adonaios has received instruction or revelation from Wisdom of Hope concerning a figure from the world above.

Within this same stream of vulgar Gnosticism, as is evidenced by the fall of Wisdom and by the figures of Faith-Wisdom and Ialdabaoth, there is a group of writings that are closely related to one another, namely, the two *Books of Jeu* in Codex Brucianus and *Pistis Sophia* in Codex Askewianus.[106] The studies of C. Schmidt have shown that the two *Books of Jeu* derive from the early third century Egypt, that

---

[105] Cf. Gibbons, *A Commentary on GrSeth*, 180, who correctly writes : "This would assume that the race of Adonaios equals the Jews, a quite possible secondary interpretation of the text. The text as it stands, however, refers to Adonaios' race of angels." In the development of this mythologoumenon we might add that the race of Adonaios, as Adonaios himself, probably originally represented the Jews and only secondarily lost this association as here in GrSeth.

[106] The texts are available in C. Schmidt, *Gnostische Schriften in koptischer Sprache aus dem Codex Brucianus* (TU 8; Leipzig 1892) and C. Schmidt, *Pistis Sophia* (Coptica, Consilio et Impensis Instituti Rask-Oerstediani Edita, 2; Hauniae 1925). The translation used here is that of C. Schmidt and W. Till in *Koptisch-gnostische Schriften* (GCS 45, 3. Aufl.; Berlin 1962), where the German translation is referred to; the English translation, when provided, is my own.

Book 4 of *Pistis Sophia* was originally a separate work from the first half of the third century in Egypt, and that Books 1-3 derive from the second half of the third century in Egypt.[107] These writings are of interest to us in that they also contain the figure of Sabaoth.

First of all, we encounter the figure of Sabaoth in the *2 Book of Jeu*. Within the pleromatic world of this *Book of Jeu* there is the highest realm, the Second Light Treasury. Below this pleromatic world appear then the 14 Aeons with their rulers. Within the First Light Treasury the figure of the Great Sabaoth is placed in the following passage :

> Again (πάλιν) you will go to the inside, to the order (τάξις) of the great Sabaoth, who belongs to the Light. When you reach his order (τάξις), he will seal (σφραγίζειν) you with his seal (σφραγίς) and he will give you his mystery (μυστήριον) and the great name.[108]

The document also introduces another figure with the name of Sabaoth, i.e. Sabaoth-Adamas, who is less benevolent than the Great Sabaoth and probably resides in the twelfth Aeon as the leader of the evil rulers :[109]

> Hear me and compel (ἀναγκάζειν) Sabaoth-Adamas and all his leaders (ἀρχηγός) so that they will come and take away their evil (κακία) in my disciples (μαθητής).[110]

Within these *Books of Jeu* the problem of the OT is not posed. Sabaoth is not clearly identified as the God of the OT nor is he related to the revelation in the OT or to the people of the OT. In the only other reference to Sabaoth, Taricheas, the son of Sabaoth-Adamas, is said to be worshipped by some who falsely claim to have known the true knowledge and to worship the true God.[111] It is unclear as to who is meant by this polemical remark. Possibly orthodox Christians rather than Jews are intended.[112] The main concern of

---

[107] C. Schmidt (TU 8) 580-98. Schmidt's attempt to make precise the derivation of the *Books of Jeu* and *Pistis Sophia* as coming from the Severians, however, is unacceptable (596). His criterion, the ruler Sabaoth, is not limited to the Severians as NatArch and OnOrgWld demonstrate. His more general derivation from the large group of Barbelo-Gnostics, within which he includes Nicolaitans, Ophites, Cainites, Sethians and Archontics is more acceptable but in itself raises again the question as to whether the criteria for separation into sects are any longer valid.

[108] *2 Book of Jeu* 50. Ed. Schmidt (TU 8) 119; cf. Schmidt (GCS 45) 316.

[109] Cf. Schmidt (TU 8) 395.

[110] *2 Book of Jeu* 48. Ed. Schmidt (TU 8) 115; cf. Schmidt (GCS 45) 313.

[111] *2 Book of Jeu* 43. Tr. Schmidt (GCS 45) 304.

[112] In the *1 Book of Jeu* 3f (tr. Schmidt; GCS 45; 258ff) Jesus contrasts his true

the *2 Book of Jeu* is rather with the reception of the mysteries and the ascent of the soul through the Aeons after its separation from the body.[113] Sabaoth then functions here not as the God of the OT. He has been released from his original function within gnostic circles and now merely represents a figure or figures in the celestial world. It is thus evident that the *2 Book of Jeu* with its benevolent Great Sabaoth and evil Sabaoth-Adamas represents a late stage of development in which various traditions have been compiled, those considering Sabaoth, the God of the OT, as righteous or in some sense good and those considering him as thoroughly evil. However, the specific tradition that Sabaoth is the repentant son of Ialdabaoth, who is enthroned in the seventh heaven, is not reflected here.

Book 4 of *Pistis Sophia* presents an even more complex set of figures with the name of Sabaoth. But, first of all, its system is also more complex. The highest realm is that of the Light Treasury below which appear in descending order the Right, the Middle, the Left —which is comprised of 13 Aeons, the Heimarmene, the Spheres, and the Way of the Middle. Within this framework the highest God within the Light Treasury can be addressed in prayer by Jesus as ïєоγ саваωе.[114] In the realm of the Right there appears the Great Sabaoth, the Good, who looks down upon the places of Paraplex, the first ruler of the Way of the Middle, and thereby destroys his place of punishment for souls.[115]

Within the Middle, there also appears the Small Sabaoth, the Good, who plays an important role in establishing the planetary system and in effecting the salvation of the righteous soul, who has not received the mysteries. First, when Jeu was establishing the five planets in their position, he noticed that the rulers needed a star to direct the world and the aeons so that the rulers would not destroy the world in their evil. Thus he took a power from the Small Sabaoth, the Good, and placed it in Zeus.[116] Secondly, the soul of a thief, when it comes from the body, is punished in the Way of the Middle, given a cup of forgetfulness, and reincarnated in a lame, curved, blind body.[117] But the soul of one who has committed no sin,

---

apostles with those who have known him after the flesh, i.e. in ignorance, and thus have no hope for the kingdom of God.

[113] E.g. c. 43 and c. 51-52. Tr. Schmidt (GCS 45) 304f and 321ff.

[114] P.S. Bk. 4.136. Tr. Schmidt (GCS 45) 232.

[115] P.S. Bk. 4.139. Tr. Schmidt (GCS 45) 238.

[116] P.S. Bk. 4.137. Tr. Schmidt (GCS 45) 234f.

[117] P.S. Bk. 4.146. Tr. Schmidt (GCS 45) 249.

performed good but not found the mysteries is placed by the Small Sabaoth, the Good, the one from the Middle. In addition to the cup of forgetfulness he is given by a παραλήμπτης of the Small Sabaoth a cup filled with thoughts, wisdom and sobriety and then sent back into a body which cannot sleep but which drives the heart to ask about the mysteries of Light until it finds them. Thus this soul will inherit the eternal Light.

Within the Left as the leader of six of the Aeons there is also Sabaoth-Adamas. In contrast to the preceding Sabaoths he is evaluated entirely negatively. While Jabraoth, the leader of the other six Aeons, has believed and ceased, Sabaoth-Adamas has persisted in sexual intercourse and thus been bound in the Sphere.[118] In a recurrent refrain it is also Jaluham, the παραλήμπτης of Sabaoth-Adamas, who brings the cup of forgetfulness to each soul.[119]

Lastly, within the realm of the Sphere one also encounters the planet Zeus, which receives a power from the Small Sabaoth, which thus can be named Sabaoth-Zeus, and which delivers the rulers from their own evil:

> He went into the middle (μέσος); he drew a force (δύναμις) from the small Sabaoth, the one from the middle (μέσος); he bound it to Zeus, since he is good (ἀγαθός), to guide them with his goodness (-ἀγαθός), and he appointed the course of his order (τάξις) with these that he should spend thirteen months in each Aeon (αἰών) as he is strengthening (στηρίζειν) so that every ruler (ἄρχων) upon whom he comes should be released from the evil (κακία) of their badness (πονηρία).[120]

Secondly, when the planets Zeus and Aphrodite, which were considered as benevolent to men in ancient astrology,[121] reach a favorable position, the places of punishment ruled over by the rulers of the Way of the Middle are destroyed and the souls undergoing punishment are released and cast into the Sphere.[122]

---

[118] P.S. Bk. 4.136. Tr. Schmidt (GCS 45) 234.

[119] P.S. Bk. 4.144; tr. Schmidt (GCS 45) 247. Cf. c. 144 (p. 248); c. 146 (p. 249); c. 146 (p. 250); c. 147 (p. 252).

[120] P.S. Bk. 4.137. Text Schmidt, *Pistis Sophia* (Coptica 2) 357; cf. Schmidt (GCS 45) 235. Cf. c. 136 (Schmidt; GCS 45; 234) for Zeus as a planet and c. 139 (Schmidt; GCS 45; 238) for the name Sabaoth-Zeus.

[121] Sextus Empiricus, *Adv. astrol.* 29, ed. and tr. R. G. Bury (LCL; Cambridge 1949) 4. 334-35. Cf. Schmidt (TU 8) 386, n. 2.

[122] P.S. Bk. 4.139. Tr. Schmidt (GCS 45) 238; c. 140 (4×), tr. Schmidt (GCS 45) 238-41. Within these five occurrences, the planet is first named "the Small Sabaoth-Zeus," and then "the Small Sabaoth, the Good, who is named Zeus upon earth" (2×) and also "the Small Sabaoth, the Good, the one from the Middle, who is named Zeus

Although there are five figures who bear the name of Sabaoth in Book 4 of P.S., nevertheless the problem of the OT is not raised—as was the case in the *Books of Jeu*. Neither the God of the OT, the revelation in the OT, nor the people of the OT are considered. The closest approximation to raising the problem is the discussion concerning the righteous soul which has never sinned, constantly performed good but never received the mysteries.[123] While one might consider this description as applying to the people of the OT, there is no clear reference or restriction to them. Rather, the concern within this book is with the various data of astrology, the punishment of sinners and the ascent of the soul, which has received the mysteries, to the Light Treasury.

As in the *Books of Jeu*, it is clear that Book 4 of P.S. represents a late stage of development in which various traditions about Sabaoth have been incorporated. In some Sabaoth represented a benevolent deity or ruler; in others he represented the evil ruler. Again the specific tradition of NatArch and OnOrgWld, that Sabaoth is the repentant son of Ialdabaoth, who is enthroned in the seventh heaven, is not reflected here.

The first three books of P.S. exhibit again a more developed system. In addition to the Light Kingdom, there are in descending order: the Light Treasury, the place of the Right, the place of the Middle, the place of the Left—which includes the 13 Aeons, Heimarmene, the Sphere, the Rulers of the Middle and the Firmament—the Cosmos, and the Underworld—which encompasses Amente, Chaos, and the Outer Darkness.[124]

Within this system there appear only two figures with the name of Sabaoth. First, there is the Great Sabaoth, the Good, in the place of the Right. He and the others in the place of the Right are there in order to gather up the particles of light from the Aeons; and at the end Sabaoth and those of the Right with him are to be kings.[125] In the meantime, in place of a soul of the rulers a power has been taken

---

upon earth" (2×). It is clear that these passages speak about the planet Zeus—witness the association with the planet Aphrodite—rather than about the figure of Sabaoth from the realm of the Middle. However, since it is a power from the Small Sabaoth, the Good, the one from the Middle, which has been given to the planet Zeus, the planet Zeus in these passages has taken over the nomenclature proper to the figure in the realm of the Middle.

[123] P.S. Bk. 4.147. Tr. Schmidt (GCS 45) 251-53.
[124] Cf. Schmidt (TU 8) 347-48.
[125] P.S. 86. Tr. Schmidt (GCS 45) 125.

by Jesus from Sabaoth and placed in Mary to provide for his soul.[126] Thus Sabaoth can be identified as the father of Jesus;[127] and the reference to Sabaoth in Isa 19:12 can be allegorically interpreted as applying to Jesus because of the power from Sabaoth within him.[128]

The second figure with the name of Sabaoth is the Small Sabaoth, the Good, who is probably placed within the Middle.[129] His only described function is to receive the power from the Great Sabaoth, which is the soul of Jesus, and to send it further into the matter of Barbelo.[130]

Within the first three books of P.S., the problem of the God of the OT is not raised.[131] However, the books of the OT and the

---

[126] "It happened afterwards that by the command (κέλευσις) of the first Mystery (μυστήριον) I looked upon the world (κόσμος) of mankind and found Mary, who is called my mother according (κατά) to the material (ὕλη) body. I spoke with her in (κατά) the form (τύπος) of Gabriel; and when she turned to the height to me, I cast into her the first power, which I had received from Barbelo, i.e. the body (σῶμα) which I bore (φορεῖν) in the height. And in place of the soul (ψυχή) I cast into her the power, which I received from the Great Sabaoth, the Good (ἀγαθός) who is in the place of the Right." P.S. 8; text Schmidt, Pistis Sophia (Coptica 2) 13-14; cf. tr. Schmidt (GCS 45) 8f. Cf. also the repeated use of this theme in the various exegetical interpretations of Ps 84:10-11, offered in c. 62 and 63; cf. tr. Schmidt (GCS 45) 79ff.

[127] "But Sabaoth, the Great and Good (ἀγαθός), whom I have named my father, has come forth (προέρχεσθαι) from Jeu, the overseer (ἐπίσκοπος) of light." P.S. 86; text Schmidt, Pistis Sophia (Coptica 2) 195; cf. tr. Schmidt (GCS 45) 125f.

[128] "Before you came, the power in the prophet (προφήτης) Isaiah prophecied (προφητεύειν) about you that you would take the power of the archons (ἄρχοντες) of the aeons (αἰῶνες) and would change their sphere (σφαῖρα) and their fate (εἱμαρμένη), so that from now on they would not know anything. Therefore, it has also said, 'Then you will not know what the Lord Sabaoth will do,' i.e. none of the archons (ἄρχοντες) will know what you will do from now on; they are Egypt, since they are matter (ὕλη). Now the power in Isaiah prophecied (προφητεύειν) at that time about you when it said, 'You will not know from now on what the Lord Sabaoth will do.' Because of the light power, which you received from Sabaoth, the Good (ἀγαθός), who is in the place (τόπος) of the Right, and which is now in your material (ὑλικός) body (σῶμα), therefore you Lord Jesus once said to us, 'Who has ears to hear let him hear,' so that you might know whose heart is directed strongly to the kingdom of heaven." P.S. 18; text Schmidt, Pistis Sophia (Coptica 2) 28; cf. tr. Schmidt (GCS 45) 17.

[129] In P.S. one also finds the figure of Adamas over the 12 Aeons. However, he is not referred to as Sabaoth Adamas. Cf. P.S. 27; tr. Schmidt (GCS 45) 23.

[130] "But the truth is the power of Sabaoth, the Good (ἀγαθός) which was joined to you and which you cast to the Left—you, the first mystery (μυστήριον) which looks down. And the Small Sabaoth, the Good (ἀγαθός), took it and cast it into the matter (ὕλη) of Barbelo." P.S. 63; text Schmidt, Pistis Sophia (Coptica 2) 127-28; cf. tr. Schmidt (GCS 45) 82.

[131] As we indicated above, the Sabaoth passage Isa 19:12 in c. 63 has been referred to Jesus rather than, for example, to the Great Sabaoth or the Small Sabaoth as the God of the OT. It is further doubtful that P.S. would consider all references to Sabaoth in the OT as applying to Jesus.

pseudepigraphical Odes of Solomon are accepted as inspired and containing revelation concerning both Faith-Wisdom[132] and Jesus.[133] The power or light-power of Jesus is said to have prophecied through Moses,[134] David in the Psalms,[135] Isaiah,[136] and Solomon in his Odes.[137] However, it is doubtful whether all parts of the OT were accepted as having equal value.

The place of the people of the OT in the divine economy is also considered within P.S. However, the contrast is not among Gentile, Jew, Christian and gnostic. Rather, the contrast is among sinners, the righteous who have not received the mysteries—which would include some of the people of the OT among others—and the gnostics.[138] The righteous will be reincarnated in bodies, which will receive the mysteries, and thus the righteous will eventually be saved.[139]

In P.S. then the problem of the God of the OT is not a concern, although the books of the OT and the righteous of the OT are considered. The main concern in P.S., instead, is focused upon reception of the saving mysteries, sinners, and the ascent of the soul through the Aeons after its separation from the body.

Once again, although the specific tradition concerning Sabaoth witnessed in NatArch and OnOrgWld is not encountered in P.S., this document incorporates previous speculation concerning Sabaoth in which he is evaluated as a good ruler, who is other than the high God.

---

[132] E.g. concerning the repentance of Faith-Wisdom in P.S. 33; tr. Schmidt (GCS 45) 32ff.

[133] P.S. 18; tr. Schmidt (GCS 45) 16f.

[134] P.S. 43; tr. Schmidt (GCS 45) 45.

[135] E.g. P.S. 36 and 38 inter alios; tr. Schmidt (GCS 45) 36f and 38f.

[136] P.S. 18; tr. Schmidt (GCS 45) 16-17.

[137] E.g. Odes Sol 19 in P.S. 58; tr. Schmidt (GCS 45) 73f.

[138] Cf. P.S. 135; tr. Schmidt (GCS 45) 229f.

[139] "When I came to the place (τόπος) of the aeons (αἰῶνες), I caused the other patriarchs (πατριάρχα) and righteous (δίκαιοι) from the time of Adam to (ἕως) now, who were in the aeons (αἰῶνες) and orders (τάξεις) of the archons (ἄρχοντες), to return through the light-virgin (-παρθένος) to bodies (σώματα), which would be righteous (δίκαια). Those which will find all the mysteries (μυστήρια) of light will enter and inherit (κληρονομεῖν) the light kingdom." P.S. 135; text Schmidt, Pistis Sophia (Coptica 2) 351-52; cf. tr. Schmidt (GCS 45) 230.

CHAPTER FIVE

CONCLUSION

As a contribution to the scholarly discussion of the origins of Gnosticism, our analysis of the Sabaoth accounts in NatArch and OnOrgWld has shown indeed that they are examples of the contribution of Judaism to Gnosticism. Specifically, apocalyptic and sapiential Judaism are the segments of Judaism, which have mainly contributed to these accounts. We have seen that these accounts derive not just from the OT but from later Judaism and that they have neither influenced nor been influenced by the NT. The only specifically Christian element in these accounts is the reference to Sabaoth's creation of Jesus Christ and the Holy Spirit in OnOrgWld. Our study has further shown that the traditions drawn upon for the presentation of Sabaoth are those of heavenly enthronement and the ascent of the apocalyptic visionary. Passages concerning the son of man in Dan 7, Enoch in 1 Enoch 69-71, and Moses in Ezekiel Tr and in Philo, provide the immediate and appropriate History-of-Religions background for understanding the composition and function of these Sabaoth accounts.

Since the editors of both NatArch and OnOrgWld had observed that these documents were related and called for a closer examination of that relationship, we compared in detail the two Sabaoth accounts. We found that the wording was identical in some portions and that the pattern in both accounts consisted of the same elements: the repentance of Sabaoth, the ascent and enthronement of Sabaoth, creation of the throne/chariot of Sabaoth, creation of angels, the instruction of Sabaoth, and the separation into right and left. From that analysis it is clear that the Sabaoth accounts in NatArch and in OnOrgWld derive from a common tradition. However, it is impossible to establish a literary dependency in either direction or to determine more exactly whether that common tradition was oral and/or written. From that examination it also became evident that the Sabaoth account in NatArch exhibits the typologically earlier stage. In contrast, the Sabaoth account in OnOrgWld exhibits inner contradictions, reduplications, and redactional features, which mark it as typologically later.

Since the Sabaoth account in NatArch showed forth the typologically earlier form, we then exegeted that account first. We discovered that the figure Ialdabaoth, the father of Sabaoth, derives from the God of the OT, the leader of the fallen angels, and the god ʿÔlam/Aiōn of ancient Canaanite myth. The figure of Sabaoth himself arises as a conflation of three figures: obviously that of the God of the OT, but also that of a leading angel (e.g. Michael) and that of the apocalyptic visionary (e.g. Enoch or Moses). It is odd within gnostic, mythological patterning to have three rather than two gods, i.e. the transcendent God, the evil god Ialdabaoth, and as his repentant offspring the god Sabaoth. However, the second century debate, particularly within Marcionite and Valentinian circles, over the God of the OT as a righteous deity and over the value of the OT provides a clue to the function of this Sabaoth account. Sabaoth, as a repentant deity with the angel of punishment at his left side, is the righteous God of the OT. Because he has been instructed by Wisdom's daughter Life about the Eighth, the books of the OT which derive ultimately from him are authenticated as possessing some truth about the perfect realm. The people of the OT then are associated with this god Sabaoth. In contrast, the true gnostics are associated with the highest God and know how to discover the true information contained in the books of the OT. Further, since Sabaoth is enthroned over the seventh heaven, he is king over all below. Thus his rule and the rule within the world are ultimately derived from evil matter and at best repentant or righteous. The gnostics, on the other hand, stem from the realm of imperishability and belong to the kingless race. This proposed function has been confirmed by an analysis of the views in other Nag Hammadi documents, among the Marcionites and Valentinians, and within related groups such as the Gnostikoi, the Archontics and the Severians. Because of the importance of this debate within the second century, a proposed date of the latter half of the second century has been offered for the composition of the Sabaoth account and NatArch.

In our analysis of the Sabaoth account in OnOrgWld, we have shown that the Sabaoth account is greatly expanded. The description of the chariot is amplified with material drawn from Jewish tradition; the author's own contribution is particularly visible in the motif of light versus darkness, which is part of the announced theme of the tractate. In terms of its function, the Sabaoth account in OnOrgWld serves an anthropological rather than a theological function. Three types of men have been enumerated in this tractate: the pneumatic, the psychic, and the choic. Within this framework Sabaoth then represents the psychic. On the other hand, the immortal Light-Man represents the pneumatic, and Ialdabaoth symbolizes the choic. In another passage, the choic man is said to be the man of Law, i.e. the Jews. Sabaoth also fashions an angelic church as well as Jesus Christ and thus represents the orthodox Christian Church. Since the Jews and Christians form a church of unrighteousness and righteousness to which the world is subject, the world and the churches of Jews and orthodox Christians are rejected. The immortal Light-Man then typifies the gnostics, who are free from this righteous and/or unrighteous rule. Interestingly enough, in one passage a further, fourth category is introduced—that of the perfect. Thus the anthropology of this document seems to be moving in the direction of Manichaeism, which distinguished the elect from the remainder of the Manichaeans. Because of its developed mythology, its familarity with other gnostic literature, and its proposed influence from Valentinianism, a date in the early third century has been offered as the time of composition for OnOrg Wld.

Lastly, further documents from Gnosticism have been considered to determine whether the specific tradition of these Sabaoth accounts is reflected in them. A positive answer to that question was found in the *Second Treatise of the Great Seth* (CG VII, 2). Here the figure is named Adonaios, however, and he is instructed by Hope rather than Life. The function of this Adonaios account is also less clear than that of the Sabaoth accounts; however, it appears to serve a Christological purpose. Examination of the two *Books of Jeu* and the various books of *Pistis Sophia*, on the other hand, yielded only a negative answer. The figure of Sabaoth fulfills a variety of roles in these late works; and, indeed, there is a variety of Sabaoth figures in these documents. However, the specific tradition of a repentant Sabaoth who is enthroned in the seventh heaven is not mirrored in them.

In conclusion, the discovery of the Nag Hammadi documents has provided us with an opportunity for a greater understanding of Gnosticism itself, the religious world of antiquity, and also the development of early Christianity. As the documents are made available to the scholarly public, thanks to the labors of the editors, detailed analysis of them is necessary before their treasures can be assimilated. Hopefully our research into the Sabaoth accounts in NatArch and OnOrg Wld will make a contribution to that investigation.

SELECT BIBLIOGRAPHY

Adam, Alfred. "Ist die Gnosis in aramäischen Weisheitsschulen entstanden?" *Le Origini dello Gnosticismo* : Colloquio di Messina 13-18 April 1966. Ed. U. Bianchi. Numen, Supplements 12. Leiden : Brill, 1967, 291-301.

Adamantius. *Dialog.* Ed. W. H. van de Sande Bakhuyzen. Griechischen Christlichen Schriftsteller 4. Leipzig : Hinrichs, 1901.

Albright, William F. "What Were the Cherubim?" *The Biblical Archaeologist Reader.* Ed. G. E. Wright and D. N. Freedman. New York : Doubleday, 1961, 95-97.

Baltzer, Klaus. "Considerations Regarding the Office and Calling of the Prophet," *Harvard Theological Review* 61 (1961) 567-81.

Behm, Johannes. ἐκχέω, ἐκχύν(ν)ω. *Theological Dictionary of the New Testament.* Tr. G. W. Bromiley. Grand Rapids : Eerdmans, 1964, vol. 2. 467-69.

Behm, Johannes and Würtheim, Ernst. μετανοέω, μετάνοια. *Theological Dictionary of the New Testament.* Tr. G. W. Bromiley. Grand Rapids : Eerdmans, 1967, vol. 4. 975-1008.

Beltz, Walter. *Die Adam-Apokalypse aus Codex V von Nag Hammadi : Jüdische Bausteine in gnostischen Systemen.* Habilitationsschrift, Humboldt-Universität, Berlin, 1970.

Betz, Otto. *Der Paraklet.* Arbeiten zur Geschichte des Spätjudentums und des Urchristentums 2. Leiden : Brill, 1963.

——. "Was am Anfang Geschah," *Abraham Unser Vater, Festschrift für Otto Michel.* Ed. O. Betz, M. Hengel and P. Schmidt. Leiden : Brill, 1963, 24-43.

Bianchi, Ugo, ed. *Le Origini dello Gnosticismo* : Colloquio di Messina 13-18 April 1966. Numen, Supplements 12. Leiden : Brill, 1967.

Böhlig, Alexander, "Der jüdische und judenchristliche Hintergrund in gnostischen Texten von Nag Hammadi," *Le Origini dello Gnosticismo* : Colloquio di Messina 13-18 April 1966. Ed. U. Bianchi. Numen, Supplements 12. Leiden : Brill, 1967, 109-40.

——. "Die Adamapokalypse aus Codex V von Nag Hammadi als Zeugnis jüdisch-iranischer Gnosis," *Oriens Christianus* 48 (1964) 44-49.

——. *Mysterion und Wahrheit.* Arbeiten zur Geschichte des späteren Judentums und des Urchristentums 6. Leiden : Brill, 1968.

Böhlig, Alexander and Labib, Pahor, *Koptisch-gnostische Apokalypsen aus Codex V von Nag Hammadi im Koptischen Museum zu Alt-Kairo.* Wissenschaftliche Zeitschrift der Martin-Luther-Universität Halle-Wittenberg, Sonderband. Halle-Wittenberg : Martin-Luther-Universität, 1963.

——. *Die koptisch-gnostische Schrift ohne Titel aus Codex II von Nag Hammadi im Koptischen Museum zu Alt-Kairo.* Berlin : Akademie-Verlag, 1962.

Bousset, Wilhelm. *Die Himmelsreise der Seele.* 1901; reprint Darmstadt : Wissenschaftliche Buchgesellschaft, 1971.

Bousset, Wilhelm and Gressmann, Hugo. *Die Religion des Judentums.* 4. Aufl. Foreword by E. Lohse. Handbuch zum Neuen Testament 21. Tübingen : Mohr, 1966.

Bousset, Wilhelm. *Hauptprobleme der Gnosis.* Forschungen zur Religion und Literatur des Alten und Neuen Testaments 10. Göttingen : Vandenhoeck and Ruprecht, 1907.

Box, George H., tr. *The Apocalypse of Abraham.* London : Society for Promoting Christian Knowledge, 1919.

——. *The Testament of Abraham.* London : Society for Promoting Christian Knowledge, 1927.

Broek, R. van den. *The Myth of the Phoenix according to Classical and Early Christian Traditions.* Tr. I. Seeger. Études Préliminaires aux Religions Orientales dans l'Empire Romaine 24. Leiden : Brill, 1972.

Brooks, E. W. tr. *Joseph and Asenath*. London : Society for Promoting Christian Knowledge, 1918.

Bullard, Roger A., ed. *The Hypostasis of the Archons*. With a contribution by M. Krause. Patristische Texte und Studien 10. Berlin : De Gruyter, 1970.

Bultmann, Rudolph. *Primitive Christianity*. Tr. R. H. Fuller. New York : Meridian, 1957.

——. *Theology of the New Testament*. Tr. K. Grobel. 2 vols. New York : Scribner's Sons, 1951-55.

Burkitt, Francis C. *Church and Gnosis*. Cambridge : University Press, 1932.

Casey, Robert P. "Gnosis, Gnosticism and the New Testament," *The Background of the New Testament and its Eschatology, in honour of C. H. Dodd*. Ed. W. D. Davies and D. Daube. Cambridge : University Press, 1956, 52-80.

——. "The Study of Gnosticism," *Journal of Theological Studies* 36 (1935) 45-60.

Cerfaux, Lucien. "Influence des Mystères sur le Judaisme Alexandrin avant Philon," *Le Muséon* 37 (1924) 54-58.

Charles, Robert H., Tr. *The Book of Enoch*. 2d ed. Oxford : Clarendon, 1912.

——. *The Greek Versions of the Testament of the Twelve Patriarchs*. 1908; reprint Darmstadt : Wissenschaftliche Buchgesellschaft, 1966.

Clapham, Lynn R. *Sanchuniathon : The First Two Cycles*. Ph.D. Dissertation, Harvard University, 1969.

Clemens Alexandrinus, *The Excerpta ex Theodoto of Clement of Alexandria*. Ed. and tr. R. P. Casey. Studies and Documents 1. London : Christophers, 1934.

——. *Opera*. Ed. O. Staehlin. 4 vols. Griechischen Christlichen Schriftsteller 12, 15, 17, 39. Leipzig : Hinrichs, 1905-36.

Colpe, Carsten. *Die religionsgeschichtliche Schule*. Forschungen zur Religion und Literatur des Alten und Neuen Testaments 78. Göttingen : Vandenhoeck and Ruprecht, 1961.

——. ὁ υἱὸς τοῦ ἀνθρώπου. *Theological Dictionary of the New Testament*. Tr. G. W. Bromiley. Grand Rapids : Eerdmans, 1972, vol. 8. 400-77.

Conybeare, Frederick C., tr. "Testament of Solomon," *Jewish Quarterly Review* 11 (1898) 1-45.

Cross, Frank M., Jr. *The Ancient Library of Qumran and Modern Biblical Studies*. Revised ed. New York : Doubleday, 1961.

——. *Canaanite Myth and Hebrew Epic; Essays in the History of the Religion of Israel*. Cambridge : Harvard University, 1973.

——. "The Council of Yahweh in Second Isaiah," *Journal of Near Eastern Studies* 12 (1953) 274-77.

——. "The Priestly Tabernacle," *The Biblical Archaeologist Reader*. Ed. G. E. Wright and D. N. Freedman. New York : Doubleday, 1961, 201-28.

Cross, Frank M., Jr. and Freedman, David N. "The Song of Miriam," *Journal of Near Eastern Studies* 14 (1955) 237-50.

Damascius. *Problèmes et Solutions touchant Les Premiers Principes*. Trad. A.-Ed. Chaignet. 2 vols. Reprint Bruxelles : Culture et Civilization, 1964.

Daniélou, Jean. "Review of A. Böhlig and P. Labib, *Koptisch-gnostische Apokalypsen aus Codex V von Nag Hammadi im Koptischen Museum zu Alt-Kairo*," *Recherches de Science Religieuse* 54 (1966) 285-93.

Delling, Gerhard. ὕμνος κτλ. *Theological Dictionary of the New Testament*. Tr. G. W. Bromiley. Grand Rapids : Eerdmans, 1972, vol. 8. 489-503.

Dölger, Franz J. "Zur Symbolik des altchristlichen Taufhauses," *Antike und Christentum* 4 (1934) 153-87.

Doresse, Jean. *The Secret Books of the Egyptian Gnostics*. Tr. P. Mairet. New York : Viking, 1960.

Eliade, Mircea. *Mephistopheles and the Androgyne : Studies in Religious Myth and Symbol*. Tr. J. M. Cohen. New York : Sheed and Ward, 1965.

Emerton, J. A. "The Origin of the Son of Man Imagery," *Journal of Theological Studies*, *New Series* 9 (1958) 225-42.

Eusebius. *Historia Ecclesiastica*. Ed. E. Schwartz and T. Mommsen. Griechischen Christlichen Schriftsteller 9.1-3. Leipzig : Hinrichs, 1903-08.

———. *Praeparatio Evangelica*. Ed. K. Mras. Griechischen Christlichen Schriftsteller 43.1-2. Berlin : Akademie-Verlag, 1954-56.

Epiphanius. *Panarion*. Ed. K. Holl. Griechischen Christlichen Schriftsteller 25 and 31. Leipzig; Hinrichs, 1915 and 1922.

Fallon, Francis T. "The Law in Philo and Ptolemy : A Note on the Letter to Flora," *Vigiliae Christianae* 30 (1976) 45-51.

Faye, Eugène de. *Gnostiques et gnosticisme*. 2ᵉ éd. Paris : Geuthner, 1925.

Filastrius. *Diversarum Hereseon Liber*. Ed. F. Heylen. Corpus Christianorum, Series Latina 9.207-324. Turnhout : Brepols, 1957.

Fitzmyer, Joseph A. *The Aramaic Inscriptions of Sefire*. Rome : The Pontifical Biblical Institute, 1967.

Förster, Werner. ἁρπάζω. *Theological Dictionary of the New Testament*. Tr. G. W. Bromiley. Grand Rapids : Eerdmans, 1964, vol. 1. 472-73.

———. *Gnosis : A Selection of Gnostic Texts*. Tr. R. McL. Wilson. Vol. 1. Oxford : Clarendon, 1972.

———. σατανᾶς. *Theological Dictionary of the New Testament*. Tr. G. W. Bromiley. Grand Rapids : Eerdmans, 1971, vol. 7. 151-63.

Förster, Werner and Rad, Gerhard von. διάβολος. *Theological Dictionary of the New Testament*. Tr. G. W. Bromiley. Grand Rapids : Eerdmans, 1964, vol. 2. 71-81.

Friedrich, Gerhard. σάλπιγξ κτλ. *Theological Dictionary of the New Testament*. Tr. G. W. Bromiley. Grand Rapids : Eerdmans, 1971, vol. 7. 71-88.

Fuchs, Ernst. ἐκτείνω. *Theological Dictionary of the New Testament*. Tr. G. W. Bromiley. Grand Rapids : Eerdmans, 1964, vol. 2. 460-63.

Gibbons, Joseph. *A Commentary on the Second Logos of the Great Seth*. Ph.D. Dissertation, Yale University, 1972.

Gifford, Edwin H., ed. and tr. *Eusebii Pamphili, Evangelicae Praeparationis*. 4 vols. Oxford : University Press, 1903.

Goodenough, Erwin R. *An Introduction to Philo Judaeus*. 2ᵈ ed. Oxford : Blackwell, 1962.

———. *By Light, Light : The Mystic Gospel of Hellenistic Judaism*. New Haven : Yale University, 1935.

———. *Jewish Symbols in the Greco-Roman Period*. 10 vols. New York : Pantheon, 1953-69.

———. "The Political Philosophy of Hellenistic Kingship," *Yale Classical Studies* 1 (1928) 55-102.

Grant, Robert M. *Gnosticism and Early Christianity*. Revised ed. New York : Harper and Row, 1966.

Grundmann, Walter. δύναμαι, δύναμις κτλ. *Theological Dictionary of the New Testament*. Tr. G. W. Bromiley. Grand Rapids : Eerdmans, 1964, vol. 2. 284-317.

Guterbock, Hans G. "The Hittite Version of the Hurrian Kumarbi Myths : Oriental Forerunners of Hesiod," *American Journal of Archaeology* 52 (1948) 123-34.

———. *Kumarbi : Mythen von churritischen Kronos, aus den hethitischen Fragmenten, zusammengestellt, übersetzt und erklärt*. Istanbuler Schriften 16. Zürich-New York : Europaverlag, 1946.

———. "The Song of Ullikummi : Revised Text of the Hittite Version of a Hurrian Myth," *Journal of Cuneiform Studies* 5 (1951) 135-61 and 6 (1952) 8-42.

Hanson, Paul D. *The Dawn of Apocalyptic*. Philadelphia : Fortress, 1975.

———. "Jewish Apocalyptic Against its Near Eastern Environment," *Revue Biblique* 78 (1971) 31-58.

———. "Old Testament Apocalyptic Reexamined," *Interpretation* 25 (1971) 454-79.

Harnack, Adolph von. *Marcion: Das Evangelium vom fremden Gott.* 2. Aufl. Darmstadt: Wissenschaftliche Buchgesellschaft, 1960.

Hesiod. *The Homeric Hymns and Homerica.* Ed. and tr. H. G. Evelyn-White. Loeb Classical Library. Cambridge: Harvard, 1959.

Hippolytus. *Refutatio Omnium Haeresium.* Ed. P. Wendland. Griechischen Christlichen Schriftsteller 26. Leipzig: Hinrichs, 1916.

Hofius, Otfried. *Der Vorhang vor dem Thron Gottes,* Wissenschaftliche Untersuchungen zum Neuen Testament 14. Tübingen: Mohr, 1972.

Irenaeus. *Adversus haereses.* Tr. and ed. A. Roberts and J. Donaldson. The Ante-Nicene Fathers 1. Grand Rapids: Eerdmans, 1956.

——. *Libros Quinque Adversus Haereses.* Ed. W. W. Harvey 1857. Reprint Ridgewood: Gregg, 1965.

James, Montague R., tr. *The Biblical Antiquities of Philo.* Prolegomenon by L. H. Feldman. 1917; reprint New York: Ktav, 1971.

Jonas, Hans. "Delimitations of the Gnostic Phenomenon," *Le Origini dello Gnosticismo:* Colloquio di Messina 13-18 April 1966. Numen, Supplements 12. Leiden: Brill, 1967, 90-108.

——. *Gnosis und spätantiker Geist.* Bd. 1, 3. Aufl. Forschungen zur Religion und Literatur des Alten und Neuen Testaments 51. Göttingen: Vandenhoeck and Ruprecht, 1964.

——. *Gnosis und spätantiker Geist.* Bd. 2/1, 2. Aufl. Forschungen zur Religion und Literatur des Alten und Neuen Testaments 63. Göttingen: Vandenhoeck and Ruprecht, 1966.

——. *The Gnostic Religion.* 2d ed. Boston: Beacon, 1963.

——. "Response to G. Quispel," *The Bible in Modern Scholarship.* Ed. J. Philip Hyatt. Nashville: Abingdon, 1965, 279-93.

Josephus. *Works.* Tr. H. St. J. Thackeray, R. Marcus, A. Wikgren and L. H. Feldman. 9 vols. Loeb Classical Library. Cambridge: Harvard University, 1950-66.

Kapelrud, Arvid S. *Baal in the Ras Shamra Texts.* Copenhagen: Gad, 1952.

Kappelmacher, Alfred. "Zur Tragödie der Hellenistischen Zeit," *Wiener Studien: Zeitschrift für Klassische Philologie* 44 (1924-25) 68-86.

Kasser, Rodolphe. "Brèves remarques sur les caractéristiques dialectales du Codex Gnostique Copte II de Nag Hammadi," *Kemi* 20 (1970) 49-55.

——. "L'Hypostase des Archontes: Propositions pour Quelques Lectures et Reconstitutions Nouvelles," *Essays on the Nag Hammadi Texts in honour of Alexander Böhlig.* Ed. M. Krause. Leiden: Brill, 1972, 22-35.

——. "Textes Gnostiques: Remarques A Propos des Éditions Récentes du Livre Secret de Jean et des Apocalypses de Paul, Jacques, et Adam," *Le Muséon* 78 (1965) 71-98.

Kippenberg, Hans G. "Versuch einer soziologischen Verortung des antiken Gnostizismus," *Numen* 17 (1950) 211-31.

Kisch, Guido, ed. *Pseudo Philo's Liber Antiquitatum Biblicarum.* Publications in Medieval Studies 10. Indiana: Notre Dame, 1961.

Koester, Helmut and Robinson, James M. *Trajectories Through Early Christianity.* Philadelphia: Fortress, 1971.

Krause, Martin. "Zur 'Hypostase der Archonten' in Codex II von Nag Hammadi," *Enchoria* 2 (1972) 1-20.

Krause, Martin and Labib, Pahor. *Die drei Versionen des Apokryphon des Johannes im Koptischen Museum zu Alt-Kairo.* Abhandlungen des Deutschen Archäologischen Instituts Kairo, Koptische Reihe, Band 1. Wiesbaden: Harrassowitz, 1962.

Lambert, Wilfred G. and Walcot, Peter. "A New Babylonian Theogony and Hesiod," *Kadmos* 4 (1965) 64-72.

Layton, Bentley. "Critical Prolegomena to an Edition of the Coptic 'Hypostasis of the Archons' (CG II, 4)," *Essays on the Nag Hammadi Texts in Honour of Pahor Labib*. Nag Hammadi Studies 6. Leiden : Brill, 1975.

——. "The Hypostasis of the Archons or 'The Reality of the Rulers'," *Harvard Theological Review* 67 (1974) 351-426 and 68 (1976) 31-101.

Lieberman, Saul. *Greek in Jewish Palestine*. New York : Jewish Theological Seminary, 1942.

——. *Hellenism in Jewish Palestine*. 2d ed. New York : Jewish Theological Seminary, 1962.

Lohse, Edward. *Die Texte aus Qumran*. 2. Aufl. Darmstadt : Wissenschaftliche Buchgesellschaft, 1971.

Lueken, Wilhelm. *Michael*. Göttingen : Vandenhoeck, 1898.

MacRae, George. *Some Elements of Jewish Apocalyptic and Mystical Tradition and their Relation to Gnostic Literature*. Ph.D. Dissertation, Cambridge University, 1966.

——. "The Apocalypse of Adam Reconsidered," *The Society of Biblical Literature : One Hundred Eighth Annual Meeting, Seminar Papers*. 2 vols. Ed. Lane C. McGaughy. Society of Biblical Literature, 1972, vol. 2. 573-80.

——. "The Coptic Gnostic Apocalypse of Adam," *Heythrop Journal* 6 (1965) 27-35.

——. "The Jewish Background of the Gnostic Sophia Myth," *Novum Testamentum* 12 (1970) 86-101.

Magne, Jean. *La Naissance de Jésus-Christ : L'exaltation de Sabaôth dans Hypostase des Archontes 143, 1-31 et l'exaltation de Jésus dans Philippiens 2, 6-11*. Cahiers du Cercle Ernest-Renan, N° 83. Paris : Cercle Ernest-Renan, 1973.

Maier, Johann. *Vom Kultus zur Gnosis*. Kairos : Religionswissenschaftliche Studien 1. Salzburg : Müller, 1964.

Malinine, Michel; Puech, Henri-Charles; Quispel, Gilles; Till, Walter C.; Kasser, Rodolphe; Wilson, Robert McL.; and Zandee, Jan; eds. *Epistula Jacobi Apocrypha : Codex Jung F. Iʳ-F. VIIIʳ*. Zürich and Stuttgart : Rascher, 1968.

Meeks, Wayne. "Moses as God and King," *Religions in Antiquity : Essays in Memory of Erwin Ramsdell Goodenough*. Ed. J. Neusner. Leiden : Brill, 1968, 354-71.

——. *The Prophet-King : Moses Traditions and the Johannine Christology*. Novum Testamentum, Supplements 14. Leiden : Brill, 1967.

Meyer, Wilhelm, ed. *Vita Adae et Evae*. Abhandlungen der philosophisch-philologischen Classe der königlichen Bayerischen Akademie der Wissenschaften 14. Munich : Verlag der königlichen Akademie, 1878, 187-250.

Millar, William R. *Isaiah 24-27 and the Origin of Apocalyptic*. Ph.D. Dissertation, Harvard University, 1970.

Nagel, Peter. *Das Wesen der Archonten*. Wissenschaftliche Beiträge der Martin-Luther-Universität Halle-Wittenberg. Halle-Wittenberg : Martin-Luther-Universität, 1970.

——. "Grammatische Untersuchungen zu Nag Hammadi Codex II," *Die Araber in der alten Welt*. Hrsg. F. Altheim and R. Stiehl. Berlin : De Gruyter, 1969. Vol. 2. 393-469.

Nickelsberg, George W. E., Jr. *Resurrection, Immortality and Eternal Life in Intertestamental Judaism*. Harvard Theological Studies 26. Cambridge : Harvard University, 1972.

Nock, Arthur D. *Essays on Religion and the Ancient World*. Ed. Z. Stewart. 2 vols. Cambridge : Harvard University, 1972.

Oepke, Albrecht. καθίστημι. *Theological Dictionary of the New Testament*. Tr. G. W. Bromiley. Grand Rapids : Eerdmans, 1965, vol. 3. 444-46.

Oldenburg, Ulf. *The Conflict Between El and Ba'al in Canaanite Religion*. Numen, Supplements, Altera Series 3. Leiden : Brill, 1969.

Orbe, Antonio. "Review of A. Böhlig and P. Labib, *Koptisch-gnostische Apokalypsen aus Codex V von Nag Hammadi im Koptischen Museum zu Alt-Kairo*," *Gregorianum* 46 (1965) 169-72.

——. "Spiritus Dei ferebatur super aquas. Exegesis gnóstica de Gen 1:2b," *Gregorianum* 44 (1963) 691-730.

Origen. *Contra Celsum*. Tr. H. Chadwick. Revised ed. Cambridge : University Press, 1965.

Pagels, Elaine. *The Johannine Gospel in Gnostic Exegesis : Heracleon's Commentary on John*. Society of Biblical Literature Monograph Series 17. Nashville : Abingdon, 1973.

——. "Gnostic Theology : A Sociological Approach," *The Society of Biblical Literature, One Hundred Ninth Annual Meeting, Abstracts*. Ed. G. MacRae. Society of Biblical Literature, 1973, 39.

Pearson, Birger. "Jewish Haggadic Traditions in the Testimony of Truth from Nag Hammadi (CG IX, 3)," *Ex Orbe Religionum : Studia Geo Widengren oblata*. Ed. J. Bergman, K. Drynjeff and H. Ringgren. Leiden : Brill, 1973, vol. 1. 457-70.

Perkins, Pheme. "Apocalyptic Schematization in the Apocalypse of Adam and the Gospel of the Egyptians," *The Society of Biblical Literature, One Hundred Eighth Annual Meeting, Seminar Papers*. Ed. Lane C. McGaughy. Society of Biblical Literature, 1972, vol. 2. 591-96.

Philo Judaeus. *Opera Quae Supersunt et Indices*. Ed. L. Cohn, P. Wendland, and J. Leisegang. 7 vols. Berlin : Reimer and de Gruyter, 1896-1930.

——. *Works*. Tr. F. H. Colson, G. H. Whitaker, and R. Marcus. Loeb Classical Library. 10 vols. and 2 supplements. Cambridge : Harvard University, 1958-68.

Philonenko, Marc, ed. *Joseph et Aséneth*. Studia Post-Biblica 13. Leiden : Brill, 1968.

——. "Remarques sur un hymn essénien de caractère gnostique," *Semitica* 11 (1961) 43-54.

Plato. *Timaeus*. Tr. R. G. Bury. Loeb Classical Library. Cambridge : Harvard University, 1966.

Pliny. *Historia Naturalis*. Tr. H. Rackham and W. H. S. Jones. 10 vols. Loeb Classical Library. Cambridge : Harvard University, 1938.

Polotsky, Hans J. "Manichaeismus," *Real-Enzyklopädie der classischen Altertumswissenschaft*. Ed. A. Pauly, G. Wissowa and W. Kroll. Supplementband 6. Stuttgart : Metzlersche Verlagsbuchhandlung, 1935, 240-71.

Pope, Marvin H. *El in the Ugaritic Texts*. Vetus Testamentum, Supplements 2. Leiden : Brill, 1955.

Puech, Henri-Charles. "Archontiker," *Reallexikon für Antike und Christentum*. Ed. T. Klauser. Stuttgart : Hiersemann, 1950, vol. 1. 633-43.

——. "Les nouveaux écrits gnostiques," *Coptic Studies in honor of Walter Ewing Crum*. Boston : the Byzantine Institute, 1959, 91-154.

Rad, Gerhard von. "Das judäische Königsritual," *Gesammelte Studien zum Alten Testament*. Munich : Kaiser, 1958, 205-13.

Rehm, Bernhard, ed. *Die Pseudoklementinen : 2 Rekognitionen*. Griechischen Christlichen Schriftsteller 51. Berlin : Akademie Verlag, 1965.

Reitzenstein, Richard. *Das iranische Erlösungsmysterium*. Bonn : Marcus and Weber's Verlag, 1921.

Rengstorf, Karl H. ἀποστέλλω. *Theological Dictionary of the New Testament*. Tr. G. W. Bromiley. Grand Rapids : Eerdmans, 1964, vol. 1. 398-406.

——. ὑπηρέτης, ὑπηρετέω. *Theological Dictionary of the New Testament*. Tr. G. W. Bromiley. Grand Rapids : Eerdmans, 1962, vol. 8. 530-44.

Roberts, Alexander and Donaldson, James, eds. *The Ante-Nicene Fathers*. 10 vols. 1885; reprint Grand Rapids : Eerdmans, 1956.

142   BIBLIOGRAPHY

Rudolph, Kurt. "Gnosis und Gnostizismus, ein Forschungsbericht," *Theologische Rund-schau* 34 (1969) 121-75, 181-231, 353-61; 36 (1971) 1-61, 89-124; 37 (1972) 289-360; 38 (1973) 1-25.
——. "Randerscheinungen des Judentums und das Problem der Entstehung des Gnosti-zismus," *Kairos* 9 (1967) 118-22.
——. "Review of A. Böhlig and P. Labib, *Koptisch-gnostische Apokalypsen aus Codex V von Nag Hammadi im Koptischen Museum zu Alt-Kairo*," *Theologische Literatur-zeitung* 90 (1965) 359-62.
Sagnard, François M.-M. *Extraits de Théodote.* Sources Chrétiennes 23. Paris : Cerf, 1948.
——. *La gnose valentinienne et le témoignage de Saint Irénée.* Études de Philosophie Médiévale 36. Paris : Librairie Philosophique J. Vrin, 1947.
Schenke, Hans-Martin. "Das Problem der Beziehung zwischen Judentum und Gnosis," *Kairos* 7 (1965) 124-33.
——. "'Das Wesen der Archonten': Eine gnostische Originalschrift aus dem Funde von Nag Hammadi," *Theologische Literaturzeitung* 83 (1958) 661-70.
——. "Hauptprobleme der Gnosis," *Kairos* 7 (1965) 114-23.
——. "Review of A. Böhlig and P. Labib, *Koptisch-gnostische Apokalypsen aus Codex V von Nag Hammadi im Koptischen Museum zu Alt-Kairo*," *Orientalistische Literatur-zeitung* 61 (1966) 23-34.
——. "Review of Bullard and Nagel," *Orientalistische Literaturzeitung*, forthcoming.
——. "Vom Ursprung der Welt. Eine titellose gnostische Abhandlung aus dem Funde von Nag Hammadi," *Theologische Literaturzeitung* 84 (1959) 243-56.
Schmidt, Carl. *Gnostische Schriften in koptischer Sprache aus dem Codex Brucianus.* Texte und Untersuchungen 8. Leipzig : Hinrichs, 1892.
——. *Pistis Sophia.* Coptica, Consilio et Impensis Instituti Rask-Oerstediani Edita 2. Hauniae : Gyldendal, Nordisk forlag, 1925.
Schmidt, Carl and Till, Walter C., eds. *Koptisch-gnostische Schriften.* 3 Aufl. Griechischen Christlichen Schriftsteller 45. Berlin : Akademie-Verlag, 1962.
Schmidt, Francis. *Le Testament d'Abraham.* 2 vols. Dissertation Strasbourg, 1971.
Schmitz, Otto. θρόνος. *Theological Dictionary of the New Testament.* Tr. G. W. Bromiley. Grand Rapids : Eerdmans, 1965, vol. 3. 160-67.
Schoedel, William R. "Scripture and the Seventy-Two Heavens of the First Apoca-lypse of James," *Novum Testamentum* 12 (1970) 118-29.
Scholem, Gershom G. *Jewish Gnosticism, Merkabah Mysticism, and Talmudic Tradition.* 2d ed. New York : Jewish Theological Seminary, 1965.
——. "Kabbalah," *Encyclopedia Judaica.* Ed. C. Roth. Jerusalem : Keter, 1971, vol. 10. 489-653.
——. *Major Trends in Jewish Mysticism.* 3d ed. New York : Schocken, 1967.
Schottroff, Luise. "Animae naturaliter salvandae : Zum Problem der himmlischen Her-kunft des Gnostikers," *Christentum und Gnosis.* Ed. W. Eltester. Beiheft zur Zeit-schrift für die Neutestamentliche Wissenschaft 37. Berlin : Topelmann, 1969.
Schrenk, Gottlob. ἀδικία. *Theological Dictionary of the New Testament.* Tr. G. W. Bromiley. Grand Rapids : Eerdmans, 1964, vol. 1. 153-57.
Schultz, J. P. "Angelic Opposition to the Ascension of Moses and the Revelation of the Law," *Jewish Quarterly Review* 61 (1971) 282-308.
Sextus Empiricus. *Opera.* Ed. and tr. R. G. Bury. Loeb Classical Library. New York : Putnam's Sons and Cambridge : Harvard University, 1933-49.
Snell, Bruno. "Ezechiels Moses-Drama," *Antike und Abendland* 13 (1967) 150-64.
Stone, Michael E., tr. *The Testament of Abraham.* Society of Biblical Literature. Texts and Translations 2. New York : Society of Biblical Literature, 1972.

Strugnell, John. "The Angelic Liturgy at Qumran, 4 Q Serek Šîrôt ῾ôlat Haššabat," *International Organization for the Study of the Old Testament, 3d Congress, Oxford 1959, Congress Volume.* Vetus Testamentum, Supplements 7. Leiden : Brill, 1960.

——. "Notes on the Text and Metre of Ezekiel the Tragedian's 'Exagoge'," *Harvard Theological Review* 60 (1967) 449-57.

Tacitus. *Annals.* Tr. J. Jackson. 3 vols. Loeb Classical Library. Cambridge : Harvard University, 1925.

Tardieu, Michel. *Trois Mythes Gnostiques : Adam, Éros et les animaux d'Égypte dans un écrit de Nag Hammadi (II, 5).* Études Augustiniennes. Paris : Centre National de la Recherche Scientifique, 1974.

Tcherikover, Victor A. *Hellenistic Civilization and the Jews.* Tr. S. Applebaum. Philadelphia : Jewish Publication Society, 1966.

Tertullian. *Opera.* Ed. A. Kroymann. Pars III. Corpus Scriptorum Ecclesiasticorum Latinorum 47. Vienna : Tempsky, 1906.

Theodoret. *Haereticarum Fabularum Compendium.* Ed. J.-P. Migne. Patrologia Graeca. Paris : Migne, 1864, vol. 83. 335-556.

Till, Walter C., ed. *Die gnostischen Schriften des Koptischen Papyrus Berolinensis 8502.* Texte und Untersuchungen 60. Berlin : Akademie-Verlag, 1955.

Traub, Helmut and Rad, Gerhard von. οὐρανός. *Theological Dictionary of the New Testament.* Tr. G. W. Bromiley. Grand Rapids : Eerdmans, 1967, vol. 5. 497-536.

Völker, Walther, ed. *Quellen zur Geschichte der christlichen Gnosis.* Sammlung Ausgewählter Kirchen- und Dogmengeschichtlicher Quellenschriften 5. Tübingen : Mohr, 1932.

Widengren, Geo. *The Ascension of the Apostle and the Heavenly Book.* Acta Universitatis Upsaliensis 7. Uppsala : Lundequistska Bokhandeln, 1950.

Wilckens, Ulrich and Fohrer, Georg. σοφία. *Theological Dictionary of the New Testament.* Tr. G. W. Bromiley. Grand Rapids : Eerdmans, 1971, vol. 7. 465-528.

Wilson, Robert McL. *Gnosis and the New Testament.* Philadelphia : Fortress, 1968.

——. *The Gnostic Problem.* London : Mowbray, 1958.

Wisse, Frederik. "The Nag Hammadi Library and the Heresiologists," *Vigiliae Christianae* 25 (1971) 205-23.

——. "The Sethians and the Nag Hammadi Library," *The Society of Biblical Literature, One Hundred Eighth Annual Meeting, Seminar Papers.* Ed. Lane C. McGaughy. Society of Biblical Literature, 1972, vol. 1. 601-07.

Wolfson, Harry A. *Philo.* 2 vols. Cambridge : Harvard University, 1947.

Wright, George E. "The Lawsuit of God : A Form Critical Study of Deuteronomy 32," *Israel's Prophetic Heritage : Essays in Honor of James Muilenberg.* Ed. B. W. Anderson and W. Harrelson. New York : Harper, 1962, 26-67.

Yadin, Yigael. *The Scrolls of the War of the Sons of Light.* Tr. B. and C. Rabin. Oxford : University Press, 1962.

INDICES

CITATIONS

O.T.

JUDAISM

N.T.

CHRISTIAN WRITINGS

Tertullian, *Adv. Marc.*		Theodoret, *Haereticarum fabularum*	
1.2	83	compendium	
3.6	84	1.14	73
4.6	84		
4.33	84		

GNOSTIC WRITINGS

ApocAd		ApocAd	
64.6-12	71	78.15	71
64.7	71	81.16	71
64.12f	71	82.4-83.4	70
64.13f	71	82.21	71
64.17	71	83.5f	70
64.20-30	71	83.13	71
64.20f	71	83.21	71
65.13	71	84.1-3	71
65.17f	71	84.7f	70
65.31f	71	84.9f	71
66.14f	71	85.4f	71
66.17-21	71	85.5f	72
66.20f	71	85.7-11	72
66.21-23	71	85.8-13	72
66.25f	71	85.15	71
66.28	71	85.19-31	73
69.2-17	71	85.24	71
69.4	71		
69.7	71	ApocryJas	
70.6	71	3.25-27	79
70.6-15	71	10.1-5	79
70.16	71		
71.16	71	ApocryJn BG	
72.14	71	22.18	79
72.15-25	72	39.10-19	21, 100
72.25	71, 72	41.12-15	78
73.9	71, 72	44.19-45.10	30
73.15-20	72	44.19ff	97
74.3-21	72	62.12ff	113
74.3f	71		
74.3	71	ApocryJn CG II, *1*	
74.7	71 (2×)	10(58).14-19	124
74.17-21	72	10(58).33f	124
74.26f	71	13.13-21	30
76.8-27	72	24(72).20ff	113
76.15-27	71		
76.22	71	ApocryJn CG III, *1*	
77.4	71	16.8-13	21, 100
77.7-15	71		
77.16-18	70	ApocryJn CG IV, 1	
77.17f	70	20.29-21.8	30
77.19	70		

GRECO-ROMAN WRITINGS

MODERN AUTHORS